WHERE ARE THE LESSON FILES?

Purchase of this Classroom in a Book in any format gives you access to the lesson files you'll need to complete the exercises in the book.

1 Go to www.adobepress.com/PSECIB2020.

2 Sign in or create a new account.

3 Click Submit.

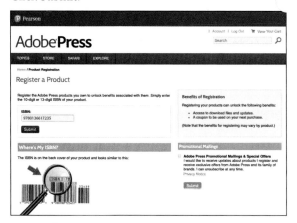

Note: If you encounter problems registering your product or accessing the lesson files or Web Edition, go to www.adobepress.com/support for assistance.

4 Answer the question as proof of purchase.

5 The lesson files can be accessed through the Registered Products tab on your Account page.

6 Click the Access Bonus Content link below the title of your product to proceed to the download page. Click the lesson file links to download them to your computer.

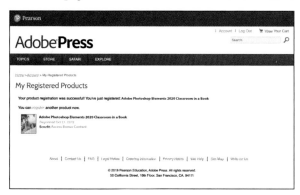

Note: If you purchased a digital product directly from www.adobepress.com or www.peachpit.com, your product will already be registered. However, you still need to follow the registration steps and answer the proof of purchase question before the Access Bonus Content link will appear under the product on your Registered Products tab.

CONTENTS AT A GLANCE

CONTENTS

Adobe Photoshop
Elements 2020

CLASSROOM IN A BOOK®
The official training workbook from Adobe

Jeff Carlson

GETTING STARTED

Adobe® Photoshop® Elements 2020 delivers image-editing tools that balance power and versatility with ease of use. Whether you're a home user or hobbyist, a professional photographer or a business user, Photoshop Elements 2020 makes it easy to produce good-looking pictures, share your stories in stylish and sophisticated creations for both print and web, and manage and safeguard your precious photos.

If you've used an earlier version of Photoshop Elements, you'll find that this Classroom in a Book® will teach you advanced skills and provide an introduction to the new and improved features in this version. If you're new to Adobe Photoshop Elements, you'll learn the fundamental concepts and a range of techniques that will help you master the application.

About Classroom in a Book

Adobe Photoshop Elements 2020 Classroom in a Book is part of the official training series for Adobe graphics and publishing software, developed with the support of Adobe product experts. Each lesson is made up of a series of self-paced projects that will give you hands-on experience using Photoshop Elements 2020.

See "Accessing the lesson files and Web Edition" on the page 3 for instructions on downloading the sample photographs and other resources used for the lessons in *Adobe Photoshop Elements 2020 Classroom in a Book.*

What's new in this edition

This edition covers many new and improved features in Adobe Photoshop Elements 2020, from improvements to the Home screen, which includes Auto Creations to make slideshows and other projects using your media, to revamped collage tools and new guided edits. Adobe has put its Sensei machine-learning technology into more tools, such as the new Smooth Skin feature, the Colorize Photo feature, and the especially useful Select Subject command that automatically creates a selection around the objects you'd otherwise spend more time selecting using other tools.

Prerequisites

Before you begin the lessons in this book, make sure that you and your computer are ready by following the tips and instructions on the next few pages.

Requirements on your computer

You'll need about 950 MB of free space on your hard disk—around 400 MB for the lesson files and up to 550 MB for the work files that you'll create as you work through the exercises.

Required skills

The lessons in this book assume that you have a working knowledge of your computer and its operating system. Make sure that you know how to use the mouse, standard menus and commands, context menus, windows, and scroll bars.

If you need to review these basic and generic computer skills, see the documentation included with your Microsoft® Windows® or Apple® macOS® software.

Installing Adobe Photoshop Elements 2020

Before you begin the *Adobe Photoshop Elements 2020 Classroom in a Book* lessons, make sure your system is set up correctly and you've installed the required software and hardware. You must purchase the Adobe Photoshop Elements 2020 software separately. For system requirements and instructions for downloading, installing, and setting up the software, refer to the topics listed under the heading "Download & install" as part of the "Troubleshooting & help" section at helpx.adobe.com/photoshop-elements.html.

Online content

Note: The sample images are provided for your personal use with this book. You are not authorized to use these files commercially, or to publish or distribute them in any form without written permission from Adobe Systems, Inc. and the individual photographers or other copyright holders.

Your purchase of this Classroom in a Book includes online materials provided by way of your Account page on adobepress.com. These include:

Lesson files

To work through the projects in this book, you will need to download the lesson files by following the instructions on the next page.

Web Edition

The Web Edition is an online interactive version of the book providing an enhanced learning experience. Your Web Edition can be accessed from any device with a connection to the Internet, and it contains:

- The complete text of the book

- Hours of instructional video keyed to the text

- Interactive quizzes

Accessing the lesson files and Web Edition

You must **register** your purchase on adobepress.com in order to access the online content:

1 Go to www.adobepress.com/PSECIB2020.

2 Sign in or create a new account.

3 Click Submit.

4 Answer the question as proof of purchase.

5 The lesson files can be accessed from the Registered Products tab on your Account page. Click the Access Bonus Content link below the title of your product to proceed to the download page. Click the lesson file link(s) to download them to your computer.

The Web Edition can be accessed from the Digital Purchases tab on your Account page. Click the Launch link to access the product.

Note: If you purchased a digital product directly from www.adobepress.com or www.peachpit.com, your product will already be registered. However, you still need to follow the registration steps and answer the proof of purchase question before the Access Bonus Content link will appear under the product on your Registered Products tab.

Creating a work folder

Now you need to create a folder to hold your downloaded and unzipped lesson files, as well as the work files you'll save in the course of the lessons in this book.

1 Create a new folder named **PSE2020CIB** inside the *username*/Documents (Windows) or *username*/Documents (maçOS) folder on your computer.

2 If you downloaded the entire Lessons folder, drag the unzipped Lessons folder into the PSE2020CIB folder on your hard disk.

3 If you downloaded the work folder for an individual lesson, first create a folder named Lessons inside the PSE2020CIB folder; then, drag the unzipped individual lesson folder to your PSE2020CIB/Lessons folder.

Now, you can create a folder to store the finished files that you'll produce as you work through the exercises.

> **Note:** In this book, the forward slash character (/) is used to separate equivalent terms and commands for Windows / macOS, in the order shown here.

4 In Windows Explorer (Windows) / the Finder (macOS), open the Lessons folder inside the new PSE2020CIB folder on your hard disk.

5 Choose File > New > Folder (Windows) / File > New Folder (macOS).
   Type **My CIB Work** as the name for the new folder.

If you follow the instructions carefully as you work through each exercise in this book, you'll preserve the original lesson file that you downloaded by saving your work with a new file name. If you do accidentally overwrite the original lesson files, you can download fresh copies at any time from your adobepress.com account.

Creating an Adobe ID

When you install Adobe Photoshop Elements 2020 (macOS) or launch the program for the first time (Windows), you'll be asked to create an Adobe ID to register your product online. If you were offline and skipped this step, Photoshop Elements will prompt you at startup. You can take advantage of one of these opportunities, or register from the Photoshop Elements Editor by choosing Help > Sign In.

Creating an Adobe ID is free and only takes a minute. Your Adobe ID will stream-line your customer support experience, making it easy to make new purchases or to retrieve a lost serial number.

With an Adobe ID, you'll also be able to log in to community forums and user groups and get access to free trial downloads, hundreds of free product extensions, members-only white papers and downloads, and more.

Understanding the catalog file

The catalog file is a central concept in understanding how Photoshop Elements works. Photoshop Elements doesn't actually "import" your images in the sense of transferring them from one place to another. For each image you import, Photoshop Elements simply creates a new entry in the catalog that is linked to the source file, wherever it is stored, but the image itself is not moved or copied.

All the work you put into organizing your photo library is recorded in the catalog file; it's updated whenever you tag, rate, or label a photo, or group images in an album.

As well as digital photographs, a catalog can include video and audio files, scans, PDF documents, and any presentations and layouts you might create in Photoshop Elements, such as slideshows, photo collages, and CD/DVD jacket designs.

The first time you launch Photoshop Elements, it creates a default catalog file (named My Catalog) on your hard disk. Although a single catalog can efficiently handle thousands of files, you can establish separate catalogs for different purposes if that's the way you prefer to work.

In the first lesson in this book, you'll create and load a dedicated catalog into which you'll import the sample images for the exercises, so that you can keep your lesson files separate from your own photo library.

Additional resources

Adobe Photoshop Elements 2020 Classroom in a Book is not intended to replace the documentation that comes with the program or to be a comprehensive reference for every feature. Only the commands and options used in the lessons are explained in this book. For comprehensive information about program features and tutorials, please refer to these resources:

Adobe Photoshop Elements 2020 Learn and Support Point your browser to helpx.adobe.com/photoshop-elements.html, where you can find hands-on tutorials, Help, answers to common questions, troubleshooting information, and more.

Adobe Photoshop Elements 2020 product home page
adobe.com/products/photoshop-elements

Photoshop Elements Forums forums.adobe.com/community/photoshop_elements lets you tap into peer-to-peer discussions as well as questions and answers on Adobe products.

Resources for educators Both adobe.com/education and edex.adobe.com offer a treasure trove of information for instructors who teach classes on Adobe software. Find solutions for education at all levels, including free curricula that use an integrated approach to teaching Adobe software and can be used to prepare for the Adobe Certified Associate exams.

Free trial versions of Adobe Photoshop Elements 2020 and Adobe Premiere Elements 2020 The trial version of the software is fully functional and offers every feature of the product for you to test drive. To download your free trial version, go to www.adobe.com/downloads.html.

1 A QUICK TOUR OF PHOTOSHOP ELEMENTS

Lesson overview

This lesson provides an overview of Photoshop Elements that will familiarize you with the basic components of the workspace while introducing many of the tools and procedures you'll use to import, manage, and edit your digital images.

The exercises in this lesson will step you through some of the skills and concepts basic to the Photoshop Elements workflow:

- Creating and loading catalogs
- Importing media
- Reconnecting missing files
- Reviewing and comparing photos
- Switching between the Organizer and the Editor
- Switching modes in the Editor
- Working with panels and the Panel Bin
- Customizing the workspace
- Using Photoshop Elements Help

 This lesson will take about 90 minutes to complete. To get the lesson files used in this chapter, download them from the web page for this book at www.adobepress.com/PSECIB2020. For more information, see "Accessing the lesson files and Web Edition" in the Getting Started section at the beginning of this book.

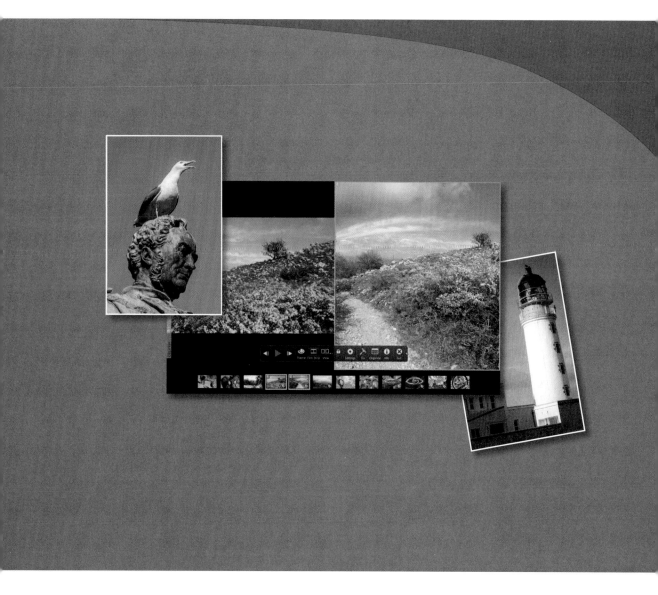

Welcome to Adobe Photoshop Elements 2020!
Take a quick tour and get to know the Photoshop
Elements workspace—you'll find all the power and
versatility you'd expect from a Photoshop application
in an easy-to-use, modular interface that will help you
keep your media files organized while you take your
digital photography to a new level.

How Photoshop Elements works

Nute. Before you start this lesson, make sure that you've set up a folder for your lesson files and downloaded the Lesson 1 folder from your Account page at www.peachpit.com, as detailed in "Accessing the lesson files and Web Edition" and "Creating a work folder" in the "Getting Started" section at the beginning of this book.

Photoshop Elements has two primary workspaces: the Elements Organizer and the Editor. You can think of the Organizer as a library and browser for your photos and other media files, and the Editor as a digital darkroom and workshop where you can adjust and enhance your images and create presentations to showcase them.

1 Start Photoshop Elements.

By default, the Home screen opens whenever you start Photoshop Elements, serving as a convenient entry point to either of the workspace modules.

This tour—like the Photoshop Elements workflow—begins in the Organizer, where you can import, sort, group, search, and share your photos. It's also where you'll find links to helpful tutorials and Auto Creations built from your media (which are covered at the end of this lesson).

2 Click the Organizer button to launch the Elements Organizer module. Review the privacy notice that appears and click OK.

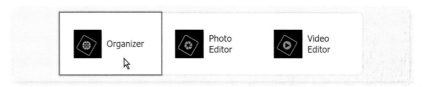

3 If you see the walkthrough screen with tips on using the Organizer, click Skip in the lower-right corner to dismiss it. As with the Home screen, you can always access the walkthrough screen from the Help menu. You may also need to dismiss (or respond to) an update notification.

The library catalog file

Behind the scenes, Photoshop Elements stores information about your images in a library catalog file, which enables you to conveniently manage all the media files on your computer without ever leaving the Organizer. When you import photos from a camera or memory card, the files are copied to your hard disk, but from there, Photoshop Elements simply registers their locations in the catalog. Or, if you add a photo that already exists on disk, wherever it is stored, the Organizer creates a new catalog entry—a link to the original file, or *source file*; the image itself is not moved or copied. All the work you put into organizing your growing photo library is recorded in the catalog file; whenever you assign a tag or a rating to a photo, or group images in a stack or an album, the catalog is updated.

As well as digital photographs, a catalog can include video and audio files, scans, PDF documents, and any presentations and layouts you might create in Photoshop Elements, such as slideshows, photo collages, and CD jacket designs.

Creating a catalog for working with this book

The first time you launch Photoshop Elements, a default catalog file (named My Catalog) is automatically created on your hard disk. Although a single catalog can efficiently handle thousands of files, you can also establish separate catalogs for different purposes—if that's the way you prefer to work. In this exercise you'll create and load a dedicated catalog to handle the sample files used for the lessons in this book, making it easy to keep them separate from your own photos.

1   When the Organizer has opened, choose File > Manage Catalogs. In the Catalog Manager dialog box, click New. Don't change the location setting, which specifies who can access the catalog file and where it is stored.

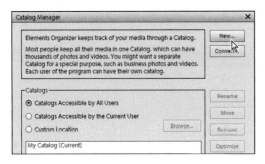

Note: On macOS, you may see a slightly different set of location options from those shown in this illustration.

2   Type **CIB Catalog** in the Enter A Name For The New Catalog dialog box. Disable the Import Free Music Into This Catalog option, if necessary, and then click OK.

3   If you see an animated walkthrough screen with tips on getting started, click Skip in the lower-right corner to dismiss it for now. You can access the walkthrough tips at any time by choosing Help > Show Walkthrough Screens.

Your new catalog is loaded in the Organizer. If you are ever unsure which catalog is currently loaded, check the catalog name displayed in the lower-right corner of the Organizer workspace.

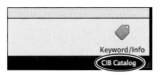

Tip: You can launch the Catalog Manager without using the menu command by simply clicking the name of the current catalog in the lower-right corner of the Organizer workspace.

Now that you have a catalog created specifically to manage the sample files that you'll use for the lessons in this book, you're ready to put some photos into it.

Importing media

Before you can view, organize, and share your photos and other media files in Photoshop Elements, you first need to import them into the Organizer in order to link them to your catalog.

You can bring photos into Photoshop Elements from a variety of sources and in a number of different ways.

1 Click the Import button, at the upper left of the Organizer workspace. The options in the Import menu vary slightly, depending on your operating system.

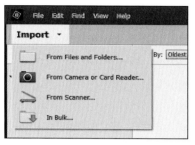

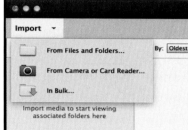

Import options on Windows   Import options on macOS

2 Click the Import button again to close the menu.

Getting photos from files and folders

If your image files are already on your computer hard disk—as is the case for the Classroom in a Book sample photos—you can either drag them directly into the Elements Organizer workspace from Windows Explorer or the macOS Finder, or import them from within Photoshop Elements using a menu command.

The import options that are listed in the Import button menu can also be accessed from the File menu.

1 Choose File > Get Photos And Videos > From Files And Folders.

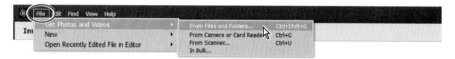

2 Navigate to and open the Lessons folder inside your PSE2020CIB folder. Open the Lesson 1 folder; then, click once to select the subfolder Import 1.

3 Make sure that the options Automatically Fix Red Eyes and Automatically Suggest Photo Stacks are disabled (see the illustration on the next page); then, click Get Media.

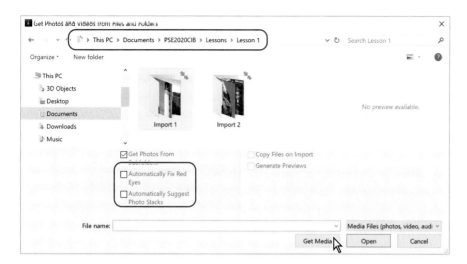

The Getting Media dialog box displays a progress bar as the photos are imported (though, if you have a fast computer, you may barely notice it).

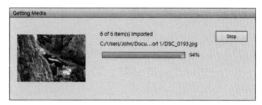

4 The Import Attached Keyword Tags dialog box appears, indicating that the photos you're importing have already been tagged with keywords. Select the box beside the Lesson 01 tag in the Keyword Tags list to confirm it for import, and then click OK.

Note: You'll learn more about keyword tags in Lesson 3.

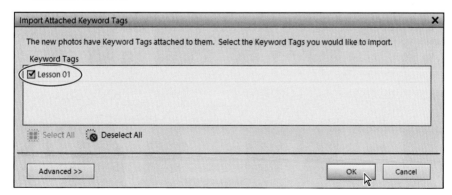

5 Thumbnails of the six imported photos appear in the Organizer's Media Browser pane. Choose View > Details. Note that each image's capture time is now displayed below its thumbnail, together with a blue tag badge indicating that the photo has attached keywords. (If you don't see the blue tag, increase the Zoom slider to make the tag appear.)

6 Repeat steps 1 through 4 for the folder Lessons / Lesson 1 / Import 2, but this time, choose From Files And Folders from the Import button menu.

Exploring the Organizer workspace

The Elements Organizer is an integral part of both Adobe Photoshop Elements and Adobe Premiere Elements video editing software. You can import, manage, and view photos and video in the Elements Organizer, which serves as a hub, allowing seamless integration of the two editing applications.

In the Organizer, the main work area is the Media Browser pane. This is where you'll review, sort, organize, and search your photos and other media files. The bars just above the image thumbnails display information about the selection of photos currently displayed; in this case, the lower bar displays the date and time of the last import. If the Media Browser were showing the results of a catalog search, the lower bar would detail the search criteria shared by that selection of images.

1   To clear the Last Import filter and view all twelve photos in your catalog, click the Clear button at the right of the search results bar above the thumbnails.

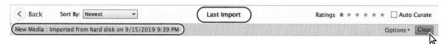

The search results bar closes. The Last Import header changes to All Media, to show that the Media Browser is now displaying all of the files in your catalog. By default, the images are sorted by capture date, arranged from newest to oldest.

2   Choose Oldest from the Sort By menu at the left of the actions bar to reverse the order. Note that you can also sort your photos by name or import batch.

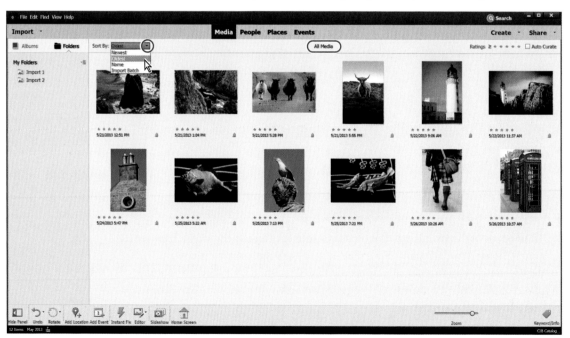

Once you've spent a little time organizing your catalog by tagging your photos, you can use the view picker above the sorting bar to move between the People, Places, and Events views, quickly filtering the images in the Media Browser so it displays only those photos that feature the faces, locations, or occasions that matter to you. The currently active view is the Media view, which is unfiltered.

Note: You'll learn more about the People, Places, and Events views, and explore a variety of ways to search the images in your photo library, in Lessons 2 and 3.

You can use the Search button (located in the menu bar on Windows, or in the application window header on macOS) to conduct a search of all the images in your catalog, or just a subset, based on text, tags, dates, folders, albums, ratings, and file type—or combine filters to set up a complex multi-criterion search.

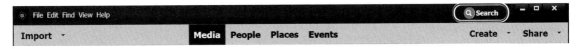

The left panel will list any albums that you create to group your photos, and also provides quick and easy access to all the files and source folders on your computer.

3   Click Folders at the top of the left panel. The default My Folders view lists only your *managed folders*: those folders that contain files you've already imported to your catalog.

4   To see your folders in hierarchy view, click the menu icon (▼☰) to the right of the My Folders header and choose View As Tree. You can expand folders in order to drill down in the hierarchy by clicking the boxes beside them. To expand the tree even further, right-click the Lessons folder and choose Show All Subfolders from the context menu. You can now see all of the subfolders inside the Lessons folder, rather than just those that contain files already managed by your catalog.

▶ **Tip:** If the left panel is not wide enough to display the folder names in the tree hierarchy, move the pointer over the panel's right edge and drag to the right with the double-arrow cursor.

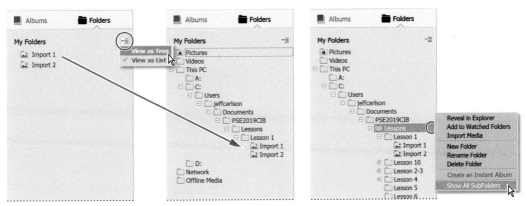

In the Folders view, you can drag and drop files and folders to new locations on your hard disk, and create, rename, and delete folders on your computer without leaving the Organizer. The catalog tracks all your work in the Folders view, making it easy to manage your media library from the ground up, and helping to avoid the hassle of locating and reconnecting missing files.

Note: You can identify a managed folder in the hierarchy by the photo folder icon (🖼). Watched folders display a binoculars icon (🔭).

When you select a folder in the Folders view, that folder, rather than your entire catalog, becomes the image source, so the Media Browser displays only the photos contained in the selected folder. Any filter or search—including the People, Places, and Events views—will be applied only to the images in the selected folder. The Media view will display the unfiltered contents of the selected folder.

5   Click the menu icon (▼≡) at the upper right of the My Folders list and choose View As List. Click between your two managed folders to see their contents isolated in turn in the Media Browser. Click All Media, at the left of the Sort By menu above the image thumbnails, to view all of the photos in your catalog.

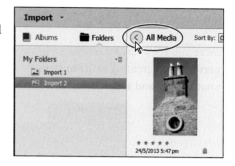

The taskbar across the bottom of the workspace presents an array of tools, giving you one-click access to some of the most common Organizer tasks.

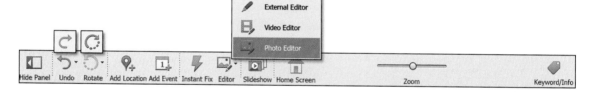

● **Note:** The Instant Fix, Editor, and Slideshow buttons are covered later in this lesson. You'll learn how to use the Add Location and Add Event buttons in Lesson 2.

6   Toggle the button at the far left of the taskbar to hide and show the left panel. The Undo / Redo and Rotate buttons are self-explanatory; click the arrow beside each of these tools to see the variant. Experiment with the full range of the Zoom slider to change the size of the image thumbnails. Leave the thumbnails set to a large enough size to see the blue keyword tag badges.

7   Select any thumbnail in the Media Browser; then, click the Keyword/Info button at the right of the taskbar to open the right panel group. The Image Tags panel at the bottom shows that the selected image is tagged with the Lesson 01 keyword. Expand the Keywords list at the top of the Tags panel; then, expand the Imported Keyword Tags category to see the Lesson 01 tag nested inside.

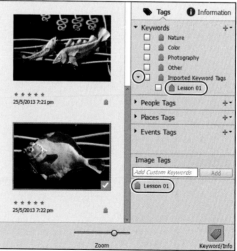

At the upper right of the Organizer workspace, above the right panel, are the Create and Share buttons.

8 Click the Create and Share buttons in turn and examine the options.

You can choose from the Create menu to begin a variety of photo projects to share and showcase your images, from personalized greeting cards to stylish photo books and slideshows.

The Share menu offers a range of ways to share your photos and videos with friends, family, and clients, or show them off to the world at large. Burn a DVD, publish to online sharing sites, attach your images to an email, or export media as a PDF slideshow.

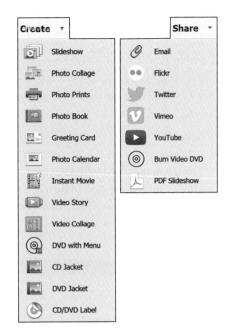

Tip: This illustration shows the Create and Share menus as they appear on Windows. You may see a slightly different set of options on macOS.

9 Double-click any thumbnail in the grid, or select it and press Ctrl+Shift+S (Windows) or Command+Shift+S (macOS), to see the image enlarged. Use the arrow keys on your keyboard to cycle through the photos in the single-image view. Double-click the enlarged image to return to the thumbnail grid view.

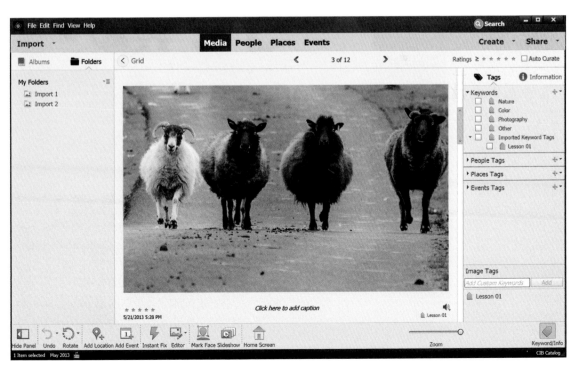

Reviewing and comparing images

Photoshop Elements provides several options for quickly and easily reviewing and comparing your photos in the Organizer. The Full Screen and Side By Side views let you examine images at any level of magnification—without the distraction of image windows, panels, and menus. In both of these views you can apply keywords, add photos to albums, and even perform a range of one-click editing tasks.

Viewing photos in Full Screen mode

You can use the Full Screen view to inspect and assess your photos in detail, or to effortlessly present a selection of images as an instant slideshow.

1 Click to select a single thumbnail image in the Media Browser, and then choose View > Full Screen. Avoid moving the pointer for a few moments until the control bar and the Quick Edit and Quick Organize panels disappear.

2 Move the pointer over the full-screen image to see the control bar again. Move the pointer over the gray tabs at the left of the screen to open the Quick Edit and Quick Organize panels. Move the pointer into the center of the screen; the control bar and panels disappear again after a few moments' inactivity.

> **Tip:** If you don't see the Film Strip, press Ctrl+F / Command+F on your keyboard, or click the Film Strip button in the Full Screen view's control bar.

The Film Strip below the main image shows all the photos from the Media Browser; if you had entered Full Screen mode with multiple images selected, the Film Strip would display only the selected photos.

> **Note:** The Slideshow button (⌗) in the standard Media view taskbar launches a slideshow with playback options as set in the Create mode's Slideshow Editor (see Lesson 9).

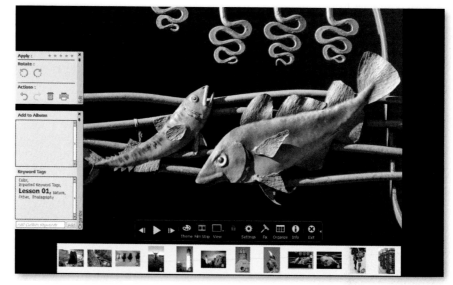

3 Use the arrow keys on your keyboard, and then the Previous Media and Next Media buttons (flanking the triangular Play button at the left of the control bar), to move backward and forward through the images in the Film Strip.

4 To view your images in a Full Screen view slideshow, press the spacebar, or show the control bar by moving the pointer over the image, and then click the Play button. To stop the slideshow, press the spacebar again, or click the Pause button in the control bar.

5   In the control bar, click the Theme and Settings buttons in turn to set a variety of options for the slideshow and the Full Screen view. Choose a style for transitions between slides, select an audio file to replace the default sound track, and set the slideshow to repeat. Play the slideshow to see the effects of your settings.

Tip: If you choose either Pan and Zoom or 3D Pixelate transitions in the Theme dialog box, you'll need to press the Esc key on your keyboard to stop the slideshow, rather than the spacebar or the Pause button in the control bar.

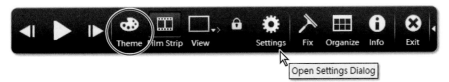

6   Stop the slideshow. Toggle the Film Strip, Fix, and Organize buttons to show and hide the Film Strip and the Quick Edit and Quick Organize panels.

Comparing photos side by side

The Side By Side viewing mode lets you keep one image fixed on one side of a split screen while you cycle through a selection of photos on the other—great for comparing composition and detail or for choosing the best of a series of similar shots.

1   Show the Film Strip, if necessary, and then click to select the first photo in the series. Click the View button in the control bar to see the alternative view options; then, choose the Side By Side view.

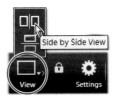

The photo you selected is displayed at the left of the screen, and the next photo in the series is shown on the right. By default, the image on the left—image #1—is active, as indicated by the blue border around the photo in the split-screen view. Any organizing or editing operation you perform will affect only the active image.

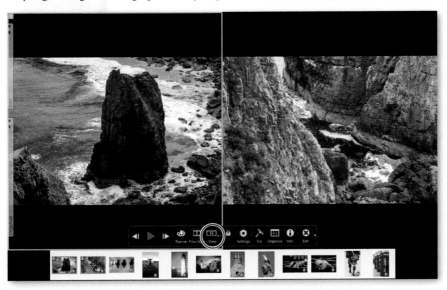

2   With the photo on the left—image #1—still active, click the first photo of the lighthouse in the Film Strip. The new selection becomes the new #1 image.

3   Press the Tab key to make image #2 (the photo on the right) the active image. Click the forward navigation (Next Media) button (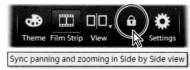) in the control bar, or press the right arrow key on your keyboard, to cycle the #2 preview to the second lighthouse photo, while the image on the left remains fixed.

4   Click either image repeatedly to toggle between fit-to-view and 100% magnification. To compare detail at higher magnification, zoom in and out in the active image using the scroll-wheel on your mouse—or by pressing the Ctrl / Command key together with the plus (+) or minus (–) key. Drag the zoomed photo with the hand cursor to see a different portion of the image.

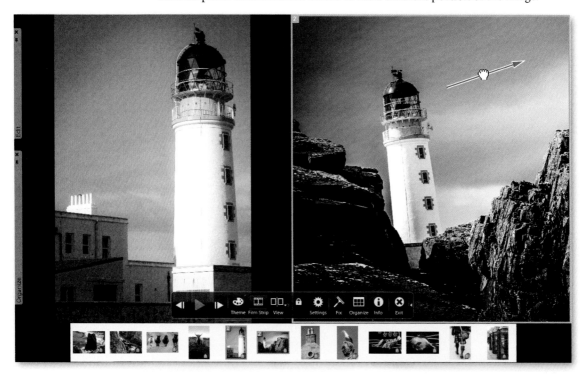

5   To synchronize panning and zooming between the two photos, click the lock icon to the right of the View button in the full screen view control bar.

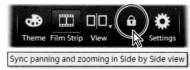

6   Click the View button and select the second split-screen layout from the fly-out menu—the horizontally divided Above And Below view.

7   Click the Exit button () at the right of the control bar, or press the Esc key on your keyboard, to close the split-screen view and return to the Organizer.

Reconnecting missing files to a catalog

When you bring a photo into Photoshop Elements, the name and location of the file is recorded in the catalog. If you wish to move, rename, or delete a photo that is already in your catalog, it's best to do so from within the Elements Organizer.

If you move, rename, or delete a file in the Windows Explorer / macOS Finder after it has been added to the catalog, Photoshop Elements searches your computer for the missing file automatically, and will usually do a great job finding it—even when the file has been renamed; however, you need to know what to do if the automatic search fails. If a file cannot be located, the missing file icon (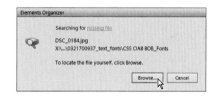) appears in the upper-left corner of its thumbnail in the Media Browser to alert you that the link between the file and your catalog has been broken.

Tip: To avoid the problem of files missing from your catalog, use the Move and Rename commands from the File menu, and the Delete From Catalog command from the Edit menu, to move, rename, or delete files from within Photoshop Elements, rather than doing so outside the application.

1 Switch to the Windows Explorer / macOS Finder by doing one of the following:

   • On Windows, minimize the Elements Organizer by clicking the Minimize button (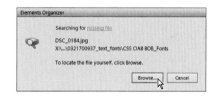) at the right of the menu bar, or simply click the Elements Organizer application button on the Windows taskbar.

   • On macOS, click the Finder icon in the Dock, or hold down the Command key and then press and release the Tab key, repeatedly if necessary, to select the Finder icon in the Application Switcher.

2 Open an Explorer / Finder window, if there's not one already available. Navigate to and open your Lessons folder. Drag the Lesson 1 folder out of the Lessons folder to the Recycle Bin / Trash. Do not empty the Recycle Bin / Trash.

3 Switch back to the Organizer, and then choose File > Reconnect > All Missing Files. Photoshop displays a message to let you know it's busy searching for the missing files. We don't expect the files to be found in the Recycle Bin / Trash, so you can stop the automatic search by clicking the Browse button.

The Reconnect Missing Files dialog box opens—as it would have done, had the search run its course without Photoshop Elements locating the missing files.

4 For this exercise, you won't follow the re-linking process through to completion, but you should take this opportunity to inspect the dialog box thoroughly (see the illustration on the next page).

At the upper left of the Reconnect Missing Files dialog box is a list of all missing files. Below the list, a preview displays a thumbnail of the currently selected missing file. To the right, you can browse the contents of your computer.

When you select a candidate, you'll see a preview thumbnail below the Locate The Missing Files pane, opposite the missing file preview, enabling you to visually verify the photo as a match, even if its name has been changed.

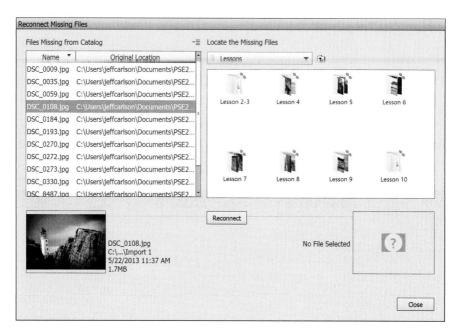

5   Once you've verified a file or series of files to be reconnected, you can click the Reconnect button. For now, click Close to cancel the operation. Note that all of the thumbnails in the Media Browser now display the missing file icon ().

6   Switch back to the Explorer / Finder; then, drag the Lesson 1 folder out of the Recycle Bin / Trash and return it to your Lessons folder.

Note: The missing file icons may persist until you next change the view or execute another command.

7   Switch back to the Organizer and choose File > Reconnect > All Missing Files. Photoshop briefly displays a message to let you know that there are no missing files to reconnect.

Switching between the Organizer and the Editor

Although the Instant Fix panel in the Organizer and the Quick Edit panel in the Full Screen view offer one-step tools for some of the most common editing tasks, you'll switch to the Editor for more sophisticated editing.

1   Select any two photos in the Media Browser.

Tip: Alternatively, right-click either of the selected images, and choose Edit With Photoshop Elements Editor from the context menu.

2   To open the selected images in the Editor, either choose Edit > Edit With Photoshop Elements Editor, or click the Editor button () in the taskbar.

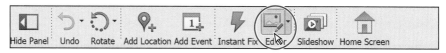

You can switch back to the Organizer from the Editor just as easily, by clicking the Organizer button () in the taskbar at the bottom of the Editor workspace.

The Editor workspace

The Editor provides a comprehensive yet intuitive editing environment, with a choice of editing modes to satisfy users of any level of expertise, and a flexible workspace that can be customized to suit the way you prefer to work.

1   If your workspace arrangement differs from the illustration below, click the word Expert in the mode picker at the top of the workspace, and then choose Window > Reset Panels. If you don't see the photo thumbnails below the main image, click the Photo Bin button in the lower-left corner of the Editor window.

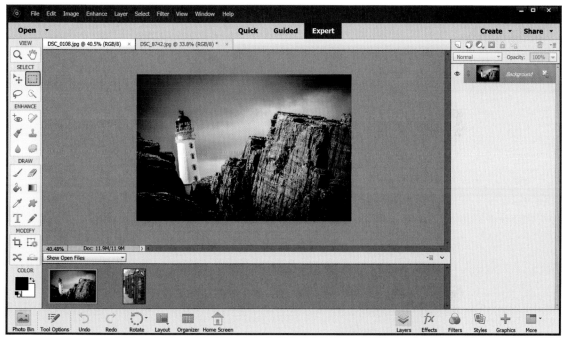

The central work area in the Editor is the Edit pane, where you'll adjust and enhance your images, and preview the projects and presentations that you create to showcase them.

2   In the edit mode picker immediately above the Edit pane, click Quick to enter Quick Edit mode. Note the simplified toolbar at the left. The right panel presents easy-to-use controls for six common image editing operations; click the small arrow beside each of the Quick Edit options in turn to expand and collapse the controls.

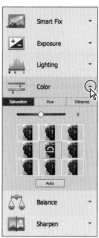

3 Click Guided in the edit mode picker above the Edit pane to switch to Guided Edit mode. The work area now shows an interactive preview for each guided edit offered. Hover the pointer back and forth over a preview to see before and after views for that procedure.

Tip: If you're new to digital imaging, the Guided Edit mode is a great place to start; you can learn new tricks and techniques as you step through each editing procedure.

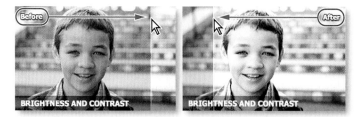

4 In the bar below the mode picker, click each category in turn to see the range of guided edits available. Click to launch a procedure from the Basics category, noting the tools and tips in the right panel. Click Cancel at the lower right, and then repeat the process for two or three edits from each of the first three groups.

5 Click Expert in the edit mode picker to switch back to the Expert mode.

6 Below the Edit pane is the Photo Bin, which provides easy access to the images you're working with, no matter how many files you have open. Click each of the thumbnails in the Photo Bin in turn to bring that photo to the front in the Edit pane and make it the active image.

7 Choose Preferences > General from the Edit / Adobe Photoshop Elements Editor menu. On the General tab of the Preferences dialog box, click the check box to activate the option Allow Floating Documents In Expert Mode; then, click OK.

8 Drag whichever image is foremost by its name tab, away from its docked position to float above the Editor workspace.

Note: Once you've activated the option to allow floating document windows, this becomes the default for any image opened in Expert Edit mode. Throughout the rest of this book, however, it is assumed that you are working with tabbed image windows docked (consolidated) in the Edit pane, unless otherwise specified. Before you complete this exercise you'll disable floating document windows so that it'll be easier for you to follow the exercises as written.

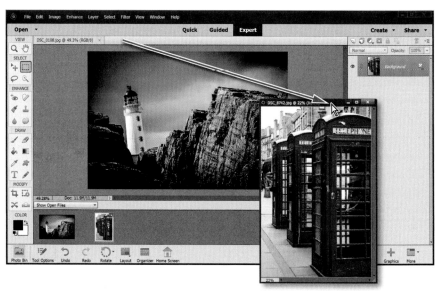

9 Explore the options for arranging image windows that are available from the Window > Images menu, and from the menu on the Layout button (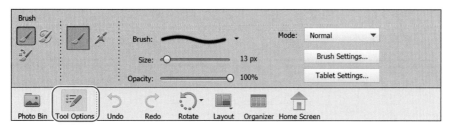) in the taskbar at the bottom of the Editor workspace. You may wish to go back to the Organizer and open more files to develop a feel for the way you prefer to work with your image windows.

10 When you're done, choose Preferences > General from the Edit / Adobe Photoshop Elements Editor menu and disable floating documents in Expert mode; then, click OK to close the Preferences dialog box.

The Edit mode toolbar includes tools for making precise selections, fixing image imperfections, drawing, painting, adding text, and creating special effects, conveniently grouped by function. You can hide and show the toolbar to free up screen space as you work by choosing Tools from the Window menu.

11 Click the Tool Options button in the taskbar at the bottom of the Editor workspace to hide the Photo Bin and show the Tool Options pane in its place. In the toolbar at the left of the workspace, click to activate several of the tools in turn, noting the settings and controls available for each in the Tool Options pane.

12 Click the Photo Bin button at the left of the taskbar to show the Photo Bin.

Working with panels and the Panel Bin

To the right of the Edit pane is the Panel Bin. In its default Basic mode, the Panel Bin displays one panel at a time.

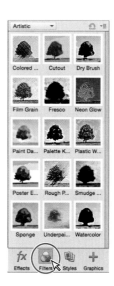

1 Use the buttons in the taskbar below the Panel Bin to switch the Panel Bin between the Layers, Effects, Filters, Styles, and Graphics panels. The illustration at the right shows the Artistic category in the Filters panel.

2 Click the More button (not the triangle beside it) at the far right of the taskbar. The rest of the Editor panels appear in a tabbed group floating "above" the workspace. Click the More button again to hide the floating panels; then, click the small triangle beside the More button and choose Histogram from the menu. The floating panels group appears once more: this time, with the Histogram panel foremost.

You can also show and hide the floating panels by choosing any panel other than the Layers, Effects, Graphics, and Favorites panels from the Window menu.

3 Drag the Histogram panel out of the tabbed panel group by its name tab, and then drag the Navigator panel onto the tab bar of the Histogram panel, releasing the mouse button when the Histogram's tab bar is highlighted in blue.

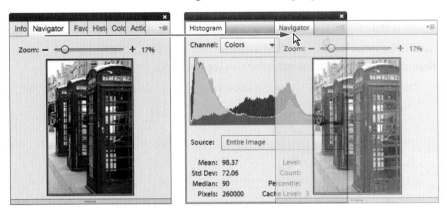

4 To close the Color Swatches panel, drag it free of the original group and click the close button (x) in its header bar (at the right on Windows, at the left for macOS), or click the small menu icon to the right of the name tab and choose Close from the Options menu. Collapse the grouped Info, Favorites, History, and Actions panels by double-clicking the name tab of any panel in the group.

5 To dock the two floating panel groups, drag the collapsed group onto the lower edge of the Histogram / Navigator group and release the mouse button when you see a blue line highlighting the connection between the two groups.
To expand the lower group, click the name tab of any of the collapsed panels.

▶ **Tip:** Single floating panels can also be grouped by docking them one above the other in this manner.

● **Note:** Photoshop Elements remembers which panels you have dismissed, and the way you've grouped those that you use most often; your arrangement will persist until you use the Reset Panels command or switch between Basic and Custom modes.

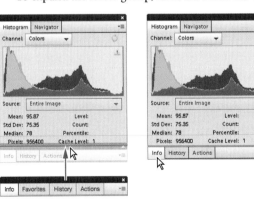
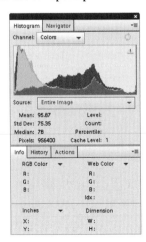

6 To separate the two tabbed panel groups again, drag the lower group away by its tab bar (not by any of the three name tabs).

Customizing the Panel Bin

If you're a dedicated user of the Expert editing mode, you may prefer to switch the workspace from Basic to Custom mode. The most important difference between the two working modes is that in Custom mode the Panel Bin can store and display more than one panel at a time—so you can dock your favorite floating panels in the Panel Bin, keeping them clear of the work area and ready at your fingertips without the need to use menu commands. You can group and arrange the panels you use most often in the Custom mode Panel Bin just as you did with floating panels in Basic mode. Panels left floating behave in the same way they do in Basic mode.

1 Click the small arrow beside the More button at the far right of the taskbar and choose Custom Workspace from the pop-up menu.

In Custom mode, the Layers, Effects, Filters, Styles, and Graphics buttons disappear from the taskbar below the Panel Bin. The panels accessed by those buttons in the Basic mode—the Layers, Effects, Filters, Styles, and Graphics panels—are now docked in the Panel Bin by default, accessible by clicking their name tabs at the top of the Panel Bin. Other panels can be opened from the Window menu or from the menu on the More button at the far right of the taskbar.

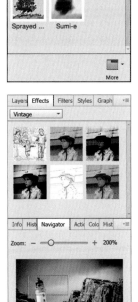

2 Click the More button at the far right of the taskbar. Drag the floating panel group to the bottom edge of whichever panel is currently foremost in the Panel Bin, and release the mouse button when you see a blue line indicating the new position.

3 Drag the Info and Color Swatches panels out of the lower panel group by their name tabs, and then close each of them by clicking the close button (x) in the header bar.

4 Choose File > Close All to close both of the open images. Bring the Editor window back to the front; then, close it by clicking the Close button (in the upper-right corner of the workspace on Windows, at the upper left on macOS).

Getting help and inspiration

Help is available in several ways, each one useful in different circumstances:

Help in the application The complete user documentation for Adobe Photoshop Elements is available from the Help menu, in the form of HTML content that displays in your default browser. This documentation provides quick access to information on using the various features in Photoshop Elements.

Depending on which module you're working in, choose Elements Organizer Help or Photoshop Elements Help from the Help menu, or simply press the F1 key.

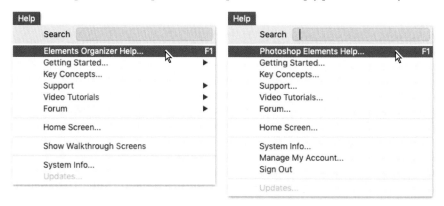

The Help menu also offers links to online community forums, video tutorials, and product support. If you're new to digital photography and image editing, choose Help > Key Concepts for explanations of basic terms and tasks, presented as an easy-to-understand visual dictionary. Click any thumbnail for an illustrated definition of a key concept and links to online Help with step-by-step instructions.

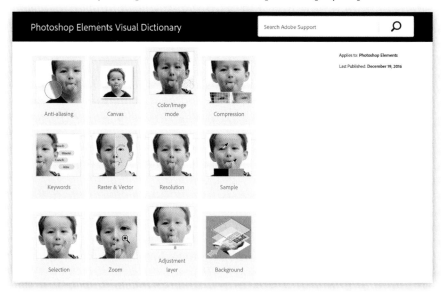

Help on the web Even without using the Help menu, you can access up-to-date documentation and community discussions via your default browser. Point your browser to https://helpx.adobe.com/elements-organizer/user-guide.html (Organizer) or https://helpx.adobe.com/support/photoshop-elements.html (Editor).

Links in the application Within the Photoshop Elements application there are links to additional help topics, such as the hot-linked tips associated with specific panels and tasks. Look for the question mark icons.

Note: Help manuals are also available as PDF documents; look for the "Help manual (PDF)" links at the bottom of the Elements Organizer Help and Photoshop Elements Help pages listed here.

Exploring the Home screen

In addition to being a launch pad for the Organizer and the Editor, the Home screen gives you access to useful and inspirational content and resources and lets you connect with the community of Photoshop Elements users.

You can switch to the Home screen at any time as you work by clicking the link in the taskbar at the bottom of the Organizer and Editor workspaces.

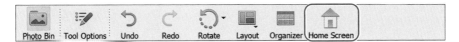

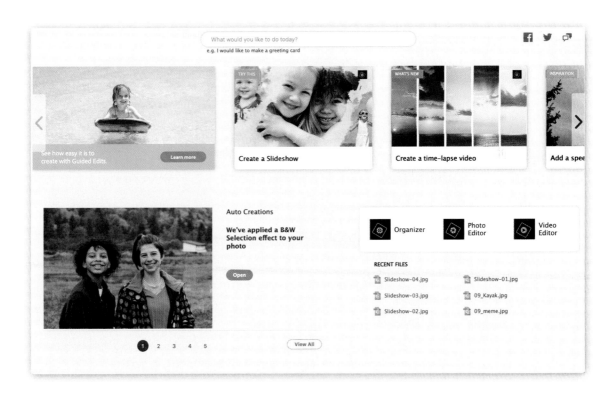

In the top row, click the button at the right side of the screen to browse available content; click any item to view tips and tutorials about features and what's new in Photoshop Elements.

The Search box draws content from Photoshop Elements Help, user community forums, online articles, and more; the Home screen makes it easy with a natural language search engine, so that you'll find the help you need even when you're unsure of the correct terminology. Try typing the word **trim** in the Search box; it offers several topics, including "Trim to a selection boundary," "Trim an image," and "Trim image Guided Edit." Choosing any of these search topics returns a choice of articles and tutorials dealing with the Crop tool and various procedures for cropping photos.

Auto Creations

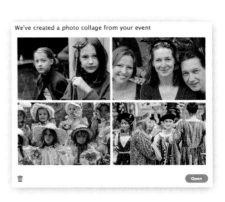

Need inspiration to get started? Photoshop Elements automatically creates collages, slideshows, stylized edits (such as the new Painterly and Depth of Field effects), and Candid Moments based on when your images and videos were captured. A group of shots taken around the same time, for instance, is likely to be an event, so Photoshop Elements assembles creations that include them.

When creations appear at the lower-left corner of the Home screen, click Open to edit one in the Organizer or the Editor. From there you can save it as a new creation or share it with others, as described in Lesson 10. Click the View All button to browse all available creations. If one doesn't interest you, click the trash icon (🗑). You may not see Auto Creations right away; as you add more media to the Organizer, it will have more material to work with while your computer is idle.

Additional resources

Adobe Photoshop Elements 2020 Classroom in a Book is not meant to replace the documentation that comes with the program, nor to be a comprehensive reference for every feature. Additional resources are listed in detail at the end of the "Getting Started" lesson in this book; please refer to these resources for comprehensive information and tutorials about program features.

You've reached the end of the first lesson. Now that you know how to import images, understand the concept of the catalog, and are familiar with the essentials of the Photoshop Elements interface, you're ready to start organizing and editing your photos in the next lessons.

Before you move on, take a few moments to read through the review questions and answers on the next page.

Review questions

1 What are the primary workspaces and working modes in Adobe Photoshop Elements?

2 What is a catalog file?

3 What are keyword tags?

4 How can you select multiple thumbnail images in the Media Browser?

Review answers

1 Photoshop Elements has two primary workspaces: the Elements Organizer and the Editor. You'll work in the Organizer to locate, import, manage, and share your photos, and use the Editor to adjust your images and to create presentations to showcase them. The Editor offers three editing modes: Quick Edit, Guided Edit, and Expert Edit. Both the Organizer and the Editor provide access to the Create and Share modes.

2 A catalog file is where Photoshop Elements stores information about your images, enabling you to conveniently manage the photos on your computer from within the Organizer. For each image you import, Photoshop Elements creates a new entry in the catalog file. Whenever you assign a tag or a rating to a photo, or group images in an album, the catalog file is updated. All your work in the Organizer is recorded in the catalog file.

   As well as digital photographs, a catalog can include video and audio files, scans, PDF documents, and any presentations and layouts you might create in Photoshop Elements, such as slideshows, photo collages, and CD jacket designs. A single catalog can efficiently handle thousands of files, but you can also create separate catalogs for different types of work.

3 Keyword tags are labels with personalized associations that you attach to photos, creations, and video or audio clips in the Media Browser so that you can easily organize and find them.

4 To select images that are in consecutive order in the Media Browser, click the first photo in the series, and then hold down the Shift key and click the last. All the photos in the range that you Shift-clicked will be selected. To select multiple non-consecutive files, hold down the Ctrl / Command key as you add files to the selection.

2 IMPORTING AND SORTING PHOTOS

Lesson overview

As your photo library grows, it becomes increasingly important that you have effective ways to organize and manage your pictures on your computer so that those valuable memories are always accessible. Adobe Photoshop Elements makes it easy to import photos from a variety of sources and provides powerful tools for organizing and searching your collection, including the People, Places, and Events views, where you can intuitively sort and search your images for the faces, locations, and happenings that mean the most to you.

This lesson will get you started with the essential skills you'll need to import images and keep track of your expanding image collection:

- Importing images from folders on your computer
- Importing photos from a digital camera
- Navigating the Media view
- Tagging faces and sorting photos in the People view
- Sorting photos by location in the Places view
- Grouping photos of special occasions in the Events view

 This lesson will take about 90 minutes to complete. To get the lesson files used in this chapter, download them from the web page for this book at www.adobepress.com/PSECIB2020. For more information, see "Accessing the lesson files and Web Edition" in the Getting Started section at the beginning of this book.

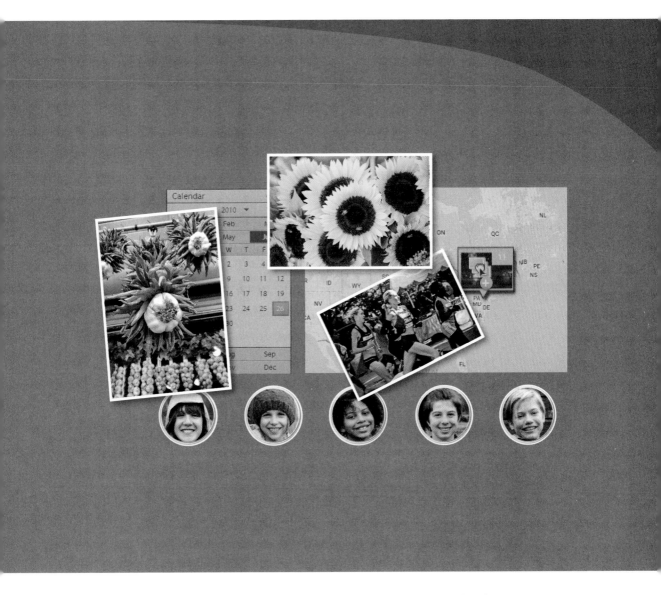

Import photos to your catalog, and then explore the People, Places, and Events views. You'll discover the many ways the Organizer can help you manage your image library so that you can always find exactly the photo you want, exactly *when* you want it—no matter how big your catalog, or across how many folders your media files are scattered.

Getting started

● **Note:** Before you start this lesson, make sure you've set up a folder for your lesson files, and downloaded the Lesson 2-3 folder from your Account page at www.peachpit.com, as detailed in "Accessing the lesson files and Web Edition" and "Creating a work folder" in the "Getting Started" section at the beginning of this book. You should also have created a new catalog (see "Creating a catalog for working with this book" in Lesson 1). You need to have completed Lesson 1 to follow the exercises in this lesson as written.

In this lesson you'll be working in the Elements Organizer, where you'll learn a variety of ways to import media into your catalog and begin to sort your image library.

1 If Photoshop Elements is still running from the previous exercise, switch to the Organizer now—if not, start Photoshop Elements, and then click the Organizer button to launch the Elements Organizer module.

2 Check the name of the current catalog, which is displayed in the lower-right corner of the Organizer workspace. On Windows, you can also see the catalog name displayed in a tooltip that appears when you hold the pointer over the Elements Organizer icon at the upper left of the Organizer window.

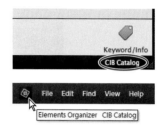

3 If the CIB Catalog that you created in Lesson 1 is not currently loaded, choose File > Manage Catalogs. Select the CIB Catalog from the list in the Catalog Manager dialog box, and then click Open.

4 If you don't see the CIB Catalog listed in the Catalog Manager, refer to the section "Creating a catalog for working with this book" in Lesson 1.

Getting photos

Before you process, print, or share your photos, the first step is to bring them into your catalog via the Elements Organizer. The Organizer provides a convenient, centralized workspace where you can browse, sort, and manage all the images in your library, no matter where the files are stored on your computer.

In the following exercises you'll import the images for this lesson into your new catalog using a variety of different methods.

Perhaps the most direct and intuitive way to bring media files into the Organizer and add them to your catalog is to use the familiar drag-and-drop technique.

Dragging photos into the Organizer

1 Use the Windows taskbar, or the macOS Dock, to switch to the Windows Explorer / macOS Finder. Open a new Explorer / Finder window. If necessary, move the Explorer / Finder window enough to see the Elements Organizer workspace behind it.

2 In the Explorer / Finder window, locate and open the PSE2020CIB / Lessons folder on your hard disk, and then open the downloaded subfolder named Lesson 2-3.

3 Inside the Lesson 2-3 folder you'll find three subfolders; drag the Import 3 subfolder onto the Media Browser pane and release the mouse button.

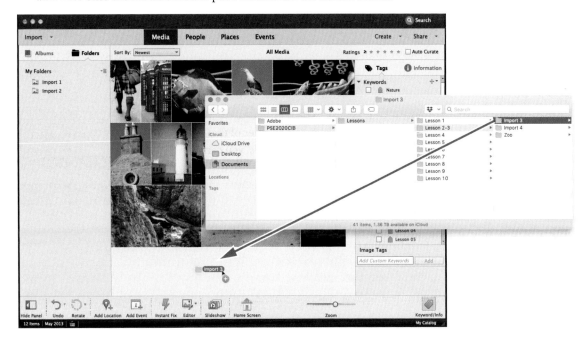

4 Click the Organizer workspace to bring it back to the front.

Photoshop Elements briefly displays a dialog box while searching inside the Import 3 folder for files to import; then, the Import Attached Keyword Tags dialog box opens.

Importing attached keyword tags

Whenever you import photos that have already been tagged with keywords, the Import Attached Keyword Tags dialog box will appear, giving you the opportunity to specify which tags you wish to import with your images.

1 In the Import Attached Keyword Tags dialog box, select the Lesson 02-03 box or click Select All; then, click OK.

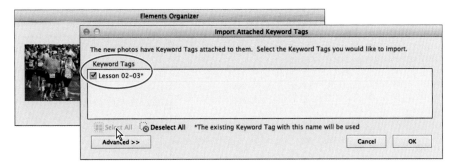

The Elements Organizer dialog box displays a progress bar as the Organizer imports the keywords. The Media Browser now shows only the newly imported images.

Tip: If you still don't see the blue badges on the thumbnails in the Media Browser after activating View > Details, use the Thumbnail Size slider above the Media Browser to increase the size of the thumbnails.

2   Make sure that the Details option is selected as activated in the View menu. Each thumbnail in the Media Browser is marked with a blue tag badge, indicating that it has keywords attached.

3   If necessary, click the Keyword / Info button at the right of the taskbar below the Media Browser to open the Tags, Information, and Image Tags panels. In the Tags panel, click the triangle beside the Imported Keyword Tags category to expand it and see the newly imported Lesson 02-03 tag nested inside, together with the keyword that you imported in the previous lesson.

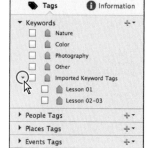

4   Click the Back button at the upper left of the Media Browser, or the Clear button at the right, to display all the media in your catalog in the Media Browser.

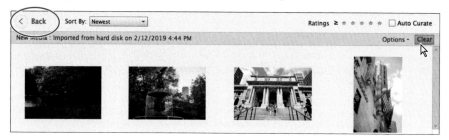

Automatically fixing red eyes during import

The term "red eye" refers to a phenomenon common in flash photography, where the retinas at the back of the subject's eyes reflect the light of the flash, so that the pupils appear red instead of black. In most cases, Photoshop Elements can fix the problem automatically during the import process, saving you the effort of further editing. This can be a substantial advantage when you're importing large numbers of images shot indoors or at night, such as photos from social occasions.

You'll import the photo for this exercise with the From Files And Folders menu command, as you did for the images in Lesson 1.

1   Click the Import button at the upper left of the Organizer workspace and choose From Files And Folders from the menu. Alternatively, choose File > Get Photos And Videos > From Files And Folders.

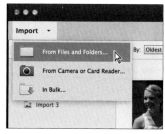

2 Navigate to and open the PSE2020CIB / Lessons / Lesson 2-3 folder. Open the subfolder Import 4; then, single-click the file Red_Eyes.jpg to select it.

3 Select the check box to activate the Automatically Fix Red Eyes option. Make sure that the Automatically Suggest Photo Stacks option is disabled; then, click Get Media.

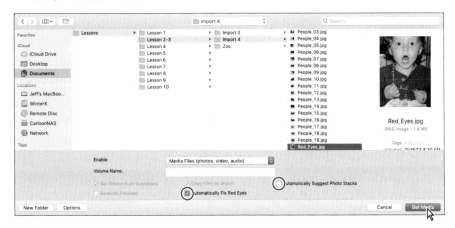

4 In the Import Attached Keyword Tags dialog box, click Select All; then, click OK.

5 The newly imported image appears in the Media Browser. If you don't see the name of the image file below the thumbnail, choose View > File Names.

The corrected photo has been stacked on top of the original in a *version set*. You can identify a version set by the badge in the upper-right corner of the thumbnail, and also by the extension to the file name, which shows that the image has been edited. You'll learn more about working with version sets in Lesson 3.

6 Click the arrow at the right of the thumbnail once to expand the version set, and then again to collapse it.

▶ **Tip:** For some images, the automatic red-eye fix may not be so effective. More tools and techniques for correcting the effect are discussed in Lesson 5.

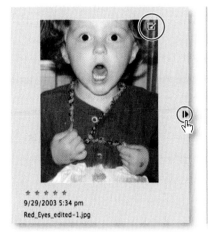

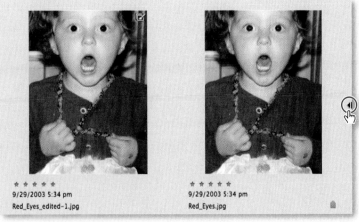

Automatic imports using watched folders

You can use watched folders to simplify and automate the process of keeping your catalog up to date. Designate any folder on your hard disk as a watched folder and Photoshop Elements will automatically be alerted when a new file is placed in—or saved to—that folder. By default, the Pictures folder is watched, but you can set up any number of additional watched folders.

You can either choose to have new files that are detected in a watched folder added to your catalog automatically, or have Photoshop Elements ask you what to do before importing the new media. If you choose the latter option, the message "New files have been found in your Watched Folders" will appear whenever new items are detected. Click Import to add the files to your catalog or click Cancel to skip them.

In this exercise you'll add a folder to the watched folders list.

1   Choose File > Watch Folders.

2   In the Watch Folders dialog, activate the Watch Folders And Their Sub-Folders For New Files option. Under Folders To Watch, click Add; then, navigate to and select your Lesson 2-3 folder and click OK.

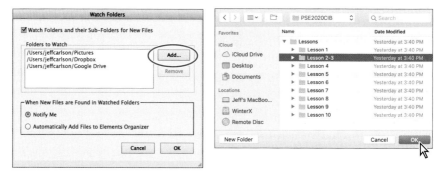

The Lesson 2-3 folder now appears in the Folders To Watch list. To stop a folder from being watched, select it in the list and then click Remove.

3   Ensure that the Notify Me option is activated, and then click OK to dismiss the Watch Folders dialog box.

Whenever a media file is placed in, or saved to, your Lesson 2-3 folder or any of its subfolders, the Watched Folders dialog will appear, giving you the opportunity to import the file or exclude it. Depending on when and how the new media is added, the notification may not appear until the next time you launch the Organizer.

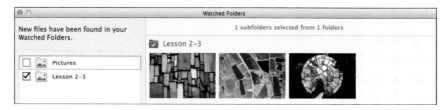

If you use online services such as Dropbox, OneDrive, or Google Drive to sync your photos from mobile devices, Elements Organizer automatically detects the cloud-based storage folders on your desktop and marks them as watched folders.

Importing images in bulk

The bulk import feature lets you browse the images in any folder on your computer, and include the files from as many folders as you wish in a single import—even though the source folders may be scattered across many locations. You can add entire folders to your bulk import, or exclude one subfolder while including another.

1 Click the Import button at the upper left and choose In Bulk from the menu. Alternatively, choose Get Photos And Videos > In Bulk from the File menu.

The Import Media dialog opens with your watched folders listed in the pane on the left. The Pictures folder is selected by default; the preview pane shows thumbnails of the images in your Pictures folder as well as those stored in the subfolders nested inside it—all selected for import.

2 Click the listing for your Lesson 2-3 folder; then, scroll the import preview pane to see the images in the subfolders that are nested inside the Lesson 2-3 folder.

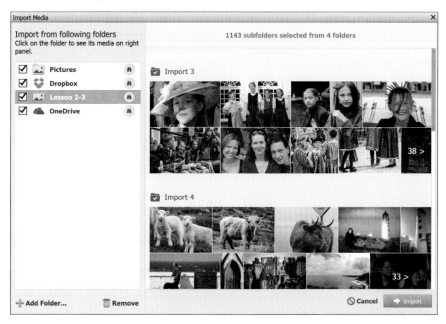

You can add folders to your bulk import by clicking the Add Folder button at the lower left. Remove a selected folder from the list by clicking the Remove button. Any new folder added to the bulk import will be marked as a watched folder by default; to disable the Watched status for a folder that's included in your bulk import, click to de-activate the adjacent Watched Folder marker ( ).

3   Click the last image in the Import 4 folder's preview selection (marked with the number) to see the rest of the images inside that folder; then, collapse the expanded subfolder by clicking Back at the upper left of the preview pane.

4   In the import preview pane, click the Import 3 subfolder to deselect it; this folder is already managed by your catalog. Leave the Import 4 folder selected, but deselect the Aquarium, Birds, Bison, Elephant, Giraffe, Monkey, and Siamang subfolders to exclude them from this import.

5   In the folders list pane at the left of the dialog, deselect your Pictures folder and any other folders to exclude their contents from this import. Check that the header above the preview pane indicates that a single subfolder is selected for import; then, click Import at the lower right.

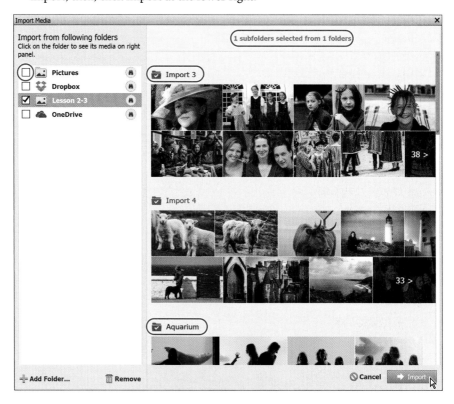

6   In the Import Attached Keyword Tags dialog box, select the check box to confirm the Lesson 02-03 tag for import, and then click OK.

7   When the import process is complete, Photoshop Elements displays a message to let you know that two of the files in the Import 4 folder (the red eyes photo and its edited copy) were already in the catalog, and were therefore not imported. Each file that was not imported is listed, together with the reason it was excluded. Click OK.

Importing from a digital camera or mobile device

If you have a digital camera, a memory card, or a mobile device at hand, you can step through this exercise using your own photos. Alternatively, you can follow the process by reading through the steps and referring to the illustrations in the book, and then return to work through this set of exercises when you are prepared.

Tip: To get the best results from this exercise, your import should include several batches of pictures taken at different times on the same day.

1 Connect your digital camera, card reader, or mobile device to your computer. If you're working on macOS, skip to step 3.

2 On Windows, the AutoPlay dialog box may appear. You could choose the option Organize And Edit Adobe Elements 18.0 Organizer (and even specify this as the default action when you connect a camera), but for the purposes of this lesson, simply click outside the dialog to dismiss it. If the Photo Downloader dialog box appears automatically, you can skip to step 4; otherwise, continue to step 3.

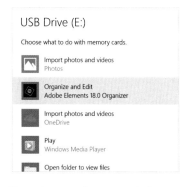

Tip: You can set AutoPlay to import to Elements Organizer by default. The AutoPlay dialog box will no longer appear when you connect your camera, but you can access the settings at any time on the Devices pane in the Windows Settings.

3 Click the Import button at the upper left of the Organizer workspace and choose From Camera Or Card Reader.

4 In the Photo Downloader dialog box, choose the name of your connected camera or mobile device from the Get Photos From menu.

5 Accept the default target folder listed beside Location, or click Browse / Choose to designate a different destination for the imported files.

6 From the Create Subfolder(s) menu, choose Today's Date (yyyy mm dd) as the folder name format; the Location path reflects your choice.

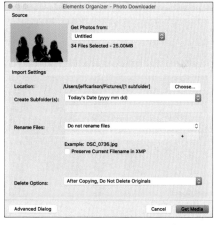

Tip: On Windows, you can activate the Automatic Download option to have the Photo Downloader download your photos automatically whenever a camera or card reader is connected to your computer, using the default settings from your Elements Organizer Preferences.

7 Make sure that the Rename Files menu is set to Do Not Rename Files, and the Delete Options menu is set to After Copying, Do Not Delete Originals. If you're working on Windows, deactivate the Automatic Download option.

8 Click Get Media.

That's all there is to it!

With these basic Photo Downloader settings, the photos will be copied from your camera to a folder named with today's date, inside your default Pictures folder. Your photos will retain their camera-generated file names.

Advanced Photo Downloader options

Note: On macOS, the Organizer properly imports the HEIC/HEVC formats captured by current iPhones and iPads. The Windows version requires that you install image extensions, found online at helpx.adobe.com/premiere-elements/using/hevc-decoding-on-windows.html. (If you try, an error message appears with that link.) If you don't want to deal with all that, you can bypass those formats: on your device, go to Settings > Camera > Format and select the Most Compatible option.

In this exercise you'll explore some advanced options for importing photos from your camera or mobile device that will help to keep your growing image library organized. You can set up your camera import so that Photoshop Elements will automatically apply tags and create groups during the import process, which means that your images will already be organized by the time they arrive in your catalog!

If you have a digital camera, a memory card, or a mobile device at hand with your own photos, you can step through this first exercise using those images; otherwise, simply read through the process and refer to the illustrations in the book, and then return to this exercise when you are prepared.

1   Repeat steps 1 through 5 from the exercise on the previous page to open the Photo Downloader, specify your camera as the import source, and accept the default destination for the downloaded files.

2   Without making any other changes to the settings, click the Advanced Dialog button in the lower-left corner of the dialog box.

In advanced mode, the Photo Downloader Dialog displays thumbnail previews of all the photos on your camera or mobile device, and also offers options for processing, tagging, and grouping your images during the import process.

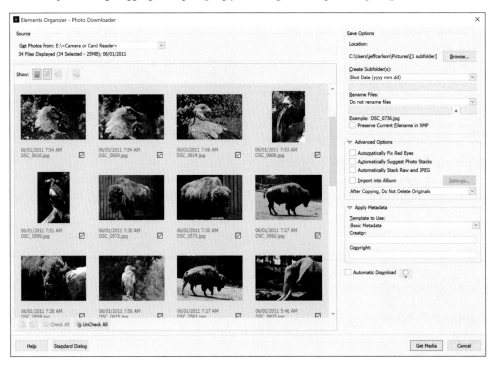

You can exclude a photo from the selection to be imported from your camera or device by clicking the check box below its thumbnail to remove the check mark.

In the next steps you'll set up the automatic creation of subfolders for files copied from your camera and apply keyword tags to the images as they are imported.

● **Note:** It may take a minute or longer for the Custom Groups (Advanced) option to appear.

3 Under Save Options, choose Custom Groups (Advanced) from the Create Subfolder(s) menu. Your selection is reflected in the Location pathname.

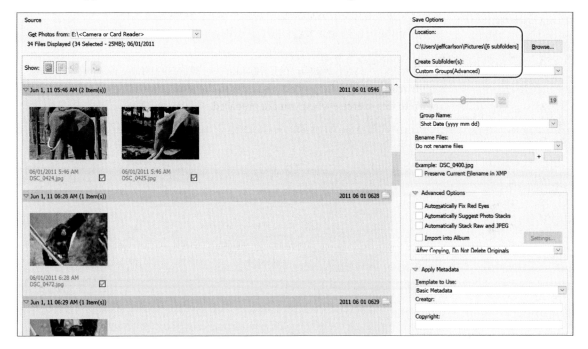

The images have been automatically divided into groups, based on capture time and date. A slider below the Create Subfolder(s) menu enables you to adjust the subdivision, and the box to the right of the slider shows the resulting number of groups. In our example, the automatic capture time grouping has produced six groups.

4 Experiment by moving the slider to the left to generate fewer groups (subfolders) or to the right to generate more. Scroll down the list of thumbnails to review the effect of the slider on the grouping of your photos. Note that the number of groups created is displayed in the box to the right of the slider.

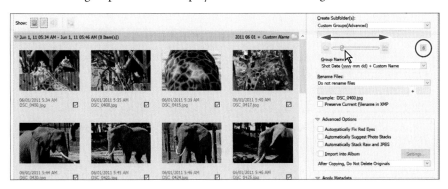

5 Next you'll specify custom names for the subfolders that will be automatically created to separate your grouped photos. From the options in the Group Name menu, choose Shot Date (yyyy mm dd) + Custom Name.

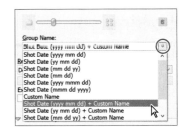

6 Click the Custom Name field at the right of the separator bar above each group in turn and type a descriptive name in the text box. In our example, we used the animal names **Giraffe**, **Elephant**, **Monkey**, and so on.

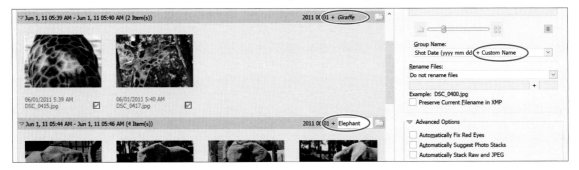

7 Under Advanced Options, activate the option Import Into Album by clicking the check box, and then click the adjacent Settings button. In the Select An Album dialog box, click the green plus sign icon, and then type a name for the new album. For now, you can click Cancel; you'll learn about creating and working with albums in Lesson 3.

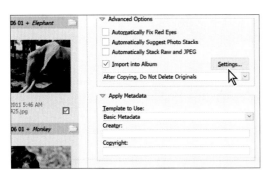
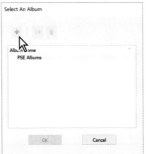
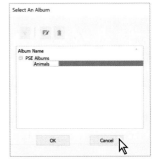

▶ **Tip:** The more you take advantage of these advanced options when importing your photos, the less time and effort you'll need to spend sorting and organizing images, and looking for the photos you want.

8 Click Get Media. The photos are copied to your hard disk, organized in subfolders named for your custom import groups. If the Files Successfully Copied dialog box appears, click Yes.

The Getting Media dialog box appears briefly while the photos are being imported into your catalog. The imported images appear in the Media Browser, and the Folders view now lists the new source subfolders, named according to the custom groups that you set up in the Photo Downloader dialog box.

Sorting your photos

When you call one of your favorite photos to mind, chances are that your first thoughts will be of the people in the picture, the location where you shot it, and the occasion that took you there. You can probably answer who, where, and when, or at least two of these questions, for the majority of your photographs. In the People, Places, and Events views in the Elements Organizer, Photoshop Elements makes it easy for you to sort, tag, and then search the photos in your library in terms of those faces, places, and happenings.

Up to this point, your time in the Organizer has been spent in the Media view, where you can review all the images in your catalog, or see the contents of a single album or folder. You'll learn more about working in the Media view in Lesson 3; for now, we'll continue our exploration of the Organizer with a look at the People view and a test-drive of Photoshop Elements' powerful face recognition tools.

Automatically finding faces for tagging

Undoubtedly, your growing photo library will include many photos of your family, friends, and colleagues. Photoshop Elements makes it quick and easy to tag the faces in your pictures with the People Recognition feature, taking most of the work out of sorting and organizing a large portion of your catalog. People Recognition automatically finds the people in your photos and makes it simple for you to tag them. Once you begin using the feature, Photoshop Elements learns to recognize the people you've already named and will automatically tag their faces whenever they appear in new photos.

Setting up People Recognition

The People Recognition feature, and also the automatic face tagging prompts that it generates, can be disabled. Before continuing with the exercises, you need to make sure that both are activated.

1   In the Organizer, choose Edit > Preferences > Media-Analysis (Windows) or Elements Organizer > Preferences (macOS).

2   In the Media-Analysis pane of the Preferences dialog box, make sure that the Run Face Recognition Automatically and Show Smart Tags And Auto Curate options are both activated. Click OK to save your settings and close the Preferences dialog box.

3   In the View menu, make sure the People Recognition option is activated.

4   For the purposes of the following exercises, make sure that the Sort By menu at the left of the bar above the Media Browser is set to Oldest. If necessary, click the adjacent Back, or All Media, button to return to the unfiltered Media view.

Tagging faces in the Media Browser

Your first experience of People Recognition will probably be the circular Add Name prompt that appears as you move the pointer over a photo in the enlarged single image view in the Media Browser.

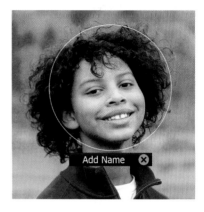

People Recognition displays these hints to help you identify and tag all the people in your photos. You can ignore or disable the hints if you wish, but remember that the more people you identify, the smarter People Recognition gets at tagging the faces of your friends and family automatically.

Note: Once People Recognition begins to recognize a particular face, the Add Name prompt changes to read "Is this *[name]*?" giving you the opportunity to confirm or cancel automatic tagging.

1 In the Folders list at the left of the Organizer workspace, click the Import 4 folder. The Media Browser is filtered to display only the contents of that folder.

2 Scroll down in the Media Browser—or reduce the size of the thumbnails using the Zoom slider in the taskbar—to locate the image People_03.jpg; then, double-click the thumbnail to see the photo enlarged in the single image view.

3 Move the pointer slowly over each of the faces in the image; white circles with the Add Name prompt appear around four of the five faces in this picture. People Recognition has failed to detect the face partially obscured by a hand.

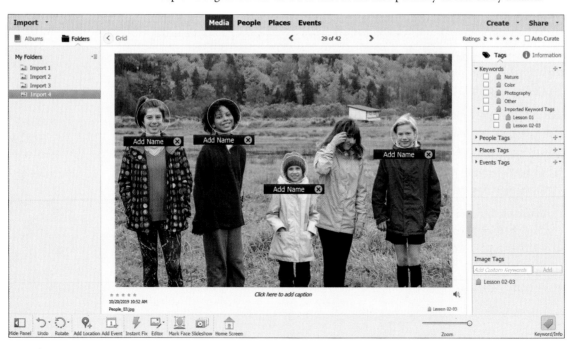

If you don't see the face tagging prompts when you move the pointer over the photo in single image view, it may be that Photoshop Elements has not yet finished analyzing your recently imported photos.

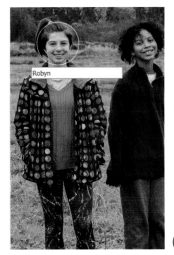 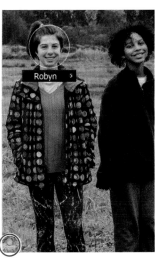

4   Click the Add Name text below the tagging circle for the girl on the left. Type the name **Robyn**, and then press Enter / Return to commit the tag.

When you press Enter / Return, a blue People tag badge appears briefly in the lower-left corner of the enlarged photo in the single image view, confirming that a new tag has been created for Robyn.

5   Type **Rhys** to tag the boy next to Robyn, **Penny** for the girl beside him, and **Simone** for the girl at the far right. Be sure to press Enter / Return to commit each tag.

6   If necessary, click the Tags/Info button at the far right of the taskbar to open the right panel group. On the Tags tab, expand the People Tags panel.

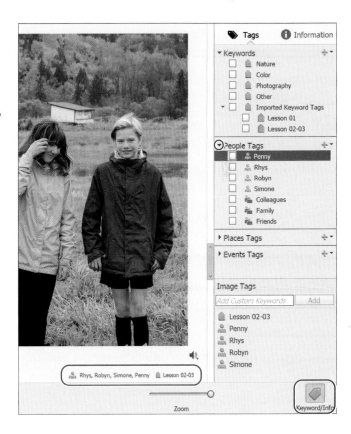

The Image Tags panel at the bottom of the right panel group shows that this photo now has five tags: the imported keyword tag Lesson 02-03, and the four new *people tags* that you created in this exercise.

These five tags are also listed at the lower right of the single image view.

As you can see, the people tags display a different badge from the standard keyword tag icon. This makes the photos that are already tagged for people easy to spot in the thumbnail grid.

7   Keep the photo open in single image view for the next exercise.

Tagging undetected faces

The People Recognition analysis occasionally misses faces that are partially obscured, "broken up" by harsh light and shadow, or photographed at an angle or in profile. You can tag undetected people manually in the single image view.

1 Click the Mark Face button in the taskbar below the enlarged image.

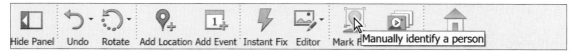

2 Drag the new tagging box onto the face that was not detected. Use the handles on the box to resize it so that it frames the face neatly, and then click the green check mark to confirm the placement. Click the Add Name text and type **Fiona** in the text box; then, press Enter / Return to confirm the new people tag.

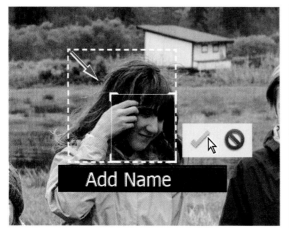
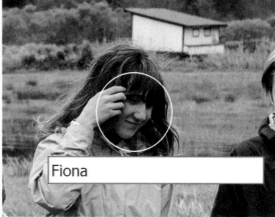

In the right panel, the Fiona tag has been added to the People Tags list, and is now listed in the Image Tags panel as one of six tags attached to this image.

● **Note:** Depending on your operating system and how much experimenting you've been doing, the results you see from People Recognition may not be exactly the same as those referred to and illustrated in these exercises; for example, in step 4, you may see an "Is This 'Penny'?" hint in place of the Add Name prompt.

3 Press the right arrow key on your keyboard once to navigate to the photo of the two sisters.

4 Move the pointer over the taller girl's face and click the Add Name prompt; then, type the letter **F**. A menu appears, suggesting the Fiona tag—the only people tag in your catalog that begins with an "F." Click the Fiona tag to accept it; then, press Enter / Return.

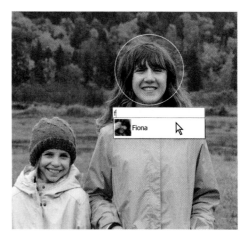

5   Press the right arrow key on your keyboard five times to navigate to the image People_09.jpg, a photo of the gang in front of a weathered wooden wall. Move the pointer over each kid's face in turn to see the tagging prompts.

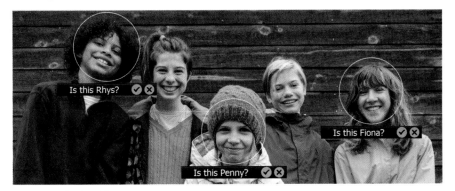

● **Note:** Remember that the People Recognition tagging suggestions may not be exactly the same as those illustrated; however, this should not affect your ability to follow the workflow.

Although you've done very little tagging at this point, People Recognition is already learning, correctly identifying two of the three faces in our example.

6   Click to confirm or dismiss the tagging suggestions (from the left, the kids are Rhys, Robyn, Penny, Simone, and Fiona). If People Recognition does not suggest the right name, click the Add Name prompt and type the first letter of the kid's name; then, click the existing people tag to accept it and press Enter / Return.

7   Double-click the image, or click Grid in the bar above the single image view, to return the Media Browser to the thumbnail view, which is still filtered to display only the photos in the Import 4 folder.

● **Note:** Even faces that are not obscured are sometimes missed. View the image People_02.jpg and identify Robyn (left) and Simone (right), if they weren't already recognized.

Welcome to the People view

Now that you've tagged a few faces in the Media Browser, let's take a look at the People view, where your library is sorted by personnel, making it easy to answer the first question you're likely to ask about the photo you're looking for: who?

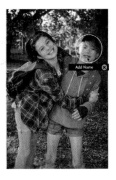

In the People view, you can let People Recognition help you bulk-process your files, rather than working through your catalog one image at a time as we did in the single image view. To keep this exercise manageable, you'll start by tagging the people in just a subset of the photos in your catalog; that way, we can avoid dealing with the faces of hundreds of marathon runners.

1   Click All Media at the left of the bar above the thumbnail grid to display all of the files in your catalog.

The Import 4 folder is no longer selected in the Folders list. The Media Browser now displays all of the photographs in your catalog; the file count in the lower-left corner of the workspace shows the total number of images in your CIB Catalog.

The file names of the photos you'll use in this exercise all include the word "people." You can start by using a filename search to isolate these images in the media Browser, and then group them as an album that you can designate as an image source while you're working in the People view.

2   Choose Find > By Filename. Type **people**; then, click OK. The search results bar immediately above the Media Browser shows that your catalog has been filtered so that you see only those items that match your filename search.

3   Choose Edit > Select All to select all the images returned by the text search; then, select the Albums tab at the top of the left panel. Click the Create New Album or Album Category button (➕) beside the My Albums header. Make sure you click the green plus sign, not the small arrow beside it.

4   In the New Album panel at the right of the workspace, type **Familiar Faces** as the name for the new album; then, click OK in the taskbar below the panel.

Navigating the People view

1   Select the Familiar Faces album in the My Albums list; then click the word People in the view picker at the top of the Organizer workspace. In the People view, make sure that you're looking at the Named tab.

Each stack in the Named people view shows a count of the photos already tagged with that person's name. A triangular notification badge (⚠) indicates that People Recognition has already found more faces that may belong in the same stack.

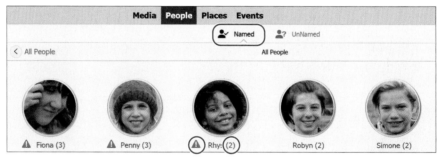

The People view displays a stack of photos for each person you've tagged. By default, the first image tagged with a new people tag becomes that person's profile picture—the photo that appears on top of their stack in the People view.

2   Move the pointer slowly across each stack thumbnail in turn to browse through all the images tagged with the same name.

3   Click the thumbnail for the Fiona stack to expand it and see the faces that are already marked with Fiona's people tag, as well as People Recognition's suggestions for inclusion in the stack. Leave the groups as they are, for the moment.

4   Click the Fiona stack again to collapse it.

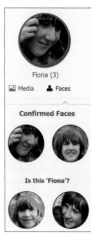

5 Click Unnamed in the bar below the mode picker to switch to the Unnamed people tab.

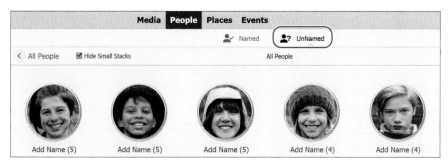

With such a small selection of photos to analyze, People Recognition shows only two or three unnamed stacks (if any at all). By default, Photoshop Elements displays only the larger groups of faces stacked by People Recognition, in order to keep the Unnamed people view uncluttered.

6 Deselect the Hide Small Stacks option in the bar above the stack thumbnails.

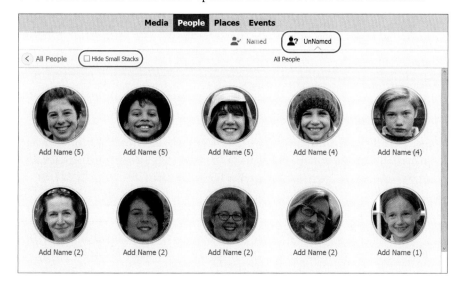

● **Note:** Depending on your operating system and how much experimenting you've been doing, the results you see from People Recognition may not be exactly the same as those referred to and illustrated in these exercises; the stacked groups and the order of the faces presented may vary, but the overall process will be the same.

Each stack in the Unnamed people view shows a count of the faces that People Recognition has judged to be similar but cannot name. Move the pointer across a stack thumbnail to quickly browse through all the images in the group.

Tagging faces in the People view

We'll start by looking at the stacking suggestions made by People Recognition in the Named people view.

1 Click Named in the bar below the mode picker to switch back to the Named people view. Click the Fiona stack to expand it again.

2   To confirm or dismiss a face, select it and click either Confirm or Not This Person in the taskbar, or hover the pointer over the suggested face to see a preview of the photo it was found in (below, right); then, click the confirm or cancel icon on the tagging thumbnail.

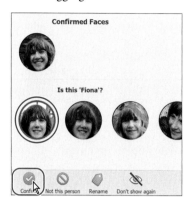 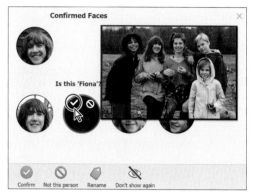

3   Click the Penny stack. Dismiss any incorrect suggestions. Shift-click the first and last thumbnails to select all the correct suggestions; then, click the Confirm button in the taskbar. Click the profile thumbnail again to collapse the stack.

4   Repeat the process for the Rhys, Robyn, and Simone stacks, confirming or dismissing the suggested additions to stacks. The Fiona, Penny, and Rhys stacks originally showed notification badges indicating that similar images had been identified; you may now find only confirmed photos. People Recognition has been learning from your actions and reanalyzing accordingly.

5   Switch back to the Unnamed people view. Click the stack with the bearded man to expand it. In our example, all of the faces in the stack belong together; click the Add Name text and type **Jeff**; then, press Enter / Return.

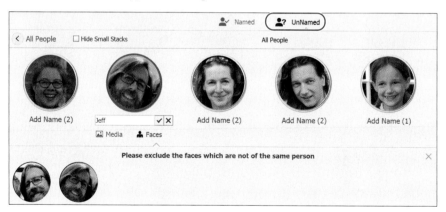

Once a stack is named, it disappears from the Unnamed people view and is added to the Named people stacks. If there is already a named stack for the same person, the two stacks are merged.

6   When you see multiple unnamed stacks for the same person, Ctrl-click / Command-click to select the matching stacks, and then click the Merge People button in the taskbar. Type the person's name (in our example it's **Tom**) in the Add A Name dialog; then, click OK.

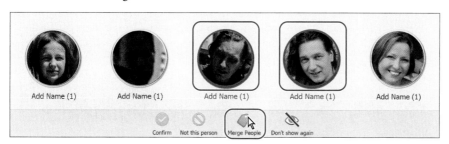

7   Select the stack with the photo of the woman with glasses. Click the Add Name text and type **Kim**; then, press Enter / Return.

8   Select all the remaining stacks and click the Don't Show Again button in the taskbar. Click OK to confirm the removal of these faces.

▶ **Tip:** If you see a blue, triangular alert badge beside a stack, click the stack to see the new faces that have been found; then, confirm or dismiss the tagging suggestions.

9   Switch back to the Named view and click each stack to check for faces that don't match. If you dismiss any faces, you'll need to revisit the Unnamed view to name them.

10 Click one of the larger stacks in the Named view to expand it. Click Media below the stack thumbnail to see the full photos rather than just the faces.

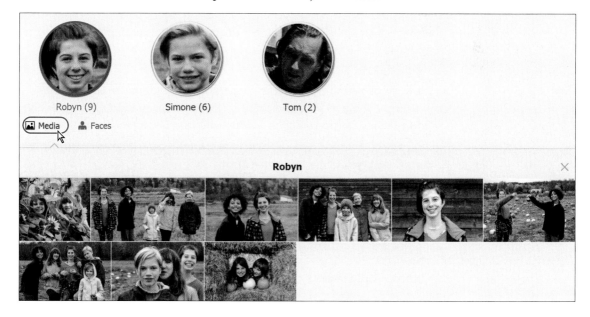

Working with people groups

You can make your people tagging more versatile by grouping your tags. You might find photos of the same person by looking in their personal stack, by filtering your Friends group, or by searching a group created for your basketball team.

1 If you don't see the Groups panel at the right of the workspace, click the Groups button (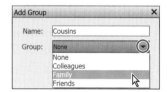) in the taskbar. Click the Ungrouped listing in the Groups panel. The header above the People stacks indicates that all the people are ungrouped.

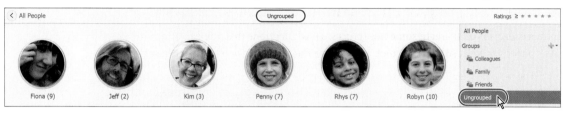

2 Shift-click to select everyone's stack except Tom's (sorry, Tom), and then drag them to the Family group in the Groups panel. Click the Family listing; the header above the People stacks shows that all seven people are now listed in that group.

3 Click the green Create New People Groups button (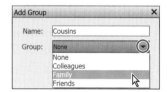)—not the arrow beside it—in the header of the Groups panel. In the Add Group dialog, type **Cousins** to name the group. Choose Family from the Group menu; then, click OK.

4 Select the stacks for the five kids, and drag them to the new Cousins group. In the Groups panel, click between the listings for the Cousins and Family groups.

5 Right-click the Cousins group in the Groups list, and choose Add Group from the menu. Name the new group **Sisters**. "Cousins" is already selected as the group inside which the new group will be listed. Click OK.

6 Select the Fiona and Penny stacks. Drag the Sisters tag from the Groups panel onto either of the selected stacks. Click between the Family, Cousins, and Sisters listings; the People view is filtered to show the members of each group.

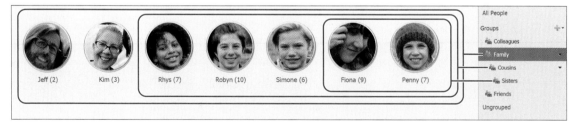

7 Click the word Media in the view picker at the top of the workspace to return to the Media Browser; then, click All Media at the upper left of the thumbnail grid. You'll learn more about the People view in Lesson 3.

Sorting photos by location

Think of that favorite photo again. You've answered "who?"—now, let's ask "where?" Photoshop Elements lets you organize your world in the Organizer's Places view, where you can put your photographs on the map (quite literally!), making it fun to follow the trail of a family road trip or revisit memories of an exotic vacation.

Adding places tags to photos from the Media view

In this exercise you'll create some new *places*: saved locations that you can attach to your photos as tags, so that it's quick and easy to find that shot you took … where?

1   Choose Find > By Filename. Type **run**; then, click OK. The search results bar immediately above the Media Browser shows that your catalog has been filtered so that you see only those items that match your filename search. Make sure the Sort By menu above the thumbnail grid is set to Oldest.

2   Shift-click, or drag a selection marquee, to select the first six photos in the Media Browser; then, click the Add Location button ( ) in the taskbar below the Media Browser.

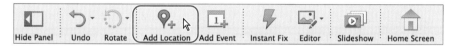

3   In the Add A Location dialog, type **New York** in the text box. If the location suggestions menu does not appear quickly, press Enter / Return. Click the suggestion New York City, New York, United States of America; then, click Apply to create the new saved location. When more than one location suggestion is offered, always choose the suggestion with the most detailed location information so that Photoshop Elements can reference it for tagging.

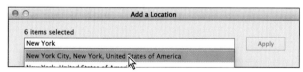

In the Media Browser, the selected photos are now marked with map pin Places badges. Click the Keyword/Info button at the right of the taskbar, if necessary, to open the right panel group. In the Tags panel, Expand the Places Tags category to see the nested listings for your new places tags.

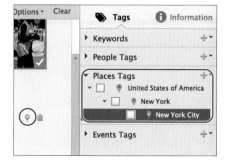

Note: In the Tags panel, the New York City places tag is colored differently from the United States tag; this indicates that it's the only tag with GPS data and a marker pin on the Places view map.

Adding photos to a saved location from the Media view

You can use the places tags in the Tags panel to search your photos, and also to quickly add more images to a group that you've already placed on the map.

1 In the Media Browser, select the next five photos from the "run" search.

2 Drag the United States of America tag from the Places Tags list to any of the selected photos. Alternatively, you could drag the photos onto the tag.

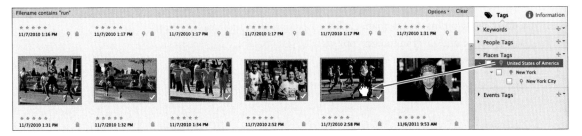

3 Hover over the places tag badge on any of the selected photos; a tooltip lists the United States of America tag; to remove it from all the selected photos, right-click the badge and choose Remove From United States of America Place.

4 With the five photos still selected, drag the New York City tag from the Places Tags list to any of the selected photos. Hold the pointer over the places tag badge; the tooltip shows that applying the New York City tag has automatically added all three tags in the hierarchy.

5 Click All Media at the left of the bar above the thumbnails to show all of the photos in your catalog in the Media Browser.

A short trip to the Places view

Just as the People view has Named and Unnamed tabs, the Places view has Pinned and Unpinned modes. The Pinned tab displays only the images in your catalog that have location data; the Unpinned view gives you access to those you've yet to place.

Now that you've added some places tags, you can begin to explore the Places view without finding either tab unpopulated.

1 Click the word Places in the view picker at the top of the workspace.

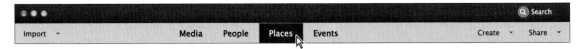

The arrangement of the Places view workspace depends on the way it was left the last time you visited. Follow the directions in the following steps to set up the work-space to match what's described and illustrated in this exercise.

2 In the Places view, click Unpinned in the bar below the view picker. Disable the Group By Time option at the left of the bar above the photo thumbnails. Use the Zoom slider in the taskbar to reduce the size of the thumbnails so that you can see as many images as possible.

3 If the Map panel appears significantly narrower in relation to the rest of the workspace than it is in the illustration below, move the pointer over the left edge of the panel; then, when the pointer changes to a double-arrow cursor, drag the edge of the map to the left to make it wider.

4 If you don't see two pins on the map, click the Minus sign icon in the corner of the map to zoom out, or drag to pan your view. If you still don't see the pins, activate the Show Existing Pins On The Map option.

● **Note:** For the sake of visual clarity, the Places view illustrations in this book show the map set to the Streets style, which looks like a road map. Use the menu at the upper left of the map to choose your preferred style.

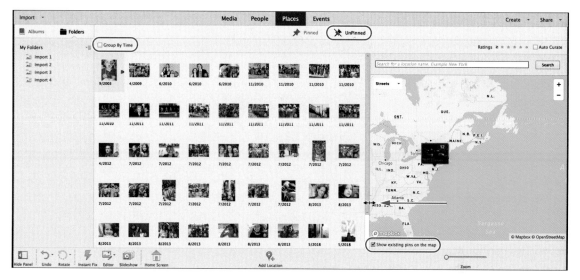

The image counts on the map pins show that there are 12 photos placed at New York and another 31 images attached to a pin located in Scotland.

5 Move the pointer over the Scottish pin, and then click the arrows at either side of the thumbnail image to see previews of all the photos pinned at that location.

6 Click the image count at the lower right of the preview to close the map temporarily and show the thumbnail grid, with all the images attached to the pin. Click Back at the upper left above the thumbnail grid to return to the split-screen Places view.

▶ **Tip:** If ever the map doesn't jump when you tell it to, or a pin seems to get lost in the move, choose View > Refresh.

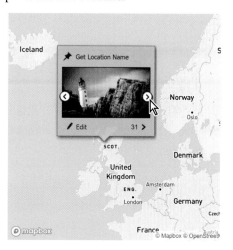

Adding photos to a saved location from the Places view

You can use the places tags in the Tags panel to search your photos, and also to quickly add more images to a group that you've already placed on the map.

Tip: You can drag photos directly onto the map from the preview pane, in either Timeline or Grid mode, even without an existing pin; however, this method may not generate a places tag in the Tags panel unless you edit the location information for the resultant pin.

1 Activate the Group By Time option at the left of the bar above the thumbnail grid. Drag the Number Of Groups slider to the maximum setting.

2 Scroll down in the preview pane until you find the November 6, 2011 group. These are the unpinned images from our "run" text search.

3 Click the check mark at the left of the group name to select all eight photos. You could click the Add Location button and do a text search for New York, as you did in the Media view, but as you already have a pin in the right place, simply drag the selected images to the New York City pin.

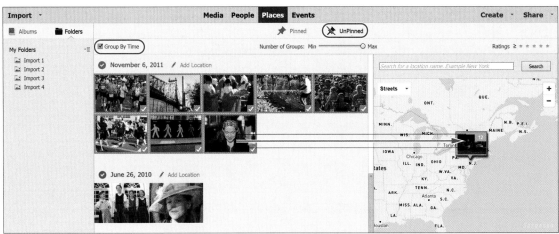

The image count on the New York City pin increases to 20, indicating that the last of our marathon photos were successfully placed. As the November 6, 2011 images are now pinned, they have been removed from the UnPinned Places preview pane.

4 Click Pinned in the bar below the view picker. Move the pointer over the New York pin to enlarge it; then click the Edit button at the lower left of the pin preview. In the Edit Location dialog, zoom in to the map, if necessary, and then drag the pin to position it on Central Park. Click the green check mark to confirm the move. If necessary, click No to dismiss the Add A Sub-location dialog; then, click Done to dismiss the Edit Location dialog.

5 Move the pointer over the New York City pin, and then click the image count at the lower right of the preview to close the map temporarily and show the thumbnail grid, with all the images that are attached to that pin.

6 Click Back at the upper left of the grid to return to the map view, then switch back to the UnPinned view in readiness for the next exercise.

Generating places tags for photos with GPS data

Places tags are created automatically for photos placed on the map using the Add Location command, as you did for the New York photos. However, when you import photos with embedded GPS coordinates—like our Pacific Northwest images—Photoshop Elements shows them on the map but does not generate searchable places tags. If you wish to generate tags for photos like these, you need to edit their location.

1   Use the map's zoom button (+) to zoom in on the Washington location until the marker splits to show two separate pins. Click the eastern pin to select the 16 photos attached to that location on the map; then, click the Edit button at the lower left of the enlarged pin preview.

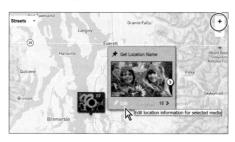

2   In the Edit Location dialog, type **Carnation** in the Search box above the map pane and click Search. Click the location suggestion **Carnation, Washington, United States of America**; then, click the green check icon to confirm the placement of 16 photos at that location. Click Done to close the Edit Location dialog.

3   If necessary, zoom out far enough to see the other pinned location to the west.

4   Zoom in to the other pin with nine or ten clicks on the map zoom control (+). Move the pointer over the pin; then click the Edit button. In the Edit Location dialog, drag the location pin north and west to position it over the Pike Place Market Area. Click the green check icon to confirm the operation. Click Done to close the Edit Location dialog.

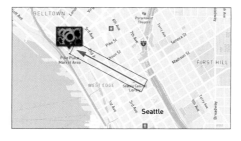

5   Zoom out enough to see both pins; then, leave the map as it is, in preparation for the next exercise that will bring you to the Places view, in Lesson 3. Click Media in the view picker to return to the Media Browser.

In the Tags panel, the new tags are listed under Places Tags. Each level is listed alphabetically, so New York appears above Washington and Carnation above Seattle.

6   Right-click the tag Downtown and choose Rename. Type **Pike Place Market** as the new name for this places tag; then, click OK.

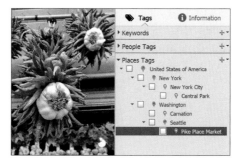

Grouping photos as events

When was your favorite photo taken? Was it at an anniversary dinner? Before your daughter's school concert? Or during a week-long tropical cruise? The enhanced Events view in Elements Organizer helps you tag your photos by occasion, making it even simpler to search your image library for all those precious memories.

Creating events from the Media Browser

You can select the images from a particular occasion in the thumbnail grid, and then create a new event to group them, without leaving the Media Browser.

▶ **Tip:** If you don't see the capture dates and file names below the thumbnails, choose View > Details, and then View > File Names. If those options are already activated, use the slider to increase the thumbnail size.

1 Choose Find > By Filename. Type **festival**; then, click OK. Make sure that the Sort By menu above the thumbnail grid is set to Oldest. The Media Browser shows 15 photos that were all captured on the same date. Select the first five photos in the series and click the Add Event button ( ) in the taskbar below the Media Browser.

2 In the Add New Event panel at the right type **Medieval Fair** to name the new event. You won't need to alter the date settings; Photoshop Elements has automatically set both the start and end dates to the capture date of the selected photos. When you click the Add Event button without first selecting a group of photos, you can set the start and end dates manually by clicking the calendar buttons at the right. Click Done at the right of the taskbar to confirm the new event.

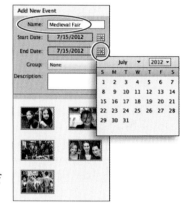

3 In the Tags panel, expand the Events Tags category to see the new event.

4 Select the next nine photos in the Media Browser, leaving the last image in the series, Festival_15.jpg, unselected. To add the selected photos to the newly created event, either drag the Medieval Fair tag from the Tags panel to any of the selected images or drag the selection from the thumbnail grid onto the tag.

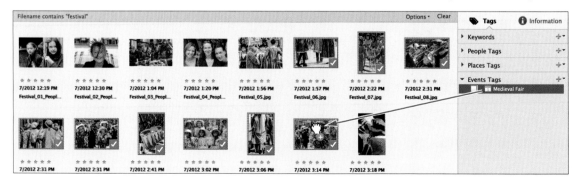

An invitation to the Events view

Do you like weddings? Sporting events? Street festivals? Road trip vacations? We've got them all … what are you waiting for?

1   Click Events in the view picker at the top of the Organizer workspace to switch to the Events view. If necessary, click Named in the bar below the view picker to switch to the default Named events view. This view mode remains unpopulated until you've saved at least one event—currently, its only occupant is your new Medieval Fair stack.

Right now, you're probably thinking "Where's the promised sports and scenic views? Bring on the travel!" Patience, *please*—we're not yet done with the parade.

2   Move the pointer slowly across the Medieval Fair stack to see all the images from this event. Stop the pointer when you see your favorite image in the set. To make this photo the top image in the stack—the cover photo—right-click it and choose Set As Cover.

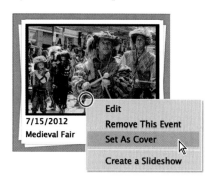

Adding photos to an event

1   Double-click the Medieval Fair event stack to see all of the photos it contains, and then click the Add Media button (⌨️) in the taskbar at the bottom of the workspace.

2   Under Basic at the left of the Add Media dialog box, make sure that All Media is set as the image source. The source images in the Add Media dialog box are ordered from newest to oldest, so you'll need to scroll down in the preview pane to find the festival photos.

3   Click to select the image Festival_15.jpg, a rear view of a parade musician in an orange jacket and plumed hat. Click Add Selected Media at the bottom of the dialog box; then, click Done.

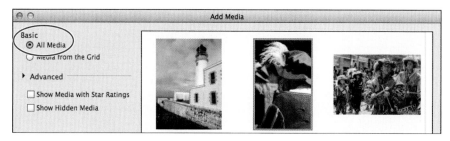

4 Check the image count in the lower-left corner of the workspace; there are now fifteen images in this Event. Collapse the event and return to the Named events view by clicking Back at the upper left.

Getting smart about creating events

You can avoid the effort of locating the images for a new event manually by letting Photoshop elements find the important occasions in your catalog automatically.

1 Select the Import 3 folder from the My Folders list in the left panel; then, click Suggested in the actions bar below the view picker to switch from the default Named events view to Suggested events mode.

2 Drag the Number Of Groups slider to the maximum setting.

In Suggested events mode, Photoshop Elements detects likely event groups amongst the photos in your catalog—or in a selected folder—on the basis of capture dates. Suggested events has separated the New York marathon photos into two stacks.

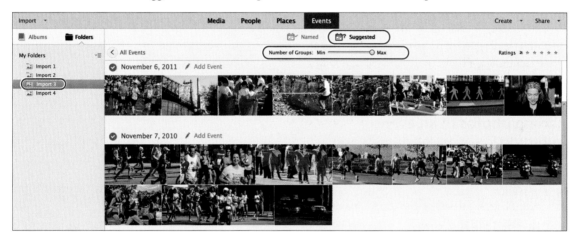

3 Click Add Event at the right of the header of each of these stacks in turn and type a name in the Name Event dialog box. Check the dates on the two stacks and name the new Events **NY Marathon 2010** and **NY Marathon 2011**. Click OK to create the new event stack.

4 The October 20, 2019 suggested stack has three photos shot during a visit to a pumpkin patch in Carnation, Washington. Make sure no other stack is selected; then, select this stack and click the Add Event button ( ) in the taskbar. Name the new Event **Pumpkins 2019**. Click OK.

5 Click the Import 4 folder in the left panel and reset the Number Of Groups slider to the maximum setting. The October 20, 2019 stack contains the rest of the photos that belong in the Pumpkins 2019 event. Select the stack and click Media in the view picker at the top of the workspace to switch to the Media view.

6   Drag the selected photos to the Pumpkins 2019 tag in the Events Tags panel; then, click All Media above the Media Browser and click Events in the view picker to return to the Events view in Suggested events mode.

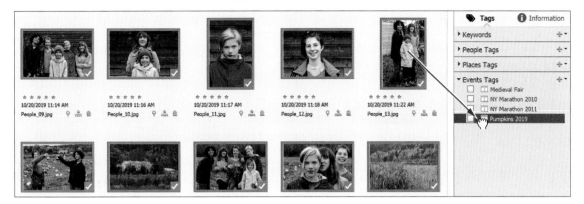

Creating long events

You can define events that span multiple days just as easily as one-time events.

1   Return to the Events view and, if necessary, click the All Events button and reset the Number Of Groups slider to the maximum setting. Then, find the Suggested event group dated July 25–24 2018.

2   Select the group, and then click Add Event to the right of the header. In the Name Event dialog box, type **Downtown Seattle Walks** to name the new event. Photoshop Elements has already set the start and end dates for the Suggested event to the capture dates of the oldest and most recent photos in the selection. Type **Pike Place and waterfront** in the Description box; then, click OK to create the event.

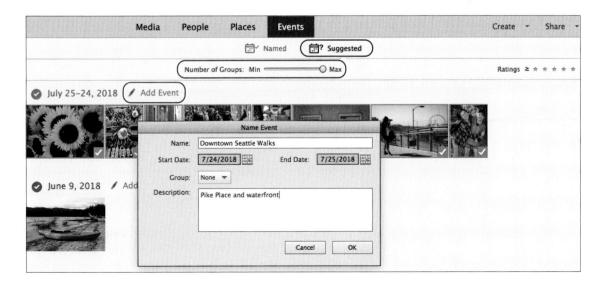

Note: You'll return to look at the Smart events mode in greater detail in Lesson 3.

3 Switch from Suggested events mode to the Named events view.

4 Move the pointer slowly across each stack to review the contents, and then right click each event to set a new cover photo. Click the Info button ((*i*)) on the Downtown Seattle Walks stack to see the description you entered.

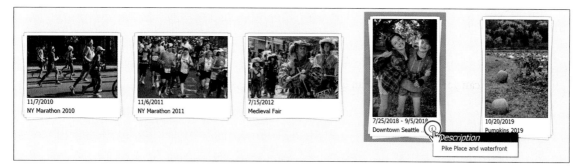

11/7/2010
NY Marathon 2010

11/6/2011
NY Marathon 2011

7/15/2012
Medieval Fair

7/25/2018 - 9/5/2018
Downtown Seattle

10/20/2019
Pumpkins 2019

Description
Pike Place and waterfront

5 Click Media in the view picker to switch back to the Media Browser.

Congratulations! In this lesson you learned a variety of ways to import media files into your Photoshop Elements catalog, and then used the People, Places, and Events views to sort and tag your images so that finding a photo will be as easy as asking "Who, where, and when?" In the next lesson you'll look at ways to add even deeper levels of organization to your catalog and discover how to locate exactly the file you want—the payoff for all this organizing! Before you move on, take a minute or two to read through the review questions and answers on the opposite page.

Review questions

1 Name three ways to import photos from your computer hard disk into your catalog.

2 What is a "watched folder"?

3 Is there a way to generate searchable places tags for photos imported with GPS data?

4 How can you add photos to an existing person, place, or event?

Review answers

1 This lesson demonstrated three ways to import photos from your hard disk:

- Drag and drop photographs from a Windows Explorer/Finder window into the Media Browser pane in the Organizer window.

- In the Organizer, choose File > Get Photos And Videos > From Files And Folders, or choose the same command from the menu on the Import button at the upper left of the workspace.

- Choose In Bulk, from either of the menus mentioned above, and then select the folders and subfolders on the hard disk that you wish to import.

2 If you designate a folder on your computer as watched, Photoshop Elements is automatically alerted when new photos are saved or added to that folder. By default, the Pictures folder is watched.

3 Although Photoshop Elements will pin photos imported with embedded GPS data on the Places view map, it doesn't automatically generate corresponding places tags, as it does for photos that you place manually. To generate searchable tags for these photos, you need to relocate them on the map. Select the photos in the Places view; then, click Edit in the enlarged pin preview. In the Edit Location dialog, either move the associated location pin slightly or use the search box to apply a known place name.

4 To add photos to an existing person, place, or event from the Organizer, select the photos you wish to include, and then either drag the selection from the Media Browser to the desired tag in the Tags panel, or drag the tag itself to any of the selected images. To add photos to an established event from the Events view, double-click the event stack to expand it; then, click the Add Media button in the taskbar at the bottom of the workspace, and browse for the photos you wish to add. In the People view, double-click to expand a person's stack, and then click the Find More button in the taskbar.

3 TAGGING, GROUPING, AND SEARCHING PHOTOS

Lesson overview

As your image collection grows larger and larger, keeping track of your photos can be a daunting task. Photoshop Elements delivers sophisticated, intuitive organizing tools that make the job enjoyable. When the time comes to search and filter your photo library for that special shot that you *know* is in your catalog *somewhere*, the same sophisticated, intuitive tools will make it just as much fun to find it.

In this lesson, you'll learn a few more techniques for sorting and grouping your photos, and a variety of ways to search your catalog:

- Using ratings to classify images by quality or usefulness
- Working with keyword tags and categories
- Using version sets and stacks to organize the thumbnail grid
- Grouping photos in albums
- Searching for people, places, and events
- Managing files in the My Folder list
- Filtering by date or import batch with the Timeline
- Finding photos by similarity, metadata, and text search

 This lesson will take about 90 minutes to complete. To get the lesson files used in this chapter, download them from the web page for this book at www.adobepress.com/PSECIB2020. For more information, see "Accessing the lesson files and Web Edition" in the Getting Started section at the beginning of this book.

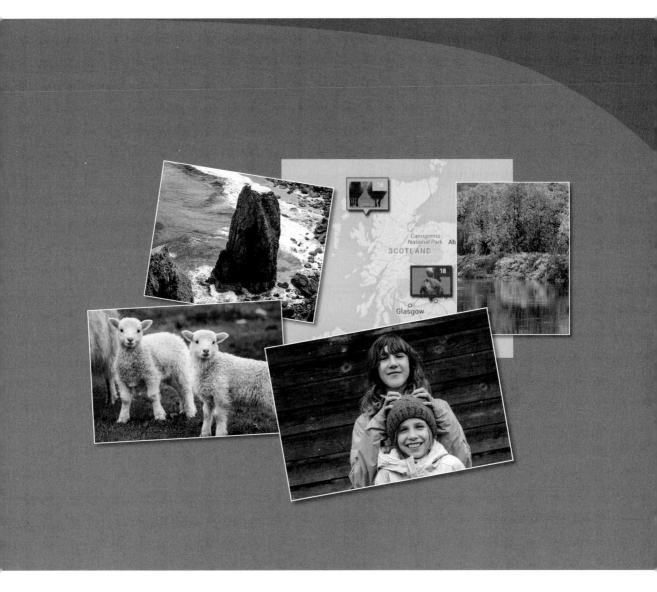

It's time to reap the rewards for all that sorting, reviewing, tagging, and organizing! Revisit the People, Places, and Events views in search-and-filter mode, where locating the photo you want is as easy as asking "Who, where, and when?" Find out how to set up complex, multi-criterion filters that can be saved and run again whenever you import new images, making it easy to keep your albums up to date.

Getting started

Before you begin this lesson you should first complete Lessons 1 and 2.

The exercises in Lesson 3 work with sample photos that were imported in the two preceding lessons, and require that the working catalog that you created in Lesson 1 is already organized with the people, places, and events tags that were applied in the course of Lesson 2.

Making it easier to find your photos

In Lesson 2, you made a start on organizing your image library by sorting and tagging the photos in terms of faces, locations, and events.

In Lesson 3, you'll learn more ways to order and "mark" your images, and discover how organizing your catalog can pay dividends by making it quick and easy to find the photos you want using the Organizer's search capabilities.

It's a good idea to make several sorting and tagging passes through each batch of photos you import, while they're still fresh in your mind, so they don't get lost in forgotten corners of your hard disk. This becomes an increasingly important strategy as you add more images to your library.

1 In the Organizer, click the Import button at the upper left of the workspace and choose From Files And Folders from the menu.

2 In the Get Photos And Videos From Files And Folders dialog box, navigate to and open the folder Lesson 2-3 and select the subfolder Zoo. Make sure the option Get Photos From Subfolders is activated and the other automatic processing options are disabled; then, click Get Media.

3 In the Import Attached Keyword Tags dialog box, click Select All; then, click OK.

4 The newly imported images appear in the Media Browser. Click the Clear button at the right of the bar above the thumbnails to clear the Last Import filter and view all of the photos in your catalog.

Rating photos

Rating your photos is a simple yet effective way to add another level of organization to your catalog. With a single click or keystroke, you can mark a photo as one of your best or relegate it to the bottom drawer—even while you're reviewing your images as a full-screen slideshow. You might choose from your five-star collection for a creative project, select from photos with a rating of three stars or higher for a presentation, or trim your catalog by removing all your unrated rejects.

1 Make sure Media is selected in the view picker at the top of the workspace. Click All Media or Back, if either is visible in the actions bar above the Media Browser, so that you see all the images in your catalog, rather than a filtered selection or the contents of a single folder.

2 Click the Import 4 folder in the My Folders list in the left panel.

3 In the Media Browser, move the pointer slowly from left to right over the stars beneath your favorite photo in this folder. When you see five yellow stars, click to apply that rating.

4 Select one of the other images in the Media Browser, and then press a number from 1 to 4 on your keyboard to apply that rating. Rate the remaining photos in the Import 4 folder, using whichever method you prefer.

5 To filter the Media Browser to display only those images from the Import 4 folder with three or more stars, click the third star in the Ratings filter at the right of the bar above the thumbnails and choose the appropriate qualifier from the adjacent menu.

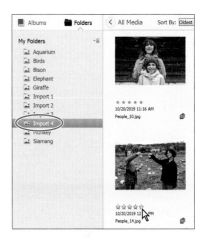

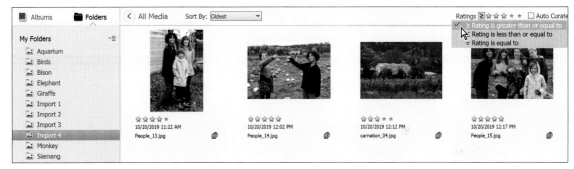

6 Click the third star in the Ratings filter once more to deactivate the filter. Select each of the other folders in the My Folders list in turn and rate about half of the photos in each folder. For the folders Import 3 and Import 4, try to rate a selection of images from each of the photo series in each folder.

7 When you're done, click All Media—at the left above the thumbnail grid—to show all the images in your catalog, rather than the contents of a single folder.

▶ **Tip:** The more photos you rate, the better for the demonstration of search features later in this lesson.

Tagging photos with keywords

Keyword tags are custom labels that you can attach to your photos and other media files, making it possible to sort them—and later, search for them—by personalized associations other than people, places, and events.

Keyword tags make it unnecessary to set up subject-specific folders or rename files with content-specific names. Both of these solutions are inflexible, confining a given photo to a single group. In contrast, you can assign multiple keyword tags to a single photo, associating it with several different groups of images simultaneously, and then use a keyword search to quickly retrieve any of those collections, even if the image files are scattered through different folders on your hard disk.

Keywords provide a perfect solution for tagging images that don't feature people you know, or where the location or event at which the photos were captured is not a particularly relevant association.

For photos that are already tagged for people, places, and events, keywords can be used to refine a search. For example, you could use people and places tags to quickly isolate all your photos of Kat and Tom together in New York, and then use keywords to filter for winter shots captured at night.

Organizing keyword tags and categories

1 If necessary, click the Keyword/Info button at the far right of the taskbar to open the right panel group.

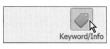

2 If you don't see a list of keywords—or at least, the collapsed Keywords header—at the top of the right panel group, click the Tags tab to bring the Tags panel to the front. If necessary, click the arrow at the left of the Keywords header to expand the Keywords list.

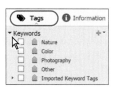

Photoshop Elements ships with a few default keywords to help get you started. In this exercise you'll convert two of the default keywords to keyword categories by creating sub-categories inside them, and then make a start on organizing your keywords by moving them into a hierarchical arrangement.

3 Select the Nature tag at the top of the Keywords list; then, click the small arrow beside the green plus-sign button ( ) to the right of the Keywords header. Examine the options available in the menu; then, choose New Sub-Category.

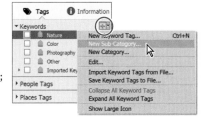

4 In the Create Sub-Category dialog box, the selected Nature keyword has been automatically set as the parent category inside which your new tag will be nested. Name the new sub-category **Animals**, and then click OK to create the new Keywords listing and close the Create Sub-Category dialog box.

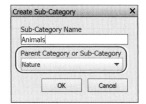

5 Right-click the Nature tag and choose Create New Sub-Category. Name the new sub-category **Scenic**, confirm that Nature is set as the parent category, and then click OK.

6   Expand the Imported Keyword Tags category, if necessary, to see all the keyword tags you've imported together with the lesson images.

7   Ctrl-click / Command-click to group-select the Aquarium, Birds, Bison, Elephant, Giraffe, Monkey, and Siamang keywords that were imported with the photos from the Zoo folder. Drag the seven selected keyword tags to the Animals tag in the expanded Nature category.

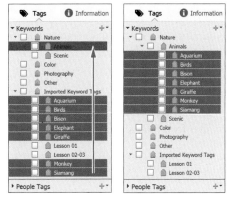

Tip: Although this procedure does not add the Nature or Animals keywords to the Zoo photos as tags, searching your catalog for either "parent" keyword will return any image tagged with any of the keywords nested inside these categories.

The seven relocated tags are now nested inside the Animals keyword sub-category.

8   Select the Animals category; then, click the small arrow beside the green plus-sign button (🞢) at the upper right of the panel and choose New Sub-Category from the menu. In the Create Sub-Category dialog box, name the new sub-category **Mammals**. The selected Animals keyword has been automatically set as the parent sub-category. Click OK.

9   Drag all of the tags in the Animals category other than the Birds keyword to the new Mammals sub-category. Right-click the Mammals keyword and choose Create New Sub-Category. Name the new sub-category **Primates**, and then click OK. Drag the Monkey and Siamang tags into the new sub-category.

Note: This approach to keywording will give you the most flexibility when searching later, but you're not required to go into this level of detail on your own images. If you feel you're getting bogged down with tags, or they're getting in the way of organizing and editing your photos, apply just one or two levels of keywords. Some people like this amount of depth, while others don't. That's okay.

Customizing the Keywords list

You can see that the Keywords list will soon become quite complex. Color-coding the categories you use most often, and assigning thumbnail images to the tags in place of the generic tag icons, may make navigating the hierarchy easier.

1   Choose Preferences > Keyword Tags And Albums from the Edit menu on Windows, or choose Preferences from the Elements Organizer menu on macOS. In the Keyword Tags And Albums pane of the Preferences dialog box, activate the picture tag option under Keyword Tag Display. Click OK to save the setting.

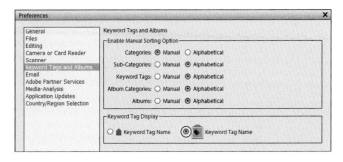

2 In the Keywords list, right-click the Nature category and choose Edit from the context menu. In the Edit Category dialog box, click Choose Color and choose a color from the picker. Leave the category name unchanged. Scroll the Category Icon menu and click to select an icon; then, click OK to close the Edit Category dialog box.

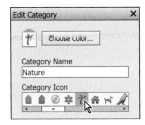

The Nature category now has a distinctive icon and color-coded badges on its sub-categories and keywords, making it stand out in the list. If you can't see the full keyword names, drag the left edge of the panel group to make it wider. If the edited Nature category changes position in the Keywords list, drag it back to the top.

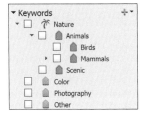

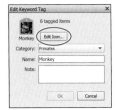

3 Right-click the Monkey tag and choose Edit. In the Edit Keyword Tag dialog box, click Edit Icon.

4 Use the arrows at the sides of the Find button in the Edit Keyword Tag Icon dialog box to cycle through all the photos tagged with the Monkey keyword. When you see the image you want, drag the handles of the bounding box to set a new keyword badge. A thumbnail at the top of the dialog box shows how the image will look applied to a tag icon. Click OK to confirm the new badge image; then click OK to close the Edit Keyword Tag dialog box.

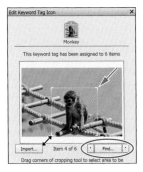

5 Click the arrow beside the plus-sign button (➕) to the right of the Keywords header and choose New Category. In the Create Category dialog box, name the new category **Travel**. Choose a tag badge color and category icon, and then click OK. Right-click the new category in the Keywords list and choose Create New Sub-Category. Name the nested sub-category **Family Trips**.

Creating and applying keyword tags

You can also work with keywords in the People, Places, and Events views.

1 Click People in the view picker at the top of the Organizer workspace. Make sure you're in the Named people mode.

2 If necessary, click All People at the top of the Groups panel to see all your people stacks. Click the Simone stack to expand it. If necessary, click Media below Simone's stack to switch from the Faces view to the Media view. Double-click the photo shown at left (People_16.jpg). If you don't see that image in Simone's stack, check the other people stacks to locate the photo and select it.

3 With People_16.jpg selected in the expanded people stack, click the Info button at the right of the taskbar; then, type **Wren Hill Farm** in the text box at the top of the Image Tags panel. Click Add to apply the new keyword. Click Back above the thumbnails grid.

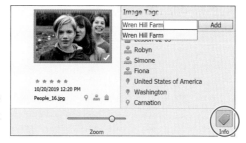

Now, you'll use the Places view to locate the other photos shot at the same location.

4 Click Places in the view picker at the top of the workspace. If necessary, pan the map to focus on the Washington marker, and then zoom in until the marker divides to show two location pins. Double-click the eastern pin to see all of the photos that are pinned at that location; then, choose Edit > Select All.

5 Click the Info button at the right end of the taskbar, and then type the letter **W** in the text box in the header of the Image Tags panel. Choose the newly created Wren Hill Farm tag from the pop-up menu. Click Add to apply the new keyword to all the selected photos.

6 Deselect all the photos, then Ctrl-click / Command-click to select just the three scenic landscape shots that do not include the kids.

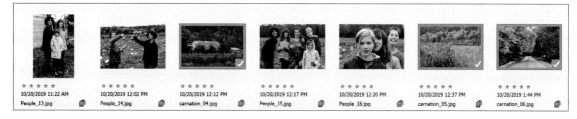

7 Type the letter **S** in the Image Tags panel text box; then, choose the Scenic tag from the tagging suggestions. Click Add to apply the new keyword to the three selected photos; then, deselect them. Click Back above the thumbnail grid to return to the Map view, and then click Media in the view picker to switch to the Media Browser, where you can organize your new tags.

8 Expand the Travel keyword category, if necessary; then, drag the Wren Hill Farm tag from the Other category into the subcategory Family Trips.

9 Drag the Travel category to the top of the Tags panel, and release the mouse button when you see a blue line indicating an insertion point just below the Keywords header.

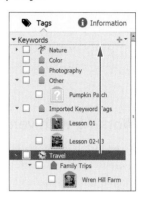

10 Right-click the Wren Hill Farm tag, and choose Edit from the context menu; then, customize the tag thumbnail as you did in the previous exercise.

Your keyword-tagging expedition ends in the Events view, where you'll tag all the images from one event, and just a selection of photos from another.

11 Click Events in the view picker. Make sure you're in the Named events view; then, double-click the Pumpkins 2019 stack to expand it. Press Ctrl+A /Command+A to select all the photos in this event; then click the Info button at the right of the taskbar, and type **Pacific Northwest** in the text box at the top of the Image Tags panel. Click Add to apply the new keyword to all of the selected photos. Click the Back button in the actions bar above the thumbnail grid to collapse the Pumpkins 2019 stack and see all of the events in your catalog.

12 Expand the Downtown Seattle Walks stack by double-clicking it. Select the image in this event that includes two girls. In the Image Tags panel, type **Cousins** in the text box; then, click Add to apply the tag.

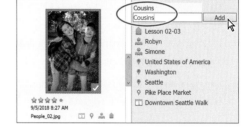

13 Click Media in the view picker to return to the Media Browser and see your new tags listed in the Keywords list. Press Ctrl+Shift+A or Command+Shift+A to deselect all the images in the current selection. Set a new thumbnail for the Cousins and Pacific Northwest tags as you did for the other new tags.

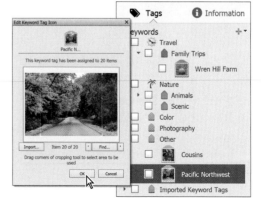

Grouping photos

As the number of files in your photo library increases, it can be more difficult to spot the image you want among the thumbnails displayed in the Media Browser.

Simply grouping some of your images in stacks and version sets can reduce the clutter in the thumbnails grid, effectively simplifying the view by hiding collections of related shots behind a single thumbnail until they're needed.

Working with version sets

A version set groups a photo in its original state with any edited copies that you've generated, so you can find all the edited versions of the image stacked behind a single thumbnail in the Media Browser, rather than scattered through your catalog.

Photoshop Elements automatically creates a version set whenever you edit a photo in the Elements Organizer. When you edit an image from your catalog in the Editor, you can choose whether or not to create a version set in the Save As dialog box.

Grouping your edited files in this way not only makes it much easier for you to find the version you want, but also lets you keep your original, unedited photo intact, easy to find and ready for a different treatment whenever you want to reuse it.

1 If the All Media button is visible in the actions bar above the thumbnails, click it to ensure that the Media Browser is showing all the images in your catalog.

2 To isolate the zoo images, click the search box beside the Nature > Animals sub-category in the Keywords list. Scroll down in the Media Browser, if necessary, and select the image DSC_0736.jpg.

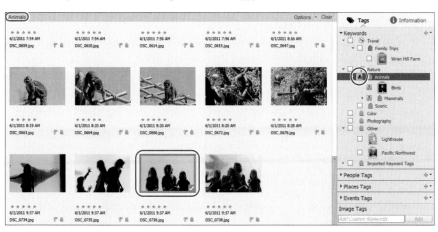

You have just made your first keyword search. With one click, you've retrieved all the photos from your last import, despite the fact that they are spread across seven folders and are tagged with as many separate keywords. The search results bar above the thumbnails grid displays a single search term: Animals.

3   Click the Instant Fix button ( ) beside the Editor button in the taskbar to open the Instant Fix editing window. Click the Smart Fix button ( ) at the right. Click Done at the lower right, and then click Yes to save the changes.

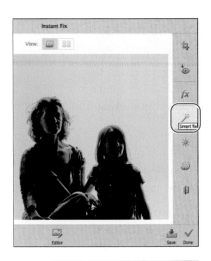

In the Media view, the edited copy is stacked on top of the original photo in a version set.

A version set can be identified by a badge (representing a stack of photos overlaid by a paint brush) in the upper-right corner of the thumbnail and by a file name extension indicating that the photo has been edited.

4   Click the Instant Fix button ( ), and then click the Crop button ( ). Choose the Custom pre-view from the cropping options; then, drag the handles of the cropping box to crop the image around the subjects. Click the green check icon; then, click Done. Click Yes to save the changes.

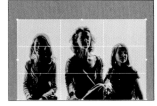

5   Click the expand button ( ) to the right of the thumbnail image to see the original and edited images in the version set displayed side by side. Select the original image, DSC_0736.jpg, and then repeat step 3.

6   There are now three photos in the version stack, with the most recent copy on top. Select the first copy, DSC_0736_edited-1.jpg—the center image in the version set—and choose Edit > Version Set > Set As Top Item. The two edited copies change places in the stack; the older version is now the "cover photo."

7   To see only the topmost photo in the version set, click the collapse button to the right of the original image, or right-click any photo in the set and choose Version Set > Collapse Items In Version Set from the context menu. Note the other commands available from the same context menu; these commands can also be found in the Edit > Version Set menu.

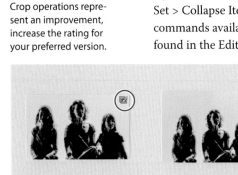

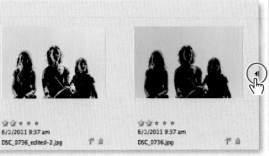

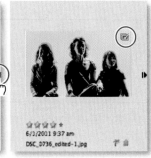

About stacks

Scrolling past rows and rows of images of the same subject to find the one you're looking for can be time-consuming and frustrating. You can reduce clutter in the thumbnail grid and make browsing for photos more enjoyable, and far more productive, by stacking related shots behind a single distinctive thumbnail.

Glancing along just one row of stacks in the thumbnails grid could save you the effort of scrolling through screen after screen of distracting images.

1 In the Media Browser, Ctrl-click / Command-click to select the four images shot at the zoo's aquarium, including the version set you created in the previous exercise.

2 Right-click the photo you edited earlier and choose Stack > Stack Selected Photos. The images are stacked, with the edited copy on top, now marked with a stack icon beside its version set badge. Click the arrow at the right side of the stack frame to expand and collapse the stack.

3 Select the four images of elephants, right-click the photo you'd like to set as the top image, and choose Stack > Stack Selected Photos from the context menu. Repeat the process for the four photos of black siamangs from Thailand and the six images of American bison.

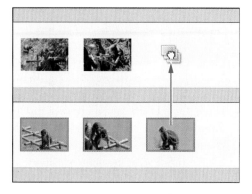

Tip: Stacks are particularly useful for managing long series of related images, such as shots taken at sports events with your camera's burst mode or auto-bracket feature. When you take photos this way you end up with many variations of what is essentially the same image—if you stack the series, you'll see only the best shot in the Media Browser.

Stacking photos automatically

You can automate the process of grouping related photos in your catalog by having Photoshop Elements suggest stacks based on visual similarities between images.

1 Press Ctrl+A / Command+A to select all of the animal photos in the Media Browser; then, choose Edit > Stack > Automatically Suggest Photo Stacks.

In the Visual Similarity Photo Search dialog box, Photoshop Elements presents groups as potential stacks. Before you go ahead and stack these groups, let's look at the options for tweaking the automatic stacking process manually.

2 To merge suggested groups of photos that belong together, Shift-click to select the images in one group and drag them into the other. In the illustration at the right, Photoshop Elements has not grouped all of the photos of squirrel monkeys.

Tip: Experiment with as many of your own photos as possible so that you get a feel for the kinds of images that perform best with this feature.

Tip: Remember that you may see different results than those illustrated, depending on your operating system.

3 Click Unique Photos at the lower left of the Visual Similarity Photo Search dialog box. The Unique Photos pane shows any photos from the selection in the Media Browser for which Photoshop Elements has been unable to suggest a stack

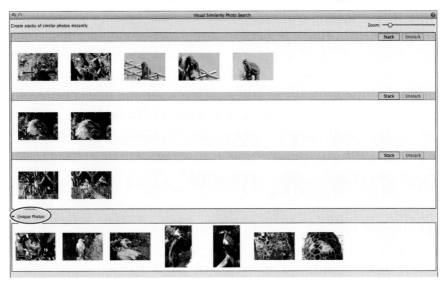

Tip: You can simply reverse this process to remove a photo from a group suggested for stacking.

4 Drag the first image in the Unique Photos pane to the top group of five shots featuring squirrel monkeys. Drag the next four images to group them with the two other photos featuring birds, and then add the last two images to the two photos of giraffes in the bottom group.

5 When you stack these groups, the first image in each group becomes the top image in the stack. Drag your favorite photo from each group to the first position in that group, and then click the Stack button at the right of the divider bar above the group. Each new stack displays the stacked photos badge.

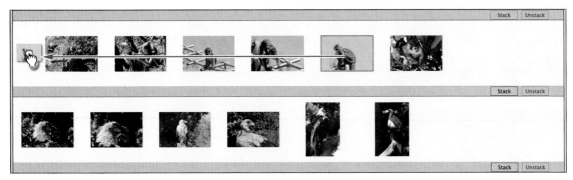

6 Click Done. In the Media Browser, the 36 photos with keywords from the Animals category are now displayed as just seven stack thumbnails. Click Media in the view picker; then click the Back button in the actions bar, if it's visible, to see all of the photos in your catalog.

Tips for working with stacks

Keep these points in mind when you're working with stacks:

- Combining two or more stacks merges them to form one new stack, with the most recent photo on top of the stack. The original groupings are not preserved.

- Many actions applied to a collapsed stack, such as editing and printing, are applied to the top item only. To apply an action to multiple images in a stack, either expand the stack and group-select the images, or unstack them first.

- If you edit a photo that you've already included in a stack, the photo and its edited copy will be grouped as a version set nested inside the stack.

- If you apply a keyword tag to a collapsed stack, the keyword tag is applied to all items in the stack. When you run a search on the keyword tag, the top photo in the stack appears in the search results marked with the stack icon. If you want to apply a keyword tag to only one photo in a stack, expand the stack first.

Tip: To access stack commands, right-click any image in a stack and choose from the Stack submenu. Alternatively, select a photo in the stack and choose from the Edit > Stack menu.

Creating albums

Another way of grouping your photos is to organize them into albums. An album is like a *virtual* folder in which you can assemble a collection of images that may be drawn from any number of *actual* folders on your hard disk. You might create a new album to collate and arrange the pictures that you intend to include in a creative project such as a photo book or a slideshow, or to group your images of a special interest subject such as flowers, classic cars, or macro photography.

A photo can be included in more than one album—the same image might be the first in a New York Architecture album and the last in a National Monuments album. You can also group albums; for example, you might group your New York and San Francisco albums together inside a Vacations album, while your Road Trips album includes the San Francisco album but not the New York album.

Tip: You can achieve similar groupings and sub-groups by using keywords tags, but your Family Trips album may contain only a subset of the photos you've tagged with the keyword Family Trips.

The principal advantage to grouping photos in an album rather than using a shared keyword tag is that in an album you can rearrange the order of the photos as you wish. In the Media Browser, each photo in an album displays a number in the upper-left corner, representing its place in the order. You can drag photos to change their position within the album, which will affect the order in which they appear in a slideshow or their placement in a project layout.

1 If necessary, click the Keyword / Info button in the taskbar to show the Tags panel. In the Keywords list, select the Animals > Mammals > Primates sub-category; then, click the search box at the left of the Primates tag to isolate all the images with tags that are included in that category. The grid displays two stacks you created earlier.

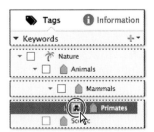

In albums, stacks are a special case; you can include a stack in an album, but only the top photo from the stack will appear in a slideshow, for instance, unless you expand the stack and select all the photos inside it before you start the slideshow.

You can't rearrange the order of stacked photos in an album, add a selection of photos from a stack to an album without adding the entire stack, or remove a stacked image from your album without removing the rest of the stack.

So you can start by unstacking the photos in the Primates category.

2   Shift-click to select both of the stacks in the Media Browser, and then choose Edit > Stack > Unstack Photos.

3   Select the best three shots of the black siamangs; then, click Albums at the top of the left panel. Click the green plus sign (![plus]) to the right of the My Albums header; make sure you click the green plus sign, not the small arrow beside it.

4   In the New Album panel at the right, type **Monkey Business** as the name for the new album; then, click OK in the taskbar below the panel.

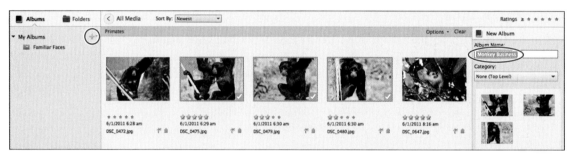

▶ **Tip:** If you don't see the album badges below the thumbnails in the Media Browser, use the Zoom slider in the taskbar to increase the size of the thumbnails. Hold the pointer over the album badge to see which album or albums a photo belongs to.

5   Your new album appears in the My Albums list, and the three siamang photos that you selected for inclusion in the album are now marked with green album badges.

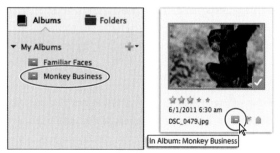

Adding more photos to an album

As you add more images to your catalog, you may have new photos that you'd like to add to existing albums—an easy way to sort and organize a fresh import—or perhaps you're assembling a collection for a photo book over several work sessions.

1   With the Media Browser still filtered to show photos with keywords in the Primates category, right-click the new album and choose Edit from the context menu. The Edit Album panel opens at the right.

2   Ctrl-click / Command-click to select the best three of the six photos featuring squirrel monkeys. Drag the selected photos into the Content pane in the Edit Album panel; then, click OK in the taskbar.

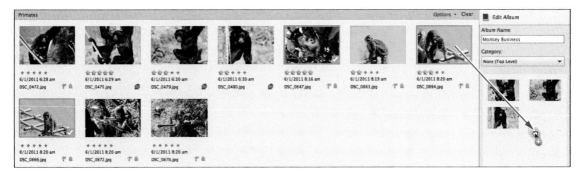

3   If necessary, click Clear in the search results bar above the thumbnails to clear the Primates filter. You can now view all of the photos in your catalog. Click the Keyword/Info button at the right of the taskbar to close the right panel group, if necessary.

4   Click the Monkey Business album in the My Albums list. Set the sorting order in the actions bar above the thumbnails grid to Album Order. Notice the counter in the upper-left corner of each image, denoting its order in the album.

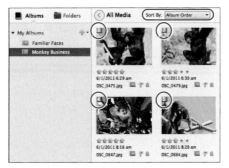

Tip: You can drag selected photos directly to an album's entry in the My Albums list, and vice versa, but using the Edit command has the advantage of providing the opportunity to rename the album or to change its place in the list hierarchy.

5   Drag the thumbnails to rearrange their order in the album, alternating the photos of siamangs and squirrel monkeys. When you're done, click All Media in the actions bar above the thumbnail grid so that the Media Browser displays all of the photos in your catalog.

Creating albums from People, Places, and Events

In Lesson 2, you used the People, Places, and Events views as aids to organizing your catalog—and your effort is already paying off. Now you can take advantage of the search and filter aspects of those views to help find the photos you need.

1   Click People in the view picker at the top of the workspace; then, make sure you're in the Named people view. If necessary, click the Groups button (icon) in the taskbar to show the Groups panel at the right; then, expand the Family group. Expand the Cousins group, and then click the listing for the Sisters group to show only the people stacks for Fiona and Penny.

2 Click the Fiona stack, and then click Media below Fiona's stack thumbnail to display full photos rather than just faces. Double-click the photo track to expand it to a grid view; then, Ctrl-click / Command-click to select the photos of the sisters together without their cousins, and any images of Fiona alone.

3 In the Albums panel, click the green plus sign (✚) (not the small arrow beside it) to the right of the My Albums header. In the New Album panel at the right of the workspace, name the new album **Double Trouble**; then, click OK in the taskbar.

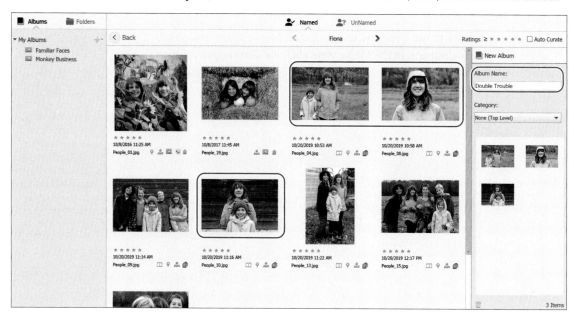

▶ **Tip:** This is a good demonstration of the advantages of grouping photos in albums rather than relying on keywords alone; a people tags search in this case returns photos with Fiona together with any number of other people, whereas an album could isolate a subset made up of pictures of Fiona alone.

Your new album appears in the My Albums list. The selected photos are marked with green album badges. If you don't see the badges, increase the thumbnail size.

4 Click the Back button in the actions bar to return to the Group view, and then click the Penny stack to expand it. Double-click a photo to view them in a grid view. Then, select the image of Penny alone and drag it directly to the Double Trouble album in the Albums list. The added photo is marked with a green album badge.

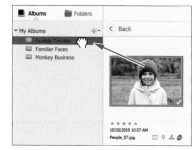

You've successfully leveraged the people tags that you attached to your photos in Lesson 2 to perform a simple people search, making use of the various viewing modes in the People view to help locate the photos you needed for the new album.

▶ **Tip:** If you don't see the map or the pins (or Washington), see the first few steps in "A short trip to the Places view" in Lesson 2.

5 Click Places in the view picker. In the Places view, double-click the western pin of the two pins positioned on Washington to show the photos pinned at that location. Select all 22 photos.

6   Click the Create New Album Or Album Category button (➕) at the top of the left panel, making sure you click the button, not the small arrow beside it. In the New Album panel at the right of the workspace, type **Washington Autumn** as the name for the new album; then, click OK in the taskbar below the panel.

7   Click Back to return to the map view, and then double-click the western pin. Select the image pikeplace_7.jpg (a bunch of sunflowers) and drag it to the newly created Washington Autumn album in the My Albums list. The selected photo is now marked with a green album badge.

▶ **Tip:** If you don't see the green album badge on completing step 7, increase the size of the thumbnails in the grid.

8   Click Back to return to the map view, and then click Media in the view picker at the top of the workspace. In the Media view, click the Washington Autumn album in the Albums panel. The image count at the lower left of the workspace shows that the album contains 23 photos—22 from a trip to the pumpkin patch in Carnation and one shot in Seattle. You've just used the Places view to filter your catalog by location to find the photos for this album. Click All Media in the actions bar to return to an unfiltered view of your catalog.

9   Click Events in the view picker. In the Named events view, shift-click to select the event stacks NY Marathon 2010 and NY Marathon 2011; then, click the green plus sign (➕) beside the My Albums header.

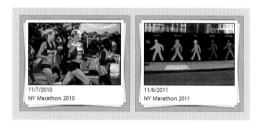

10 In the New Album panel, type **Running New York** as the name for the album. Before you click OK to create the new album, Ctrl-click / Command-click in the New Album panel's content pane to select three or four images that you'd like to exclude from the album, and then click the trash-can icon at the bottom of the panel to remove them. Click OK in the taskbar.

The new Running New York album appears in the My Albums list in the left panel, grouping the marathon photos that you located by filtering for events tags.

11 Click Media in the view picker. In the Media view, click each of the albums Double Trouble, Running New York, and Washington Autumn. If you wish, you can rearrange the order of the thumbnails in the grid for each of your newly created albums.

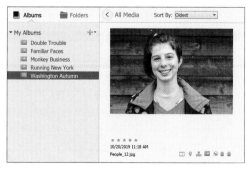

▶ **Tip:** If you're unable to re-order the photos in an album, check the Sort By setting at the left of the bar above the thumbnails grid. To customize the order of photos in an album, the sorting order should be set to Album Order.

12 When you're done, click All Media in the actions bar to see the unfiltered contents of your catalog in the Media Browser.

Filtering and finding photos

In this lesson, you've begun to take advantage of the Organizer's search and filter capabilities—even while you've been concentrating on using it to mark and manage your images. Most of the search and filter tools are so well integrated into the Elements Organizer workspace that you're barely aware of using them.

▶ **Tip:** This is what's referred to as an "and" search: "Show me items that are in the Import 4 folder *and* have a rating of three stars or higher."

At the start of this lesson you learned how to apply ratings to your photos. By the time you reached step 5, you had already performed a two-term search—with just two clicks. You filtered your catalog so you could look at the images in a single folder (by choosing from the list in the left panel), and then refined the search to show only the photos with the highest ratings (by clicking a star in the actions bar).

▶ **Tip:** This is referred to as an "or" search: "Show me any item that is tagged with this keyword *or* that one … *or* any of these five."

In the next exercise, you tidied up your keywords list by dragging keyword tags into a hierarchy of categories and subcategories. This simple housekeeping task made it possible to find the images for the exercises that followed by running a *seven*-term search—this time with just one click! A single click on the Animals category filtered your catalog for all the images of birds, bison, elephants, giraffes, monkeys, and siamangs—retrieving photos found in seven separate folders.

Finding people, places, and events

The first time you visited the Places, People, and Events views, you were learning how to sort and tag your photos. During the last exercise you discovered that each of these workspaces also serves as a filter that is capable of presenting your images in a variety of different arrangements to help you locate the photos you're looking for. In this section, you'll take another look at finding people, places, and events.

Looking for somebody?

1 Click People in the view picker. You should be in the Named people view.

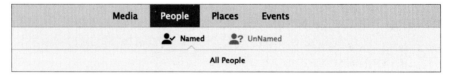

2 If you don't see stacks for all eight people you tagged in Lesson 2, the People view is either displaying images of just one of the people in your catalog or is displaying whichever people it can find in just a selected part of your catalog. To see all of the tagged people in the whole of your catalog, click the Back button or the All People button at the upper left.

3 To quickly skim through all the photos in any of your people stacks, move the pointer slowly across the stack thumbnail. Stop moving the pointer, and then right-click whichever image is currently visible to see the commands that can be applied to the stack. Skim through each people stack.

Even the All People view is a search result—the stacks displayed are the answer to the question "Which people are in my catalog?"

4 Click the Rhys stack to show all the images in the catalog tagged with Rhys's people tag. Toggle the setting below the stack thumbnail to shift between the Media and Faces views. In the Faces view, hover over any of the face thumbnails to see the full photo from which the thumbnail was extracted.

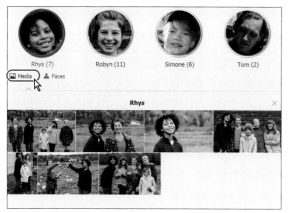 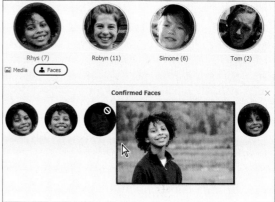

5 Double-click either a face or a full photo from Rhys's stack to see all the photos in the stack displayed in the thumbnail grid view. Double-click a photo in the grid view to see it enlarged in a single-image view. Click Grid, and then Back, in the actions bar to return to the named people stacks.

Your catalog is still small, so there are not so many pictures of any of the people you've tagged, but as your photo library grows, you may see hundreds of photos of a given person in each stack. Scanning these thumbnails may be preferable to looking through every photo in your catalog, but it can still be daunting. You can effectively filter the view by selecting individual albums or folders as the image source.

6 Note the image counts for the Penny and Fiona stacks; then, click to select Double Trouble from the Albums list in the left panel. The image count drops, as this album contains only those images of each sister alone, or the pair without their parents or cousins. To see exactly *which* pictures of Penny and Fiona are in this album, move the pointer slowly across each of the stack thumbnails.

7 Click each of the other albums to see who's inside; then, click All People at the left of the actions bar above the stacks. Switch the left panel from the Albums list to Folders and click between the Import 3 and Import 4 folders. As you switch between the folders you'll notice that the image count for each stack changes. Click the All People button in the actions bar to deselect the current folder as the image source and see the image counts for the entire catalog.

Note: When you skim the contents of a people stack with a single album or folder selected as the image source, rather than the entire catalog, remember that the photo you set as the profile picture (the image you see at the top of the people stack) may not be present in that album or folder.

The Groups mode provides yet another way to find and filter your photos in the People view.

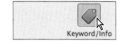

Note: All of the tagged people in your CIB catalog are included in groups. Once you're working with your own catalog, people that you've tagged but not added to any group will appear in the Ungrouped listing.

8   If you don't see the Groups panel at the right, click the Groups button (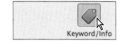) in the taskbar; then, expand all the Family and Cousins groups. Click down the Family hierarchy to the Sisters listing. Note the image counts for each stack; then open the Albums pane at the left and select the Double Trouble album to filter the search. Click the Double Trouble album again to clear the filter.

To move a person from one group to another, simply drag their people stack to a different entry in the Groups list. To remove someone from a group, right-click their stack and choose Move To Ungrouped from the context menu.

9   Click All People at the top of the Groups panel; then, click Media in the view picker to return to a view of your entire catalog.

Finding people from the Media view

You can also work with your people tags in the Media view, making it quick and easy to leverage all that tagging and grouping to find the photos you want.

1   If necessary, click the Keyword/Info button at the far right of the taskbar to open the right panel group.

2   In the Tags panel, expand the People Tags category; then, expand the Family group and the three groups nested inside it.

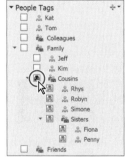

3   Click the search box to the left of the Cousins tag.

Depending on the accuracy of your face tagging and grouping, this search could return up to 19 photos. The search results bar above the thumbnails lists the Cousins tag as the single search term.

4   Right-click the Simone tag and choose Exclude From Search. The binoculars icon in Simone's search box is replaced by a barred circle, and the number of images displayed in the Media Browser is reduced. The search results bar now lists these search terms: Cousins, ~~Simone~~.

5   Click the Clear button at the right of the search results bar to clear the filter.

6   In the People Tags list, click the search box for the Simone tag. The Media Browser should display up to six photos. Click the search box for the Robyn tag. The thumbnails in the grid are reduced to those images with both people tags. Click the search box for the Penny tag; the search results bar lists the Robyn, Simone, and Penny tags as search terms.

The search returns only images including all four girls; in other words, there are no photos of Simone together with Robyn but without Fiona.

7 Click the Clear button in the search results bar to clear the filter.

Searching every place

Now you'll revisit the Places view to pin some more photos to the map before you do some searching by location.

1 Click Places in the view picker; then, click Unpinned in the bar below the view picker. The preview pane shows all the images in the catalog that do not yet have location information. Toggle the Group By Time option in the actions bar to filter this simple search by date. Set Number Of Groups to Maximum.

2 Scroll to the pictures dated June 26, 2010. Click the check mark beside the date to select all the photos in the group; then, click Add Location beside the header. In the Add A Location dialog, type **edgartown**, and then press Enter / Return. Click the location suggestion Edgartown, Massachusetts, United States of America, and then click Apply.

3 Reset Number Of Groups to Maximum, if necessary; then, locate and select the group dated July 15, 2012: photos of a Medieval Fair parade. Click Add Location and type **Kaufbeuren** in the Add A Location dialog; then, press Enter / Return and accept the location Kaufbeuren, Bavaria, Germany. Click Apply.

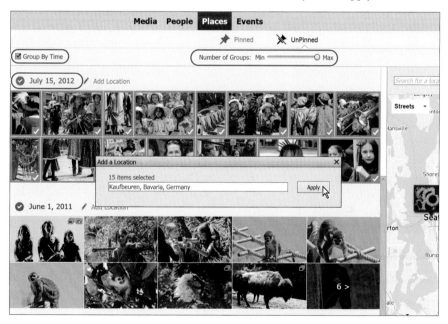

4 Repeat the process to place the selection of photos shot on June 1, 2011, at the **LA Zoo**. Accept and apply the location, LA Zoo Lights, Los Angeles, California 90027, United States of America. (Oddly, "LA Zoo" by itself doesn't come up in the location database, but "LA Zoo Lights" does.)

▶ Tip: At this zoom level, the two pins on Scotland appear to merge.

5   Switch the Places view to Pinned mode; then zoom and pan the map to see all your pins from LA to Kaufbeuren (or as much as will fit onscreen).

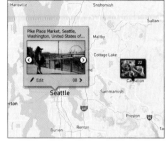

6   Zoom the map until you see the marker on the West Coast of the US divide to show separate pins for the pumpkin patch images and the trip to Pike Place Market. Hover over the Seattle pin and use the arrows at the sides of the pin preview to see the images pinned to this location.

7   Click the preview image count to expand the location stack to the thumbnail grid, where you can select photos, see them enlarged, tag faces, apply keywords, add captions, assemble albums, edit images, or view a slideshow.

8   Click Media in the view picker to return to the Media Browser. In the Tags panel, collapse the Keywords and People Tags lists and expand the Places Tags pane. Collapse the Germany and United Kingdom tags and click the search box for the United States.

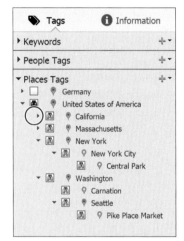

Every places tag in the United States hierarchy is included in the search. The Media Browser displays all the images returned by this search.

9   Right-click the search box for Carnation and choose Exclude From Search from the context menu. The image count in the Media Browser drops.

10 Expand the People Tags list. Click the search box for Simone. The number of photos returned by the search has been narrowed to one from Seattle.

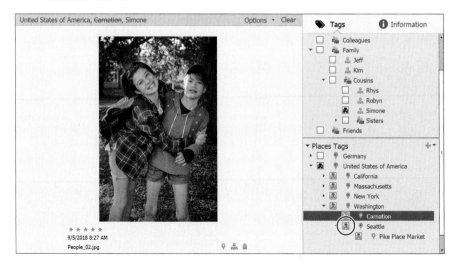

Looking for the right occasion

Let's see what you're missing in the Events view.

1 Click Events in the view picker. If the Events view is set to Suggested events, click Named in the actions bar to shift to the Named events view. The grid displays an event stack for each of the five events you created in Lesson 2.

2 If you don't see the calendar, click the Calendar button (🎛) at the right of the taskbar. The calendar's header currently reads "All Years," indicating that the Events view is displaying all the events in your catalog, regardless of their dates.

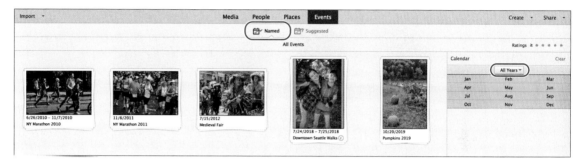

3 Click the All Years heading; the drop-down menu shows that your catalog contains events from each year from 2010 to 2019. Choose 2018 from the menu. The Events view is now filtered to show only one named event, which takes place over a two-day period in July.

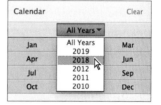

4 Click Suggested in the actions bar to shift to Suggested events mode. Use the calendar menu to focus on 2018; then click the month of July on the calendar. Set the Number Of Groups slider to Minimum. The photos are separated into two groups that cover two days.

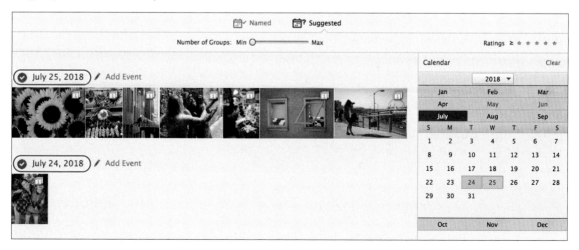

5 Select the group dated July 25, 2018; then, click Add Event. Name the event **Market Visit**; then, click OK. Choose Edit > Deselect, and then switch to the Named events view to see the new named event stack.

The two-day Downtown Seattle Walks event has not been split up; Suggested events has merely enabled you to designate a subset based on grouped capture dates as an event in its own right. The Downtown Seattle Walks event still covers the original two-day period.

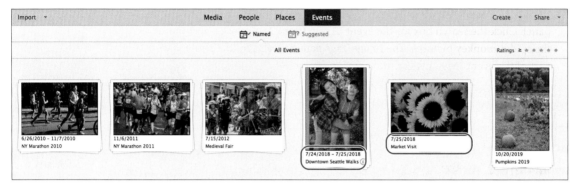

6 Switch to the Suggested events view. With the calendar set to display All Years, increase Number Of Groups to the maximum. Select the June 1, 2011, stack. Click Add Event and name the new event **A trip to the zoo**; then, click OK.

7 Choose Edit > Deselect. Choose 2011 from the calendar menu, and then click to focus on the month of June. Drag the Number Of Groups slider to a setting one stop less than the maximum, and then scroll down the preview pane.

This one-day event is now divided into clusters based on capture time. The suggested sub-events correspond to the different animals encountered during a walk around the zoo; four of the six sub-events are represented in the preview pane by stacks that you created earlier.

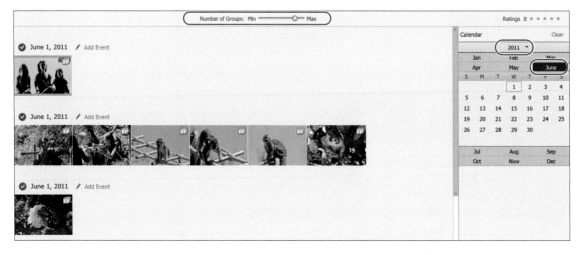

8 Select the second group, click Add Event, and type **Meeting the monkeys**; then, click OK. Choose Edit > Deselect. Switch back from Suggested events mode to the default Named events view to see your new event stacks.

9 Move the pointer slowly across each new event stack in turn to see the images inside the events. For each new event, stop the pointer when you see your favorite image; then, right-click the image and choose Set As Cover to make this photo the cover photo.

10 Click Media in the view picker, and then expand the Events Tags pane in the Tags panel. Click the search box for the event "A trip to the zoo"; then, select one of the spider monkey pictures. The Image Tags pane reveals that the photo is also part of the event "Meeting the monkeys."

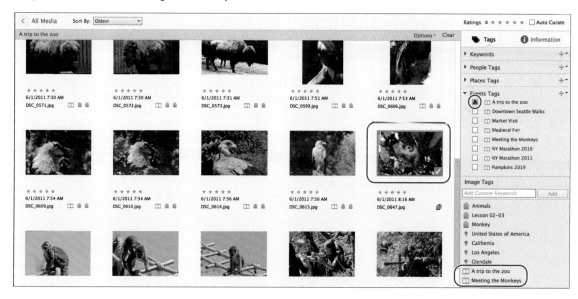

11 Click All Media in the actions bar to clear the search, and then click the search box for the two-day event "Downtown Seattle Walks." Select one of the sunflower images; the Image Tags pane shows that the photo is also tagged with the event "Market Visit." Click All Media to clear the search.

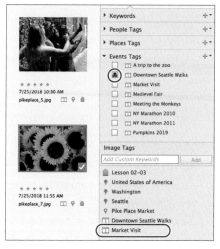

Using the Timeline to refine a search

The Timeline is an effective search tool in its own right, but you can also use it in combination with any of the other search and filter tools to help refine a search or to navigate the results. You might search for photos with a particular keyword tag and then use the Timeline to narrow the search to the files from a particular import batch, or to images captured within a specific date range.

Note: The height of the bars indicates the relative number of files captured in each month.

1 Set the Sort By menu in the actions bar to Oldest; then, choose View > Timeline to show the Timeline above the Media Browser. In this sorting order mode, the Timeline breaks your catalog down by capture date; you can see that your catalog contains images captured over a 16-year span, from the oldest entry, in September 2003, to the most recent, in October 2019.

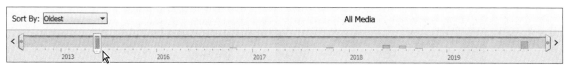

2 Click any of the bars in the Timeline, or drag the sliding frame; the thumbnails grid scrolls, if necessary, to show you the first image in the grid with a capture date that falls within that month.

3 Drag the markers at the ends of the Timeline inward to define a range of six or eight months. The grid now displays only the images captured in that period.

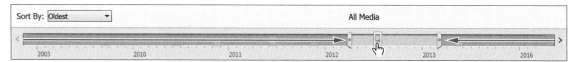

4 In the actions bar, set the Sort By option to Import Batch. The bars in the Timeline now represent import batches arranged in chronological order.

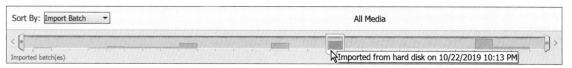

5 Click a bar in the Timeline; the view scrolls to show you the first image imported in that batch. In the grid, the photos are grouped under batch headers; select all the images in a batch by clicking the header. Hide the Timeline by choosing View > Timeline; then, reset the sorting order to show the oldest photos first. Choose Edit > Deselect.

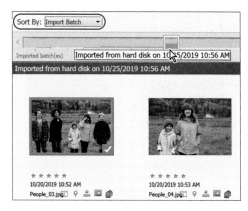

Setting up a multi-criterion search

In the course of this lesson, you've already made a few "and" and "or" searches; these are multi-criterion searches. Up to this point, you've achieved this by using a combination of filters applied via the folders, albums, and tags lists, with side trips to the People, Places, and Events views.

The Search view lets you set up a complex search with multiple filters—all on a single screen—and makes even single-criterion searches more visual and intuitive.

1   If necessary, clear any active filters and deselect any album or folder selected in the left panel by clicking Back or All Media in the actions bar. Make sure that you have no images selected.

2   Click the Search button at the upper right of the Organizer workspace.

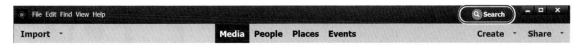

3   We'll start with a simple text search. Type the letter **T** in the text bar at the top of the search screen. Photoshop Elements shows a list of suggestions based on the people, places, events, and keyword tags that already exist in your catalog. Each kind of tag has a distinctive icon. In this case the search has found one keyword tag, one event tag, one people tag, and five Smart Tags, which are generated automatically by Photoshop Elements.

4   Swipe over the letter **T** and type **washington**; then press Enter / Return. The search screen displays all of the photos with the Washington keyword. The text bar shows your single search term. To the right of the word "Washington" in the text bar, type a minus sign (–), a space, and **Pike**. Select the Pike Place Market location tag and then press Enter / Return. The search results are reduced.

5   In the text bar, click the minus sign between the two search terms and change this from a "not" search (one that *excludes* one or more terms) to an "and" search. The search results grid now shows only those photos that have the Washington *and* Pike Place Market keywords.

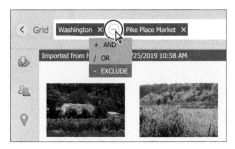
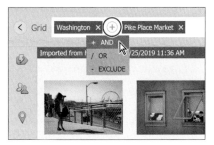

6   Click the Clear Search button (⊗) at the right of the text search bar.

> **Tip:** In several earlier exercises, you used the Find > By Filename command to isolate photos with a given word in their file names. In such cases, the menu command is preferable to a Search window text search, which may also return images tagged with Smart Tags that include the searched word. For example, a search for a series of files with the word "run" in their name would include any image that Photoshop Elements had automatically tagged with the words "run" and "running."

7 Hover the pointer over the Smart Tags icon, just below the text search bar. Scroll down through the list of tags that were automatically generated when Photoshop Elements analyzed the images at import. The list is not arranged alphabetically; it's more useful to scan the images for visual cues, rather than reading the words. Click one or two of the tags that show the highest image counts, clearing the search each time.

8 Move the pointer slowly down the column of search criteria icons, noting the way the People, Places, and Date groups are presented. Click at least one group from each criterion to see the photos marked with that people, places, or events tag. Every click adds a term to the search bar; clear the search each time before testing the next criterion.

9 Hover over the Keywords icon and click the listings for the Pacific Northwest and Wren Hill Farm tags. By default the two terms are separated in the search bar by the OR operator (/); click the forward slash between keywords to change this to an "and" search, as you did in step 5.

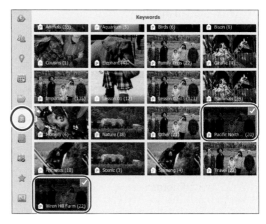

10 Inspect the Albums and Events groups without adding to the search terms; then move to the Ratings criterion and click the fourth star.

As you can see in the search bar, you've set up a search for those images that have both the Pacific Northwest and Wren Hill Farms tags, and a rating of four or more stars.

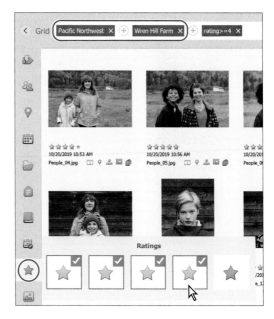

11 Click the Clear Search button ( ) at the right of the text search bar.

Letting Photoshop Elements curate your photo collection automatically

The Auto Curate feature uses the same media analysis technology that enables Face Recognition, Smart Tags, and visual searches to save you time and effort by curating your catalog automatically.

Auto Curate intelligently ranks the photos in your catalog—or the images in a selected folder, album, or search result—based not only on their quality as determined by the media analysis algorithms, but also on your own input as you sort your library using the tagging and grouping tools in the Organizer.

As well as prioritizing images that are well focused, with balanced color and lighting and useful Smart Tags, Auto Curate filters your catalog for the people that you've tagged most frequently and the pictures that you've included in albums, trips, and events—automatically finding the best of those photographs that mean the most to you.

To have Photoshop Elements curate your photos automatically, first make sure Face Recognition and Media Analysis are enabled in the Organizer preferences. Next, select an image source—either your entire unfiltered catalog, a particular folder or album, or the results of a more complex search made using any of the methods discussed in this lesson—then, click the check box at the right of the search bar above the thumbnail grid in the Media view to activate Auto Curate. Use the adjacent slider, or enter a number in the text box, to designate the number of images you wish Photoshop elements to choose for you.

For best results with newly imported photos, allow Face Recognition and Smart Tag analysis to complete before using Auto Curate.

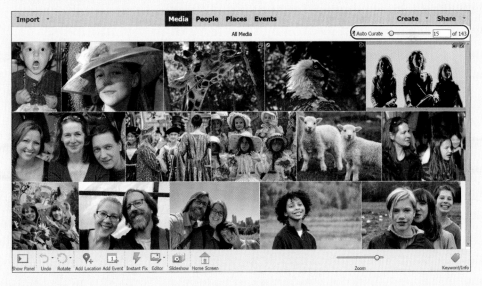

Saving complex searches

It's unlikely that the results of the search you set up would ever change, no matter how many photos you add to your library.

However, when you set up a search with more generalized criteria, it can return more images each time new matches are added to the catalog.

1 In the Search screen, select the Family Trips tag (in the Keywords category), the Sisters people tag (use a text search), and the Seattle, Washington tag (under Places). Set a rating of three stars or higher.

There are no photos in your catalog that match these criteria—but that may well change after the next school break. You can save this search and run it periodically to find the best shots to add to your happiest family album.

2 Click the Grid button to the left of the search bar; then, click Options at the right of the search result bar in the Media view and choose Save Search Criteria As Saved Search. In the Create Saved Search dialog box, name the saved search **Best of Sisters Seattle Vacations**, and then click OK.

3 Click the Back button in the actions bar to clear the three-term search; then, choose Find > By Saved Searches.

Tip: To modify the criteria that define a saved search, and even change it from an "and" search to an "or" search, select the search in the Saved searches dialog box and then click New Search Query.

4 Select your saved search in the Saved searches dialog box, and then click Open. The search results bar lists your saved search criteria. Click clear in the search results bar.

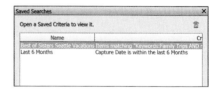

Finding photos by searching their metadata

Some metadata attached to an image file is generated automatically by the camera; more is added when you spend time organizing your catalog. Searchable metadata includes file attributes, tags, ratings, albums, version sets, captions, notes, capture date, and a range of camera model, lens, and exposure details—to mention just a few!

The Details (Metadata) search lets you leverage all that information to find exactly the files you want; run any search, and then filter for just the shots taken with a wide-angle lens.

1 Choose Find > By Details (Metadata). Choose the criteria you want from the menus provided. Any metadata search you define can be saved as a saved search by simply activating that option below the search rules. Set up a few search rules of your own, and examine the criteria menus to see the many searchable categories.

2 Click Cancel to dismiss the Find by Details (Metadata) dialog.

Finding photos by visual similarity

In Lesson 2, you saw how easy it is to tag the faces in large numbers of photos using People Recognition. In this section you'll look at another set of tools that harness the power of Photoshop Elements' automatic image analysis software.

1   In the Keywords list at the top of the Tags panel, click the search box to the left of the Animals keyword to isolate all the photos with that tag. Select all of the stacks that you see in the grid and choose Edit > Stack > Unstack Photos. Choose Edit > Deselect, or simply click an empty part of the grid.

2   Choose Find > By Visual Searches > Visually Similar Photos And Videos.

3   Drag the image DSC_0609.jpg to the Find bar. If you see a warning that your catalog has not yet been fully indexed, click OK, Start Indexing.

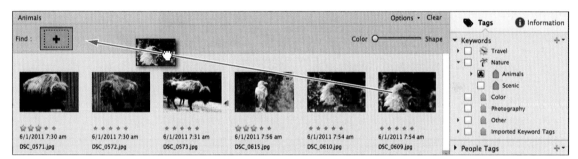

The search returns images displayed in the Media Browser in descending order of visual similarity to the photo you dragged to the Find bar. A marker displaying the calculated percentage of visual similarity for each image appears in the lower-left corner of its thumbnail, and a slider appears in the Find bar for tweaking the search results. The optimum position for the slider will vary for each image searched.

Note: The search results you see onscreen may vary from those illustrated here, depending on your operating system.

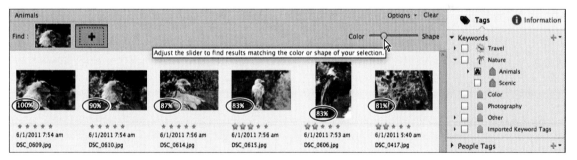

4   Experiment with the Color–Shape slider. A move to the left weights the analysis toward similarities in color, texture, and pattern; moving the slider to the right returns images that share more in terms of shape, proportion, and composition.

5   Right-click the thumbnail in the Find bar and choose Remove From Search. Make another image the object of a new search. Experiment with the Color–Shape slider, and then repeat the process for several more images.

In some cases it may be helpful to add a second reference photo to your visual search. You can either drag a second image to the Find bar or click the plus sign (+) to the right of the first reference photo in the Find bar and select a second image from the Media Browser. The search will look for a combination of visual attributes.

6   Click Clear at the right of the actions bar; then, isolate the Animals photos again, as you did in step 1.

Finding objects in photos

You can search your photo library for a specific object.

1   In the Media Browser, select the image DSC_0472.jpg, a photo of a siamang.

2   Choose Find > By Visual Searches > Objects Appearing In Photos.

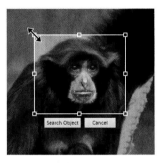

3   In the enlarged view, drag the bounding box to the ape's head. Use the handles at the corners of the bounding box to fit it neatly around the shape, and then click Search Object.

Once again, the results are ranked by similarity to the reference object. As for all visual searches, you can refine the search results by tweaking the Color–Shape slider.

4   When you're done, click the Back button at the left of the actions bar.

Finding and removing duplicate photos

▶ **Tip:** The Duplicate Photos search can be particularly helpful for dealing with long series of photos captured with a camera set to the auto-bracketing or burst mode.

The last of the visual search options finds and groups duplicated, or very similar, images, and then gives you the opportunity to either stack them or delete them from your catalog—great for housekeeping as your image library gets bigger.

The process is very similar to the automated stacking workflow (see "Stacking photos automatically" earlier in this lesson). You'll be presented with groups of similar photos; for each group, you can stack the photos and keep them in the catalog, confirm them for removal, or do nothing.

You can search an individual folder for duplicates, or run the search on a selection of images in the Media Browser. If there is no folder or album selected as the image source, no filter in operation, and no active selection in the Media Browser, Photoshop Elements searches your entire catalog for duplicates.

Congratulations—you've reached the end of Lesson 3! In this lesson, you've created version sets, stacks, and albums, and discovered more techniques for finding and managing your files.

Review questions

1 Do you need to be in the Media view to add keyword tags to an image?

2 What are version sets and stacks?

3 What is the main difference between grouping files using shared keyword tags and grouping them in an album?

4 What is the purpose of the Timeline view?

5 Why would you save search criteria as a saved search?

Review answers

1 Although the Tags panel in the Media view offers the most keyword tagging options, you can add keywords to your photos in any of the other three Organizer views by typing in the text box in the Image Tags panel. To show the Image Tags panel in the People and Events views, you'll first need to expand a stack and then click the Info button at the right of the taskbar. In the Places view, the Info button is available at all times.

2 A version set automatically groups an original photo and its edited versions. Stacks can be created manually or automatically to group similar or related photos. A version set can be nested inside a stack; if you edit a photo that's in a stack, the photo and its edited copy are put in a version set nested inside the stack. Both version sets and stacks make it easier to locate photos by reducing the clutter in the thumbnail grid.

3 The main difference between grouping files in an album, rather than with a shared keyword tag, is that in an album you can rearrange the order of the files.

4 The Timeline is an effective search tool in its own right, but it's very useful in combination with other search and filter tools to help you to refine a search or to navigate the results. You might use the Timeline to narrow search results to files from a particular import batch, or images captured within a specific date range.

5 For many searches, you can easily "save" the results—in other words, preserve the grouping of images that match the search criteria—by creating an album or by tagging all the photos returned by the search with the same keyword, place tag, or event tag. Once established, these groupings are static; their content will not change over time unless you manually add or remove photos or tags. A saved search, on the other hand, can be more versatile; you can run the same complex search again and again, returning more images that match the search criteria each time you add photos to your catalog.

4 IMAGE EDITING BACKGROUND AND BASICS

Lesson overview

Photoshop Elements offers a comprehensive suite of easy-to-use tools and a choice of three editing modes, so it's simple to achieve impressive results, whatever your experience level. Guided Edit mode helps novices learn as they work, Quick Edit mode presents an array of one-touch controls for correcting common image problems, and Expert Edit mode delivers all the power and sophistication experienced users expect.

This lesson begins with an overview of the core concepts behind image correction, and then introduces a range of approachable techniques to help you get more from your photos in just a few clicks:

- Making quick and easy edits in the Organizer
- Understanding the histogram, levels, and white balance
- Working in the Quick Edit, Guided Edit, and Expert Edit modes
- Correcting an image using Smart Fix and Auto Smart Tone
- Turning frowns into smiles and opening closed eyes
- Applying editing presets selectively with the Smart Brush
- Working with camera raw images

 This lesson will take about 90 minutes to complete. To get the lesson files used in this chapter, download them from the web page for this book at www.adobepress.com/PSECIB2020. For more information, see "Accessing the lesson files and Web Edition" in the Getting Started section at the beginning of this book.

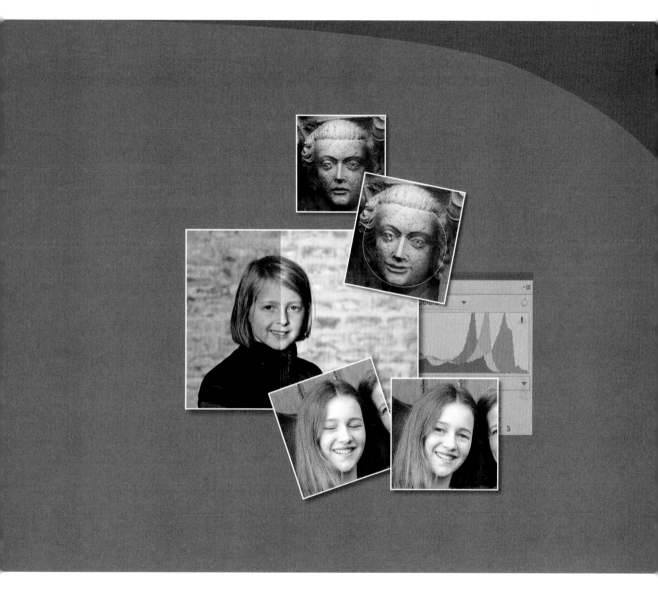

Explore the many powerful and versatile editing tools that make it easy to get more from your photos in Photoshop Elements—even if you're a beginner. Start with a few of the easy-to-use, one-step image-correction features, and then experiment with some more advanced techniques, such as layering preset adjustments with the Smart Brush.

Note: Before you start this lesson, make sure you've set up a folder for your lesson files and downloaded the Lesson 4 folder from your Account page at www.peachpit.com, as detailed in "Accessing the lesson files and Web Edition" and "Creating a work folder " in the "Getting Started" section at the beginning of this book. You should also have created a new work catalog (see "Creating a catalog for working with this book" in Lesson 1).

Getting started

You'll start by importing the sample images for this lesson to your CIB Catalog.

1 Start Photoshop Elements and click Organizer in the Home screen. Check the lower-right corner of the Organizer workspace to make sure the CIB Catalog is loaded—if not, choose File > Manage Catalogs and select it from the list.

2 Click the Import button at the upper left of the Organizer workspace and choose From Files And Folders from the drop-down menu. In the Get Photos And Videos From Files And Folders dialog box, locate and select your Lesson 4 folder. Disable the option Get Photos From Subfolders and the automatic processing options; then, click Get Media.

3 In the Import Attached Keyword Tags dialog box, click Select All and then click OK.

Editing photos in the Organizer

You can fix a range of common image problems without even leaving the Organizer.

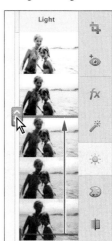

1 In the Media Browser, select the image DSCN0532.jpg. Click the Instant Fix button (⚡) in the taskbar to open the image in Instant Fix mode, and then click the Light button (☀) in the actions bar at right.

Tip: On a small screen, the entire range of an Instant Fix adjustment may be represented by only seven preview thumbnails, whereas a larger screen may show 11; what you see onscreen may differ from the illustrations.

2 Experiment with the slider; as you work, the original state of the image is indicated by a red marker. Drag the slider upward from its original position about two thirds of the way to the top. Click Save at the lower right of the workspace, and then click Done.

The edited file is grouped with the original in a version set and will appear in the media browser as the top image.

3 Click the arrow at the right of the image frame to expand the version set. In the expanded version set, select the unedited original, DSCN0532.jpg. Click the Instant Fix button (⚡) in the taskbar; then, click the Color button (🎨) in the actions bar. Experiment with the slider; then, drag it upward from its original position about two thirds of the way to the top. Click Save, and then click Done.

Note: The most recent version always appears at the left in an expanded version set and becomes the image displayed on top of the collapsed version set.

4 Making sure that you select the original image each time, repeat the process for the Clarity (🎛) and Smart Fix (🪄) adjustments, saving the results as you did in step 3. Drag the Clarity slider to its minimum setting to give the image a soft, "dreamy" look. There is no slider for the Smart Fix edit; Smart Fix is a one-click tool that analyzes the image and then combines multiple adjustments to correct exposure, contrast, color balance, and saturation automatically.

5   Double-click the original image to see it in the single image view. Use the left arrow key on your keyboard to compare the unedited photo with the results of your single-click adjustments. Double-click the enlarged image to return to the thumbnail view. Select all four edited versions; then, right-click any of the selected thumbnails and choose Delete Selected Items From Catalog.

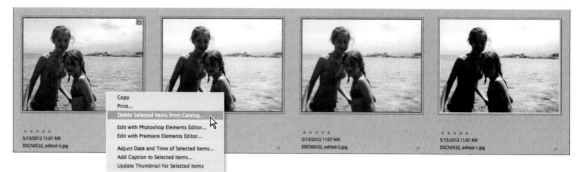

6   In the Confirm Deletion From Catalog dialog box, click to activate the option Also Delete Selected Item(s) From The Hard Disk; then, click OK. You'll use different techniques to edit this photo later in the lesson.

7   In the Media Browser, select the image DSC_3607.jpg, and then click the Instant Fix button ( ). Click the Light button ( ), and then drag the slider up about halfway to the top from where it started. Click the Color button ( ), then drag the slider down about halfway to the bottom. Toggle the switch in the taskbar to compare before and after views.

You've improved this photo dramatically in just a few moments—without even leaving the Organizer.

▶ **Tip:** If you have a group of photos that all need to be cropped to the same size or converted to antique sepia—or a series of shots from the same shoot that all require similar lighting adjustments—select them and then click the Instant Fix button to work on them as a set.

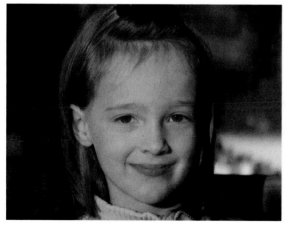 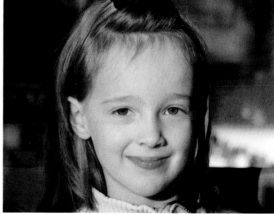

8   Click the Back button ( ) at the upper left of the Instant Fix workspace; then, click No in the Save Changes dialog. You'll work more with this photo in the next exercise.

Recognizing what your photo needs

For some photos, the instant fixes in the Organizer will be enough, but for more control—and access to the full power of Photoshop Elements editing tools—you'll work in the Editor. Before you explore the Editor's three working modes, we'll look at some of the basic concepts behind image adjustment and correction.

Recognizing and understanding a photo's problems and deficiencies makes the task of correcting and enhancing the image much faster and easier—even when you're simply choosing from automatic fixes as you did in the full screen view.

1   In the actions bar above the Media Browser, make sure the Sort By order is set to Oldest. Ctrl-click / Command-click to select both of the photos that you've already worked with in this lesson; then add the image DSC_0212.jpg to the selection. Click the Editor button (not the arrow beside it) in the taskbar.

Note: The Editor opens in whichever edit mode was active when you last exited the application.

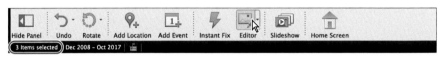

2   If you're not already in Expert Edit mode, click Expert in the mode picker at the top of the Editor workspace; then, choose Window > Reset panels.

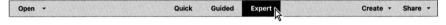

3   Click the arrow beside the More button (⬛) at the right of the taskbar and choose Histogram from the menu.

Note: The triangular alert icon will reappear on the histogram each time you change an image; click the icon to refresh the graph.

4   If necessary, change the Channel setting in the Histogram panel from the default Colors to RGB; then click the triangular alert icon (⚠) at the upper right of the black and white Histogram curve to refresh the histogram graph with uncached information.

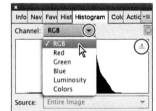

Understanding the histogram

A histogram is a graph that maps the distribution of tonal values in an image, from the shadows (at the left end of the curve) through the midtones to the highlights (at the right of the curve).

A peak in the curve shows that the corresponding part of the tonal range is well represented—in other words, the image contains plenty of detail in that area. Inversely, a trough in the histogram curve can indicate a deficiency of image detail.

You can use the histogram both as a "diagnostic" tool that can help you recognize where corrections need to be made and also as a source of dynamic feedback that enables you to assess how effective an adjustment will be, even as you set it up.

1 If you don't see the Photo Bin at the bottom of the Editor workspace, click the Photo Bin button (⌷) in the taskbar.

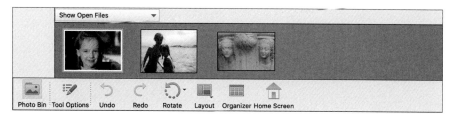

2 Watch the curve in the Histogram panel as you click each of the thumbnails in the Photo Bin in turn to bring that image to the front in the Edit pane.

▶ **Tip:** Refresh the histogram for each image as it becomes active.

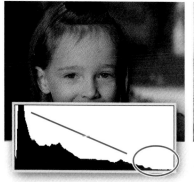

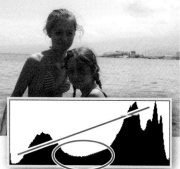

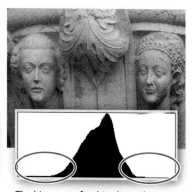

This histogram is heavily weighted toward the left and deficient in the midtones; the image is overly dark, with a lack of tonal depth and definition in the girl's face.

With plenty of information at the ends of the curve, the overall contrast is good, but the central trough indicates a lack of midtone detail that gives the shaded skin a dull, underexposed look.

The histogram for this photo shows almost no information at either end and a somewhat lopsided spread of midtones. The image lacks contrast; it appears flat and slightly overexposed.

3 For each of the photos you've already worked with, click the thumbnail in the Photo Bin to bring the image window to the front; then, choose Enhance > Adjust Smart Fix. Watch the image and its histogram change as you drag the Fix Amount slider to set a value of 60% (for Auto Smart Fix, the value is 40%). Click OK to close the Adjust Smart Fix dialog box.

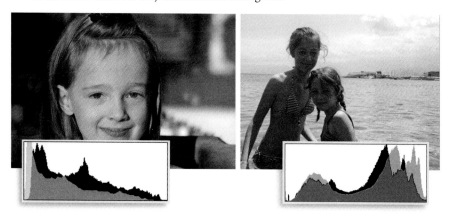

The changes in the images are reflected in their histograms (shown here with the original curves overlaid in gray for comparison). In both cases there is more information in the midtone range, boosting detail and definition in skin tones, and a better spread of tones from dark to light, improving the overall contrast.

4 Bring the image DSC_3607.jpg to the front and choose File > Save As. Name the new file **DSC_3607_AutoSmart.jpg**, to be saved to the My CIB Work folder and included in the Organizer, but not in a version set. Click Save, then click OK to accept the JPEG quality setting and close the file. Repeat the process for the image DSCN0532.jpg, making sure to add **_AutoSmart** to the file name.

Adjusting levels

Once you're familiar with the histogram, the Levels dialog box provides a direct way to adjust the distribution curve in order to improve an image's tonal range.

1 You should still have the photo DSC_0212.jpg open from the previous exercise. Choose Enhance > Adjust Lighting > Levels. In the Levels dialog box, make sure the Preview option is activated.

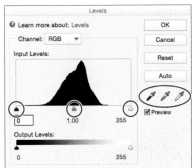

In the Levels dialog box, you can use the shadows, midtones, and highlights sliders below the Input Levels histogram graph (left, middle, and right, respectively), or the Set Black Point, Set Gray Point, and Set White Point eyedroppers at the right, to redefine the end points of the curve and adjust the distribution of image information along its length.

Although the midtones range is most in need of adjustment in this image, it's important to get the shadows and highlights right first.

2 Select the Set Black Point Eyedropper tool; then, watch the histogram as you click the dark area in the lower-left corner of the image. The white line and gray area in the histogram indicate the shape of the curve prior to this adjustment.

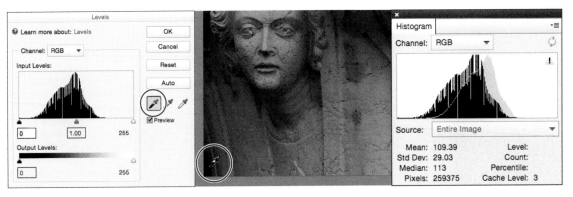

The black point eyedropper has not worked well on our lesson photo; it should ideally be used to sample a black area rather than a colored shadow. The deeper shadows have been "clipped" to black and the color has become much cooler as the warm hues have been removed to produce a pure black at the sampled point.

3 In the Levels dialog box, click Reset and we'll try another method for adjusting the shadows. Hold down the Alt / Option key as you drag the shadows slider to the right to set a value of 70, just inside the left end of the tonal curve. The clipping preview shows you where the darkest parts of the image are.

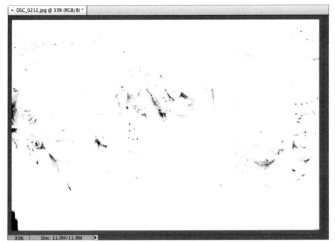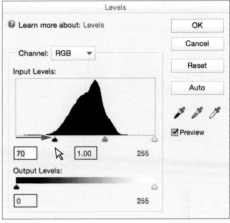

4 Watch the histogram as you release first the Alt / Option key and then the mouse button. The histogram curve shifts to the left—possibly a little too much. You can see that the left end of the curve has become truncated. In the Levels dialog box, use the shadows slider to reduce the value to 45. The curve in the histogram is adjusted so that there is minimal truncation (clipping).

5 Hold down the Alt / Option key; then, drag the highlights slider to 185. The clipping preview begins to show significant clipping of image detail in the brighter parts of the photo, as shown in the illustration below. Correct the adjustment by dragging the highlights slider back to 195, where the clipping is minimal; then release the Alt / Option key and the mouse button.

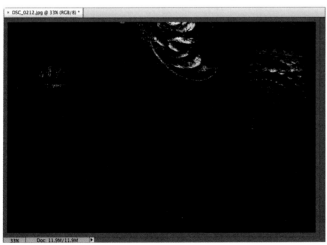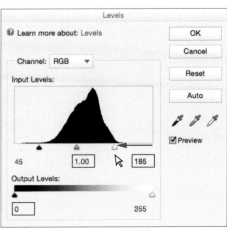

6 In the Levels controls, drag the midtones slider (the gray triangle below the center of the graph) to the right to set the midtones value to 0.8.

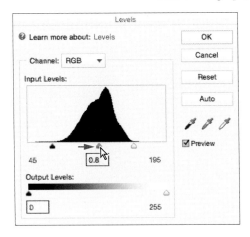

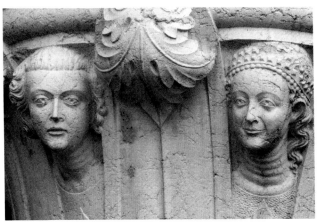

7 In the Histogram panel, click the yellow alert icon to refresh the display.

▶ **Tip:** Your edits have caused some gaps and spikes in the histogram curve. Where possible, avoid adjustments that create large gaps; even if the image still looks good onscreen, gaps indicate a loss of image data that may be apparent as color banding when printed.

8 Compare the original histogram (the red overlay) to the adjusted curve. Information has spread outward, widening the midtones range as well as filling out both the highlights and shadows.

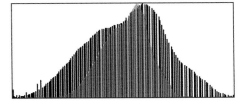

9 Click OK to close the Levels dialog box. Select Edit > Undo Levels, or press Ctrl+Z / Command+Z, to see how the image looked before editing. Choose Edit > Redo Levels, or Press Ctrl+Y / Command+Y to reinstate your corrections.

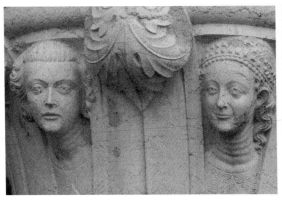 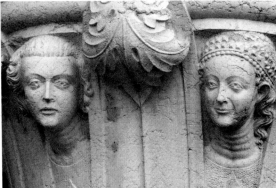

10 Choose File > Save As. Name the new file **DSC_0212_Levels.jpg** and set your Lessons / My CIB Work folder as the destination. Activate the option Include In The Elements Organizer and disable Save In Version Set With Original. Click Save; then click OK to accept the JPEG settings. Choose File > Close.

Assessing a photo's color balance

Artificial light, unusual shooting conditions, and incorrect camera settings can all result in unwelcome color casts in an image. Unless your camera is properly set up to compensate for current weather conditions, photos shot on an overcast day may have a flat, bluish cast due to a deficiency in the warmer colors, while the "golden" light of late-afternoon sunshine can produce an overly warm appearance. Fluorescent lighting is notorious for producing a dull, greenish tint.

In this exercise, you'll work with an image that has the opposite problem: a warm yellow-red cast commonly seen in indoor shots captured under tungsten lighting. We'll start with a look at the Balance controls in the Quick Edit mode.

1   To switch to Quick Edit mode, click Quick in the view picker above the editing pane. In Quick Edit mode, choose Window > Reset panels.

2   Choose File > Open. Navigate to your Lesson 4 folder; then, select the image DSC_0241.jpg, and click Open.

3   In the Adjustments panel at the right of the Quick Edit workspace, expand the Balance panel. Color imbalances are defined in terms of an image's *temperature* and *tint*; the Balance panel has a separate control pane for adjusting each of these attributes. For now, make sure that the Temperature tab is selected just below the panel's header.

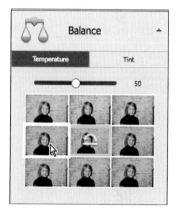

The grid of preview thumbnails shows the full range of variation possible with this control. Clicking the central thumbnail resets an image to its original state—a blue frame highlights the currently selected setting.

4   Move the pointer over each preview thumbnail in the grid in turn to see that level of adjustment applied temporarily to the image in the work area. A white frame highlights the setting currently previewed.

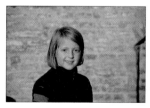 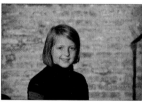 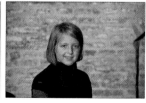

▶ **Tip:** You can preview and apply incremental settings between the levels represented in the preview thumbnails by dragging the slider left or right.

5   Click the Tint tab above the slider control and explore the variations.

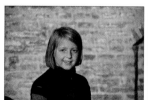 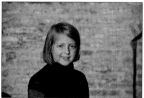 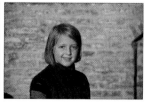

The color temperature of an image accounts for casts ranging from cool blue to hot orange-red; "tint" refers to casts ranging from yellow-green to magenta-pink.

Working with the Temperature and Tint settings

If you're new to color correction, the preview thumbnails provide a useful visual reference for understanding what's behind an unwanted color cast. Before we take a closer look at the issue in the Expert Edit mode, you can correct this photo using the Balance controls and save the results for comparison to other techniques.

1 In the Temperature pane, click the preview to the left of the central thumbnail.

Note: When you switch panes, the Editor doesn't retain the original value. So if you want to adjust the Temperature value again after changing Tint, you'll find that Temperature is set back to the original value of 50. The image retains the edit you made, but the slider resets each time.

2 Switch to the Tint pane. Move the pointer over the preview to the right of the central thumbnail. For the Tint controls, moving by one preview in this direction increases the value by an increment of 25—a little too far for our lesson photo. Instead, drag the slider to set a value of 2, or click the number itself and type a new value of **2**.

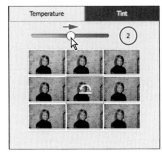

3 Choose File > Save As. Activate the option Save As A Copy. Name the copy **DSC_0241_QuickBalance.jpg**, to be saved to your My CIB Work folder and included in the Organizer but not in a version set; then, click Save. Click OK to accept the default JPEG quality settings.

4 In the Adjustments panel header, click the Reset Image button to reset all the controls, reverting the image to its original state.

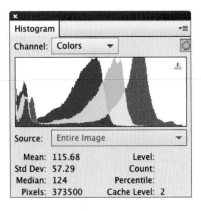

Consulting the color histogram

Let's see what the histogram has to say about this photo.

1 Click Expert in the mode picker at the top of the Editor workspace.

2 If the Histogram panel is not already open, choose Window > Histogram. If necessary, set the Channel menu at the top of the Histogram panel to Colors.

The histogram corroborates the visual evidence: this photo has a serious imbalance in the spread of color information. Rather than a largely unified curve, there is a marked separation of colors; reds and yellows are over-represented in the upper midtones and highlights, while greens and blues are lacking.

In the next exercise, you'll learn how to correct a color cast by adjusting the photo's *white balance*—or redefining the *white point*—to re-calibrate the image's color.

Adjusting the white balance

A color cast has the appearance of a tinted transparency overlaid on all the colors in your photograph. For example, the yellow-red cast commonly associated with indoor shots captured under tungsten lighting will be visible even on objects that should appear white, and even white paper photographed under fluorescent lighting will have a blue-green tint.

To adjust the white point, or white balance, you need to identify what should be a neutral tone in your photo—either a white object or an area of gray that should appear neither noticeably cool nor warm. Photoshop Elements will then recalculate the color values across the entire image in relation to whatever pixels you've defined as the new, color-neutral benchmark.

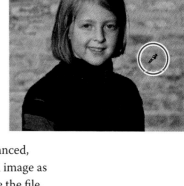

1   Choose Enhance > Adjust Color > Remove Color Cast. The Remove Color Cast dialog box appears, and the pointer becomes an eyedropper cursor (🖋).

2   Click with the eyedropper to sample a mid-gray from the mortar between the bricks in the background. If this introduces an overly cool blue cast, click the Reset button in the Remove Color Cast dialog box and try again. Try targeting a lighter tone.

3   When you're satisfied with the results, click OK to close the Remove Color Cast dialog box.

4   Examine the color histogram. The histogram curve is much more balanced, though the photo could still be improved. For now, save the corrected image as **DSC_0241_WhiteBalance.jpg**, with all the usual settings; then, close the file.

Although blue and cyan are still predominant in the lower midtones, the histogram curve is now more unified, without the dramatic separation of colors you saw earlier.

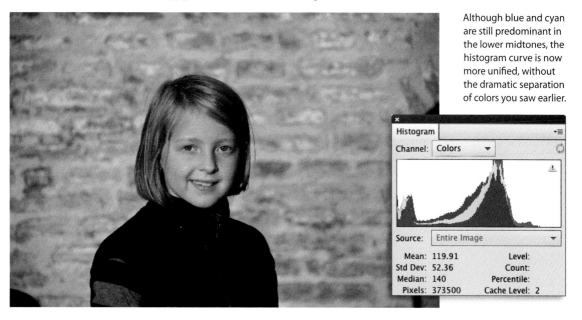

Making easy color and lighting adjustments

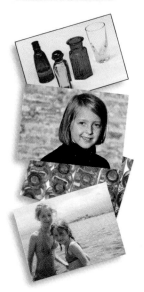

In this section, we'll begin our exploration of the Editor, taking a closer look at the tools and techniques that will enable you to get the best from your photos. Now that you've soaked up a little theory, you'll find it easier to understand the processes, whether you're using one-click fixes or making detailed selective edits.

Whether the problem is inadequate exposure, a lack of contrast, or an unsightly color cast, you can make fast fixes using the simple controls in Quick Edit mode, let the Guided Edit mode step you through a wide range of editing tasks, make detailed adjustments in Expert Edit mode—or even arrange for Photoshop Elements to batch process your photos, applying your choice of automatic corrections.

Fixing photos automatically in batches

In this exercise, you'll batch process all of the image files used in this lesson, saving the auto-adjusted photos as copies so that you can compare the results of the automatic processing to the edits you make using other techniques.

1   If the Editor is not still in Expert mode, click Expert in the mode picker. Choose File > Process Multiple Files. In the Quick Fix options, at the upper right of the Process Multiple Files dialog box, click the check boxes to activate all four auto-fix options: Auto Levels, Auto Contrast, Auto Color, and Sharpen.

2   At the upper left of the dialog box, choose Folder from the Process Files From menu. Under Source, click the Browse button. Locate and select the Lesson 4 folder as the source folder for the images to be processed. Click OK / Choose. Under Destination, click Browse to set the My CIB Work folder as the destination for the processed copies.

Note: For Windows users: if you get an alert warning that files could not be processed, ignore it. A hidden system file under some versions is the cause, which will have no impact on the success of your project.

3   Under File Naming, activate the Rename Files option. Choose Document Name from the menu on the left, and then type **_AutoFix** in the second field. This will add the appendix "_AutoFix" to the existing document names as the processed copies are saved.

4   Review the settings in the dialog box. Make sure that the resizing and file conversion options under Image Size and File Type are disabled, and then click OK.

Photoshop Elements opens, processes, and closes the images. The newly created copies are automatically tagged with the same keywords as the source files.

Adding the auto-corrected files to your catalog

When you modify an image in the Editor, the Include In Organizer option in the Save and Save As dialog boxes is activated by default. However, when you batch-edit files with the Process Multiple Files command, this option isn't part of the process—you must add the automatically edited copies to the Organizer manually.

1 Switch to the Organizer by clicking the Organizer button (⊞) in the taskbar; then, click the Import button at the upper left of the Organizer workspace and choose From Files And Folders from the drop-down menu.

2 In the Get Photos And Videos From Files And Folders dialog box, locate and open your My CIB Work folder. Ctrl-click / Command-click or marquee-select all the files with the suffix "_AutoFix." Disable any automatic processing option that is currently active; then, click Get Media.

3 In the Import Attached Keyword Tags dialog box, click Select All; then, click OK. The files are imported to your CIB Catalog and displayed in the Media Browser. Click the Back button (◀) to display all the images in your catalog.

Correcting photos in Quick Edit mode

In Quick Edit mode, Photoshop Elements conveniently groups easy-to-use controls for the most common basic image correction operations in the Adjustments panel.

Earlier in this lesson, you tried some one-click fixes in the Organizer's Instant Fix panel. Later, you applied a combination of the same automatic fixes while batch processing files. The Adjustments panel presents similar automatic adjustment options but also gives you the opportunity to preview and fine-tune the settings.

1 You should still be in the Organizer from the last exercise. If you don't see the right panel group, click the Keyword/Info button at the far right of the taskbar. If you don't see the list of keywords, click the Tags tab at the top of the right panel. Expand the Imported Keyword Tags category; then, either double-click the Lesson 04 tag or click the empty search box at the left.

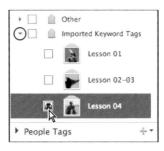

Note: In this illustration, the Lesson 04 tag icon has been customized; you may see a different thumbnail.

2 Select the original photo of the colored perfume bottles, DSC_2474.jpg, making sure not to confuse the unedited file with the AutoFix copy; then, click the Editor button (🖼)—not the arrow beside it—in the taskbar.

3 Use the mode picker to switch the Editor to Quick mode. If you don't see the Adjustments panel at the right, click the Adjustments button in the taskbar.

Applying quick fixes

All of the Quick Edit adjustments have manual controls. Automatic fixes are available for Smart Fix, Lighting, Color, and Sharpen, but not for Exposure or Balance.

Note: Smart Fix is a combination of several adjustments; it corrects overall color balance and improves shadow and highlight detail.

1 Choose Before & After - Horizontal from the View menu above the Edit pane. In the Adjustments panel, expand the Smart Fix pane and click the Auto button. Notice the immediate effect on the image in the After view.

2 Expand the Lighting pane, and then click both Auto Levels and Auto Contrast, noting the effects of the adjustments in the After view.

3 Expand the Color pane and click the Auto button; then expand the Exposure pane and drag the slider to set a value of 0.7.

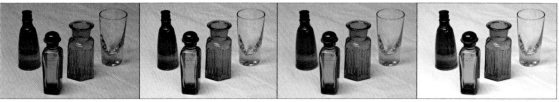

Smart Fix: Auto   + Levels and Contrast: Auto   + Color: Auto   + Exposure: 0.7

4 Choose File > Save As. In the Save As dialog box, type **DSC_2474_QuickFix.jpg** as the name of the new file, to be saved to your My CIB Work folder in JPEG format and included in the Organizer but not as part of a version set. Click Save. In the JPEG Options dialog box, accept the default quality and click OK.

> ▶ **Tip:** Click a thumbnail in the preview grid to apply that level of adjustment; then, use the slider to fine-tune the effect. The preview grids not only provide an intuitive editing interface but also serve as a great way to learn the effects of the various adjustment controls as you work with them.

5 Expand the Color pane once again and click the Saturation tab. A grid of preview thumbnails shows the range of variation possible with the Saturation slider. A blue frame highlights the central thumbnail, which represents the image in its current state. Move the pointer slowly over each thumbnail in the grid to preview your image with that level of saturation in the work area.

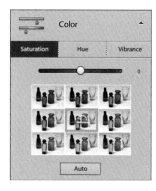

6 Repeat the process for the Color pane's Hue and Vibrance controls.

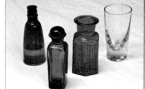

Saturation: -100

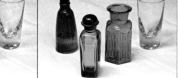

Saturation: +100   Vibrance: -100

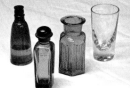

Vibrance: +100

7 Return to the Lighting pane and explore the Shadows, Midtones, and Highlights tabs in the same way. To reset a control, click the thumbnail with the Reset icon (not always the central preview).

8 To discard any changes you've made and revert the image to its last saved state, click the Reset Image button in the header of the Adjustments pane.

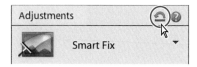

9 Choose File > Close. Don't save any changes.

Adding quick effects, textures, and frames

In Quick Edit mode, the Effects, Textures, and Frames panels present a range of one-click choices that make it easy to add a creative touch to your photos. You can access these three panels by choosing from the buttons at the right of the taskbar.

The Effects (fx) panel offers instant photo effects, which simulate nostalgic camera and film looks; a range of color, black-and-white, and duotone photo processing styles; and sketch and lithographic treatments that can turn even a boring snapshot into a work of art. The Effects panel also hosts the Smart Looks feature, which presents effect suggestions tailored to suit the image you're working with.

Choose from the Textures panel to give the surface of your photo the look of peeling paint, soft canvas, or pitted chrome. Other textures are applied with a colored pattern overlay. Add a frame to make your image really stand out. The Frames panel presents choices from simple graphic photo-print borders to the 3D, photographic look of the Aged, Scrapbook, and Flowers And Buttons frames.

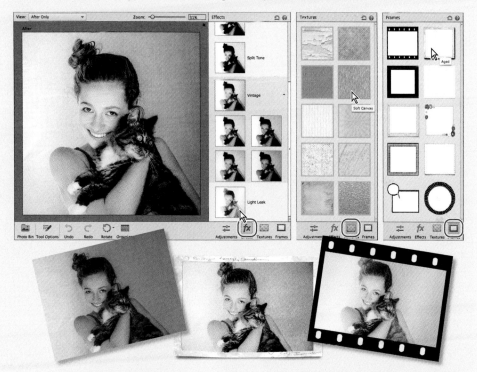

You can scale, rotate, or move a photo inside its frame without leaving Quick Edit mode. If you prefer to have more control over the way the effects and textures are applied to your image, you can take it into Expert mode, where each effect and texture has its own layer and layer mask. You can modify the opacity and blending mode for each layer, or edit its layer mask to create areas in the photo where the effect or texture is reduced or removed entirely.

Turning a frown into a smile

If your family album includes pictures of a tired toddler, temperamental teen, or grumpy grandfather, Photoshop Elements can help you cheer them up! The Adjust Facial Features tool makes it easy to turn a frown upside down, widen squinting eyes, and tweak other facial features—so everyone in your photos looks their best.

The Adjust Facial Features tool makes use of face-aware technology to identify the faces in your photo, and then lets you adjust a variety of attributes for the eyes, nose, lips, forehead, and jaw. You'll find the Adjust Facial Features command in the Enhance menu in both the Quick Edit mode and Expert mode.

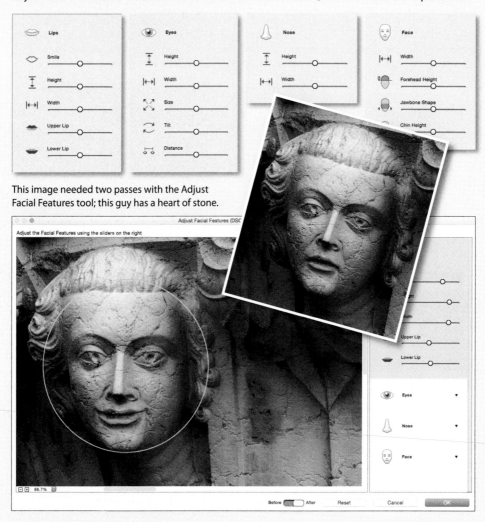

This image needed two passes with the Adjust Facial Features tool; this guy has a heart of stone.

Working in Guided Edit mode

If you're a newcomer to digital image editing and you're not sure exactly what adjustments an image needs, the Guided Edit mode is a great place to start. You'll find a range of procedures for correcting lighting and exposure, each with easy-to-follow prompts and instructions that make it simple for even a novice to get great results. You can improve your photos quickly, at the same time as learning image correction concepts and techniques that you can apply even in Expert mode.

● **Note:** For help with some of the common problems you might encounter as you try the more advanced tasks in Photoshop Elements, refer to the section "Why won't Photoshop Elements do what I tell it to do?" in Lesson 5.

1 If necessary, switch to the Editor. Click Guided in the mode picker at the top of the workspace, and then select the Basics category.

The Basics category offers solutions for many of the most common image problems, from guided Brightness And Contrast, Levels, and Lighten And Darken adjustments to fix lighting and exposure issues, to procedures for sharpening, cropping, straightening, or resizing your photos. You'll use two of these later in this lesson.

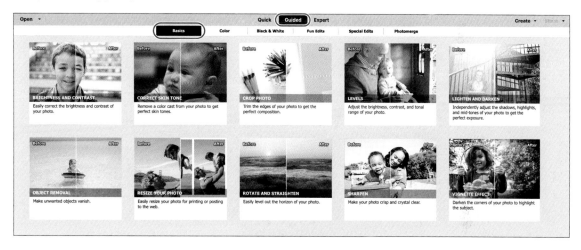

2 The guided procedure previews are interactive; hover the pointer over each preview in turn and move slowly back and forth to see before and after views for the respective adjustment.

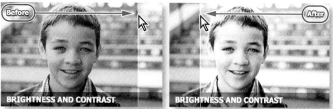

3 Explore each of the other categories. You'll use a procedure from the Color category later in this section, and another in Lesson 6. The Black & White category includes not only straight color-to-grayscale conversions, but also a number of mixed effects that let you preserve the color in part of your image while applying a black and white treatment elsewhere. You'll try several of the Fun Edits effects in Lesson 7, and four of the Photomerge projects in Lesson 8. Several categories offer guided versions of procedures you'll perform in other Editor modes.

Guided color correction

The Color category in the Guided Edit mode offers two creative film-style color treatments—the Lomo Camera and Saturated Film effects—and two procedures for technical color correction.

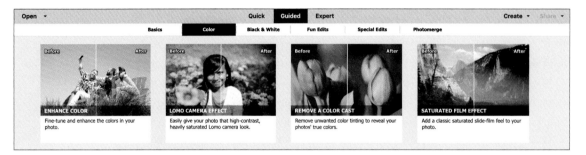

In Lesson 6, you'll use the Remove A Color Cast adjustment to balance a photo that was shot under fluorescent lighting. The Remove A Color Cast edit is a one-step procedure with the single function of correcting an image's *white point* or *white balance*—a concept you learned about earlier in this lesson. In this exercise, you'll use the Enhance Color treatment, which applies a broader color correction, combining several adjustments to not only balance, but also boost and brighten, color.

You'll work once again with the image of the old perfume bottles, which has an obvious color cast as a result of inadequate artificial lighting.

1 Click the Open button (not the arrow beside it) at the upper left of the Editor workspace. Locate your Lesson 4 folder and open the image DSC_2474.jpg.

2 Launch the Enhance Color adjustment from the Color category in Guided Edit mode. Use the View menu at the left of the bar above the Edit pane to switch to the Before & After - Horizontal view; then, choose View > Fit On Screen.

In the Guided Edit mode, the Zoom and Hand tools are the only items in the toolbar; everything you'll need for whichever editing task you choose is presented in the panel at the right.

3 Click the Auto Fix button *twice* to correct the color and contrast; the photo improves dramatically. For photos with less extreme problems, a single click produces satisfactory results.

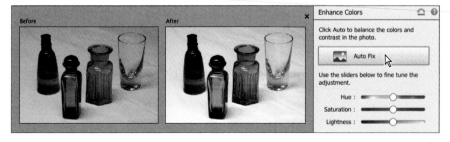

4 In the Enhance Colors pane, drag the Hue slider to the left to set a value of –32.

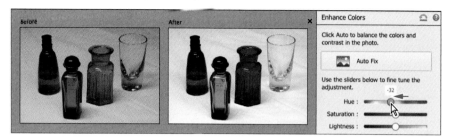

All the colors in the image are shifted along the spectrum: the red bottle becomes purple, the blue-green glass is warmed to yellow-green, the orange bottle turns red, and the violet-blue reflections in the clear glass are shifted to cyan.

5 Set the Saturation value to 40, and the Lightness to 10. The new colors become more vibrant, but the overall contrast is still inadequate.

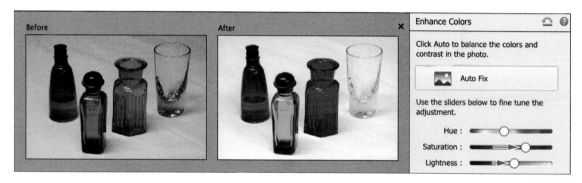

6 Click Next at the lower right; then, click Done. Switch to the Basics category, and then click Lighten And Darken. Drag the Shadows slider to 33 to retrieve detail in the dark bottle caps and bases; then set the Midtones to 100 to increase contrast by shifting the tonal spread. Click Next; then, click Save As.

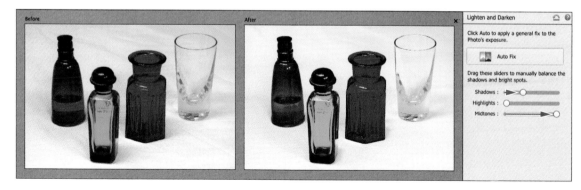

7 Name the file **DSC_2474_EC-LD.jpg** (for Enhance Colors, Lighten And Darken) and save it to the My CIB Work folder with all the usual settings. In the JPEG Options, set the Quality to 10, then click OK. Choose File > Close.

Resizing photos made easy

For many of us, resizing an image can be confusing. When we share to social networking sites or by email from our mobile devices, the work is done for us, behind the scenes—but when we need to scale a photo to meet specific requirements, the Image > Resize command presents us with an array of options for dimensions, file size, resolution, and resampling that can be difficult for a novice to understand.

In the Guided Edit mode, the Resize Your Photo panel makes the task easy, stepping you quickly through the process of scaling an image to meet specific size requirements, whether they're given in pixels, inches, or bytes.

1 In the Organizer, use the Keywords list to find all the images tagged with the Lesson 04 keyword. Select the edited photo DSC_3607_AutoSmart.jpg; then, click the Editor button ( ) in the taskbar.

2 If the Editor is not still in Guided mode, switch modes now, and then select the Basics category. Click the preview to launch the Resize Your Photo procedure.

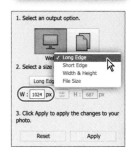

3 In the panel at the right, choose the Web output option. Choose Long Edge from the size options menu. Our lesson file is 1500 pixels wide; to reduce it to an Instagram-friendly size that retains sharpness, type **1024** in the "W" box. When you set the length of one edge, the other is automatically adjusted to maintain the aspect ratio. The correct resolution for the web is set automatically.

4 Click Apply; the new file size is displayed below the resizing controls. It's that easy! For now, click the Reset button to cancel the resize-for-web process without leaving the Resize Your Photo panel.

Note: When you resize an image for print with the Shrink To Fit option activated, the saved output file will include the white areas that you see in the resizing preview.

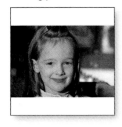

5 Under Select An Output Option, click the Print button. From the size options menu, choose Width & Height. Type **6.9** in both the W (Width) and H (Height) boxes; then click Preview. The photo is cropped to fit the square aspect ratio. Click the Cancel button ( ) on the preview image; then, repeat the process with the Shrink To Fit option activated. Click Apply. The photo is scaled so that it fits the specified dimensions without cropping.

Our lesson image has a 4 x 6 aspect ratio, so all of the predefined size options, except 4 x 6 inch, will result in cropping unless the Shrink To Fit option is activated.

6 Click the Reset button and choose "8 x 10 in" from the size options menu; then, click Preview. Drag to the left in the preview window to adjust the crop, and then click the green Commit button ( ). Click Next at the lower right and inspect the options available. For now, close the file without saving.

Working with Auto Smart Tone

The Auto Smart Tone feature provides a highly intuitive way to make the most of your photos with just a few clicks. Even if you begin with no clear idea of what adjustments an image needs, the Auto Smart Tone dialog box provides visual clues and simple controls that make the process easy.

● **Note:** The Enhance > Auto Smart Tone command is available in both Quick and Expert modes in the Editor.

Called "smart" for a good reason, the Auto Smart Tone feature uses intelligent algorithms to analyze and correct an image automatically—and then actually learns from whatever adjustments you make.

Auto Smart Tone begins by comparing your image to a database drawn from hundreds of images of all types; it then references information about how those images were corrected by different photographic professionals in order to calculate an automatic adjustment that is uniquely suited to the particular photo you're editing. Auto Smart Tone adjustments combine corrections to different aspects of both tone and color, depending on the deficiencies of the image at hand.

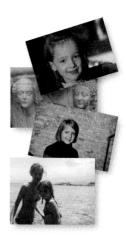

1   In the Organizer, isolate the photos for this lesson, if necessary, by clicking the Lesson 4 folder in the list at the left, or the search box beside the Lesson 04 tag in the Tags panel. Select the unedited images DSC_3607.jpg, DSCN0532.jpg, DSC_0212.jpg, and DSC_0241.jpg; then, click the Editor button in the taskbar.

2   In the Editor, click Expert in the mode picker at the top of the workspace to switch to Expert Edit mode; then bring the image DSC_0241.jpg to the front by clicking its name tab at the top of the Edit window. Choose Auto Smart Tone from the Enhance menu to open the Auto Smart Tone dialog.

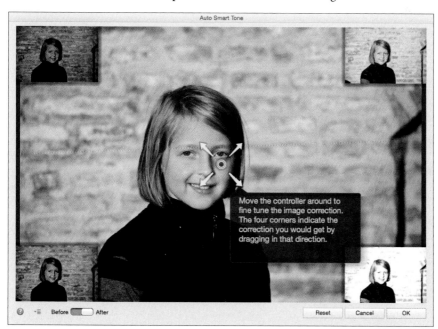

The Auto Smart Tone dialog box opens with the automatic adjustment pre-applied. In the center is a "joystick" control that can be dragged in any direction; a preview in each corner shows what to expect from dragging in that direction. For this photo, the upper-left preview is dark, low-contrast, and saturated; the thumbnail at the lower left is also dark but has more contrast and less saturated color. At the right, the upper preview is brighter, with more neutral colors; the lower is even brighter, with more contrast.

3   Click the upper-right preview—the closest to a technically balanced solution; the joystick control moves to the limit of its range in that direction. Press and hold the control pin; a reference grid appears. Drag the control pin downward by three grid divisions to increase the color saturation, and two squares left to deepen the shadows.

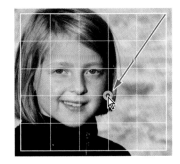

4   Toggle the Before / After switch at the lower left of the dialog box to see the photo with and without the Auto Smart Tone adjustment.

5   Click OK, and then repeat the process from step 2 for each of the other three open images. If you're unsure, drag the joystick left to right and top to bottom to become accustomed to the effects; then, refer to the illustrations below as a rough guide. Start from the points indicated, and then season to taste. Leave the last photo open in the Auto Smart Tone dialog box and read on.

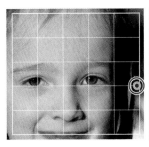 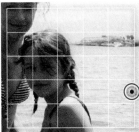 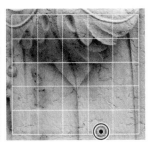

As you tweak the automatic adjustment, Auto Smart Tone learns from your actions. Each time you use the feature, your adjustments are recorded and then taken into consideration when Smart Tone is calculating a solution for the next photo. Over time, Auto Smart Tone remembers whether you tend to favor a high-contrast, color-saturated look or dreamy, high-key treatments and begins to tailor its automatic adjustments accordingly for similar images.

▶ **Tip:** Once you're comfortable with Auto Smart Tone, you can hide the corner thumbnails for a clear view of your photo. You can also disable learning for the current image.

6   Click the small menu icon (▾☰) at the lower left of the Auto Smart Tone dialog box to see the options available. For now, leave both options activated. Click OK to confirm your adjustment and return to the Editor.

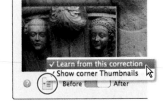

If you feel that Auto Smart Tone may be picking up your beginner's bad habits, you can reset the learning feature on the General tab in Preferences.

7   For each of the four images, choose Save As; then add the suffix **_SmartTone** to the file name and save a JPEG file to your work folder, to be included in the Organizer but not in a version set. When you're done, choose File > Close All.

Opening closed eyes

We have all had a promising group shot or portrait spoiled by closed eyes. Until now, the solution has been to replace the person with their eyes closed by combining shots using the Photomerge Group Shot tool, which you'll use in Lesson 8.

Adobe has addressed this very common problem with the Open Closed Eyes tool, which can do the job in just a few clicks.

1   In the Organizer, right-click the unedited image DSCN0555.jpg and choose Edit With Photoshop Elements Editor from the context menu. In the Editor, use the picker above the work area to switch to Quick Edit mode.

2   Select the Eye tool ( ) from the toolbar. In the tool options pane at the bottom of the workspace, click Open Closed Eyes.

Tip: The Open Closed Eyes command is also available in the Eye Tool options in Expert mode, and in the Enhance menu in both Quick and Expert mode.

3   In the Open Closed Eyes dialog, click to select the face of the girl in the center with her eyes closed. Zoom in using the controls below the preview pane; then, click each of the sample faces at the right to see the results. When you're done, click Reset at the lower right, and then re-select the girl with the closed eyes.

As a more appropriate source for the open eyes you need, you can choose one or more photos of the same girl that are already in your catalog, or images stored on your computer that are not yet managed by Photoshop Elements.

4   Under Eye Source at the right of the preview pane, click Computer. Navigate to the folder Lessons / Lesson 4 / EyeOpener, select the image DSCN0557.jpg, and click Open. Click to apply the eyes from the second face in the second row.

As you can see, the Open Closed Eyes tool has successfully substituted the eyes from the source image, even though the angle of the head is different. Photoshop Elements will also attempt to match color and tonal differences, though this was unnecessary in our example, as the source image was captured in the same lighting conditions. When there is no viable source photo from the same session, look for an image where the lighting angle is similar.

5   Click OK. Save the file to your work folder with an appropriate name, to be included in the Organizer but not in a version set; then, choose File > Close.

Selective editing with the Smart Brush

Tip: For images with a subject that is backlit, like our lesson photo, overall adjustments will never suit both the shaded subject *and* the brightly lit background. In such cases, using the Smart Brush to adjust differently lit areas in the image separately is the perfect solution.

Sometimes the best way to enhance a photo is to modify just part of the image, or to treat separate areas—such as background and foreground elements—differently, rather than applying an adjustment to the photo overall.

The quickest and easiest way to do this is to paint your adjustments directly onto the image with the Smart Brush tool. The Smart Brush is both a selection tool and an image adjustment tool—as you paint, it creates a selection based on similarities in color and texture, through which your choice of editing preset is applied.

1 Isolate the Lesson 4 images in the Media Browser. Select the unedited image DSCN0532.jpg, and then click the Editor button ( ) in the taskbar.

2 In the Editor, click Expert in the mode picker, if necessary. In Expert mode, choose Window > Reset Panels. Click the Photo Bin button ( ) at the left of the taskbar to hide the Photo Bin; then, choose View > Fit On Screen.

3 Select the Smart Brush ( ) from the toolbox. If the tool options pane doesn't open automatically at the bottom of the workspace, click the Tool Options button ( ) in the taskbar.

Tip: You'll use the tool options pane several times in this exercise. If you prefer, you can hide it as you work, and then show it again as needed by clicking the Tool Options button in the taskbar.

4 In the tool options pane, use the slider to set a brush size of 25 px (pixels); then, click the colored thumbnail to open the Smart Brush presets picker. Choose the Nature category from the Presets menu at the top of the pop-up menu, and then select the Make Dull Skies Blue preset.

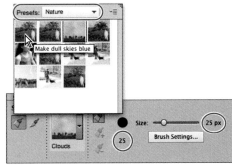

5 Press the Esc key on your keyboard to close the preset picker. Starting above and to the left of the taller girl's head, drag across the sky. If your selection expands too far, subtract areas such as the distant shoreline from the selection by holding down the Alt / Option key and painting carefully back over them. When you're happy with the adjustment area, Choose Select > Deselect so that a new stroke will create a new adjustment, rather than add to the current one.

Tip: Press the left bracket key ([ ) to decrease the brush size, and the right bracket key ( ]) to increase it. While you're fine-tuning the selection, use a small brush and make slow, short strokes.

6 Starting at the left, drag to select the water. As long as the adjustment remains active, your strokes will add to the current adjustment area. Hold Alt / Option if you need to paint out submerged legs and the highlights on the girls' arms.

7 If you don't see tabs for the Layers, Effects, Filters, Styles, and Graphics panels at the top of the Panel Bin, click the arrow beside the More button ( ) at the right of the taskbar and choose Custom Workspace. Drag the Layers panel out of the Panel Bin by its name tab, and then hide the Panel bin by un-checking its name in the Window menu.

Two new layers have been created for the adjustments; each displays a colored icon representing the gradient used for the Blue Skies effect and a black and white thumbnail representing the layer mask through which the adjustment has been applied. Colored markers—Smart Brush *adjustment pins*—mark the points in the photo where you started dragging with the Smart Brush for each adjustment.

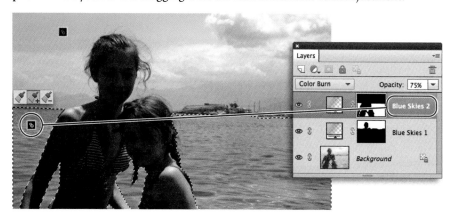

Each Smart Brush edit occupies its own layer, where it remains active and separate from the image itself—so you can add to or subtract from the selection, tweak the effect, or even change which preset is applied, without permanently affecting your original photo. The adjustment pins will be visible whenever the Smart Brush is active.

8 Deselect the Blue Skies 2 adjustment by clicking the Background layer in the Layers panel. Open the Smart Brush presets picker by clicking the Blue Skies thumbnail in the tool options pane. Select the Lighten Skin Tones preset from the Portrait category. Press Esc to close the Smart Brush presets picker.

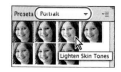

9 Drag over the two girls, including their hair and swimsuits. If your selection expands to include areas of water, hold Alt / Option as you paint out the unwanted areas. Make sure the selection includes hands, elbows, and at least a little of the base of some of the windswept wisps of hair. You won't see a dramatic effect in the selected areas yet; you'll tweak the adjustment a little later.

A new adjustment pin appears on the image; in the Layers panel, a new adjustment layer is added for the Lighten Skin Tones effect. To the left of its layer mask thumbnail, the new adjustment layer displays a different icon from the Blue Skies effect, indicating that it applies a different type of adjustment through the painted mask.

10 Right-click the new adjustment layer (not its black-and-white layer mask icon) and choose Duplicate Layer. Type **Lighten Skin Tones 2** to name the new layer; then, click OK.

11 Hold down the Alt / Option key as you carefully paint the girl on the right out of the selection completely; then, drag the new Smart Brush adjustment pin aside a little to see the marker for your original Lighten Skin Tones adjustment.

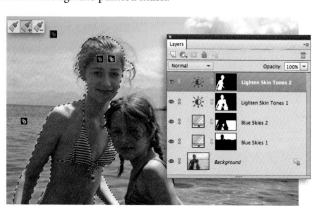

Tweaking Smart Brush adjustments

Each Smart Brush adjustment has its own set of controls that let you customize the effect—even in a later editing session, as long as you've saved the file with its layers.

● **Note:** You can use the Smart Brush on the same area in an image as many times as you wish. If you re-apply the same preset, the effects are usually cumulative; if you apply more than one effect to the same image area, their effects are combined. Adjustment layers affect all lower layers in the Layers panel; rearranging the order of different adjustments applied to the same area can alter the combined effect.

1 In the Layers panel, double-click the gradient icon (▨) on the Blue Skies 1 layer. In the Gradient Fill dialog box, you can modify the gradient's colors, angle, and fade rate. Watch the sky as you choose Reflected from the gradient Style menu; then, click OK.

2 Use the Opacity slider at the top of the Layers panel to decrease the opacity of the Blue Skies 1 layer from 75% to 30%. You can use the adjacent menu to change the blending mode, but for now, leave it set to Color Burn.

3 Select the layer Blue Skies 2—the adjustment for the sea. Double-click the gradient icon (▨) for Blue Skies 2; then, disable the Reverse option. Click OK. Reduce the opacity of the Blue Skies 2 layer from 75% to 40%.

4 Double-click the Brightness/Contrast icon (☀) on the Lighten Skin Tones 1 layer to open the Adjustments panel in Brightness/Contrast mode. Set a Brightness value of +60 and increase the Contrast to +25; then, close the control panel. Repeat the process for the layer Lighten Skin Tones 2, at the top of the list. Set both the Brightness and Contrast to a value of 15.

5 Click the Hand tool to disable the Smart Brush and hide the pins. In the Layers panel, toggle the eye icon (👁 , 👁) beside each adjustment layer's name to show and hide its effect so that you can assess just how the image has changed.

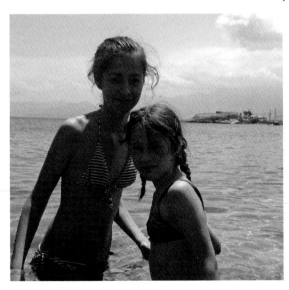 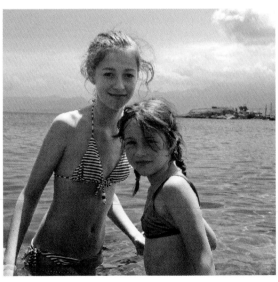

6 Choose File > Save As. Name the file **DSCN0532_SmartBrush** and set up the usual save options. This time, choose the Photoshop file format and activate the Layers option so that you can edit your adjustment layers later. Close the file.

Working with camera raw images

Raw images are high-quality image files that record the maximum amount of image data possible, in a relatively small file size. Though larger than compressed formats such as JPEG, raw images contain more data than TIFF files and use less space. Many common file formats involve in-camera processing of the incoming image data that can effectively degrade the quality of the image. In creating a compressed file, data deemed superfluous is discarded; in mapping the spread of captured data to a defined color space, the range of the color information can be narrowed. In contrast, raw images retain all of the data captured for each and every pixel.

Capturing photos in raw format gives you more flexibility and control in editing. Raw files do incorporate camera settings such as exposure, white balance, and sharpening, but this information is stored separately from the image data. When you open a raw image in Photoshop Elements, these settings become "live," so you can adjust them to get more from the raw image data, working with 12 bits of data per pixel rather than the 8 bits/channel of JPEG or TIFF formats.

In the following exercises, you'll work with a raw image in Nikon's NEF format as you explore the Camera Raw window. This section will also serve as a review of the image editing concepts and terminology that you learned earlier.

1 Isolate the Lesson 4 images in the Media Browser, if necessary, by clicking the search box beside the Lesson 04 keyword tag in the Tags panel.

2 Locate the camera raw image DSC_5683.NEF. Right-click the thumbnail and choose Edit With Photoshop Elements Editor from the menu. Photoshop Elements opens the image in the Camera Raw window.

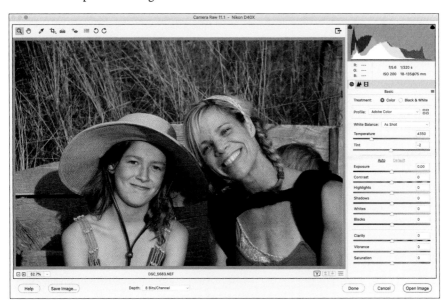

Note: Although not all digital cameras can capture raw images, the newer and more advanced models do offer this option. To see an up-to-date list of the camera models and proprietary raw file formats currently supported by Photoshop Elements, visit the Adobe website.

▶ **Tip:** If you see a message about working with raw images in Photoshop Lightroom, click Continue In Photoshop Elements.

The moment you open a raw file for the first time, the Camera Raw plug-in creates what is sometimes referred to as a *sidecar file* in XMP (Extensible Metadata Platform) format. Any modification that you make to the raw photograph is written to the XMP file rather than to the image file itself, which means that the original image data remains intact, while the sidecar file records every edit.

Getting to know the Camera Raw window

▶ **Tip.** Click the Detail tab to access controls for sharpening image detail and reducing the grainy digital artifacts known as noise.

On the right side of the Camera Raw window is a control panel headed by three tabs: Basic, Detail, and Camera Calibration. For this set of exercises you'll work with the Basic tab—the default—which presents controls for making adjustments that are not possible with the standard editing tools in Photoshop Elements.

1 Depending on your operating system and Camera Raw plug-in version, you may see a Preview check box above the image window; make sure it is activated.

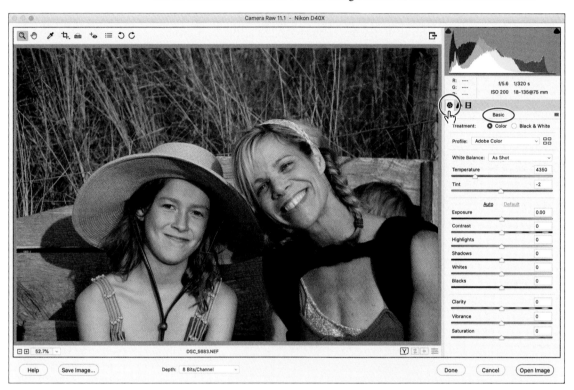

2 Hold the pointer over each tool in the toolbar to see a tooltip with the name of the tool and the respective keyboard shortcut. Click the Toggle Full Screen Mode button (⇥) at the right of the toolbar to switch to full-screen mode.

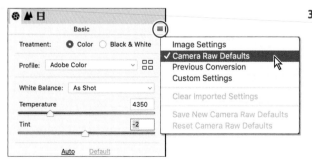

3 Click the menu icon at the right of the Basic tab's header bar to see the choices available from the Options menu. You can apply the same settings you used for the last image you worked with, have Photoshop Elements revert to the default profile for your camera by choosing Reset Camera Raw Defaults, or save your own custom settings as the new default for your camera.

Adjusting the white balance

The white balance presets can help you rectify a color cast caused by lighting conditions. You could correct the white balance of a photo shot on an overcast day, for example, by choosing the Cloudy preset. Other presets compensate for artificial lighting. The As Shot preset uses the settings recorded by your camera, while the Auto setting recalculates the white balance based on an analysis of the image data.

Note: Incandescent lighting typically causes an orange-yellow color cast, while fluorescent lighting is notorious for a dull green tint.

1   Switch between the presets in the White Balance menu, comparing the effects to the default As Shot setting. In the following pages you'll discover why setting the appropriate white balance is so important to the overall look of the image.

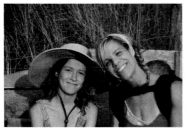
Auto preset

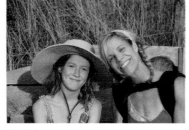
Daylight preset

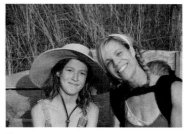
Fluorescent preset

2   For now, choose As Shot from the White Balance presets menu.

For many photos, the right preset will produce satisfactory results or at least serve as a basis for manual adjustment. When none of the presets takes your image in the right direction, you can use the White Balance tool (🖊) to sample a neutral color in the photo, in relation to which Camera Raw will recalculate the white balance. The ideal target is a light to medium gray that is neither discernibly warm nor cool. In our sample photo, the weathered wood is a potential reference, but we can probably be more certain that the steel fencing wire in the background is a neutral gray.

Tip: In some images it can be difficult to identify a neutral tone; in the absence of a definitive visual reference you may at times rely on what you know about the photo: that it was taken on a cloudy day, for example, or under fluorescent lighting. It may help to look for references such as white paper, clothing, or paint, and then sample a shaded area.

3   Zoom in to the image by choosing 100% from the Zoom Level menu in the lower-left corner of the image window or by double-clicking the Zoom tool. Select the Hand tool (✋) and drag the image downward and to the right so that you can see the thick wire to the left of the girl's hat.

4   Select the White Balance tool (🖊), right beside the Hand tool in the toolbar. Sample a medium gray from the center of the wire where it crosses a relatively dark area. If you see little effect, click a slightly different point.

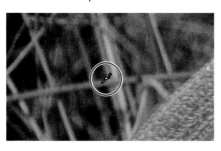

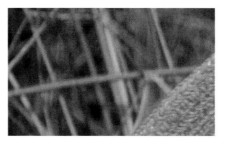

5   Zoom out by choosing Fit In View from the Zoom Level menu in the lower-left corner of the preview window.

The white balance is now set to Custom and the image has become cooler. The weathered wood in the background is a more neutral gray and the skin tones are rosier. The eyes also look clearer, having lost the original yellow-orange cast.

Note: Depending on where you clicked to set the white balance, you may see different values from those illustrated.

6   Use the White Balance menu to alternate between your custom settings and the As Shot preset, noting the change in the preview window, as well as the differences in the Temperature and Tint settings.

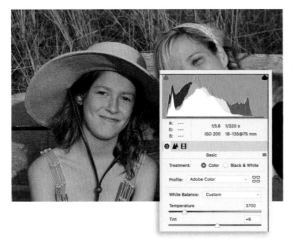
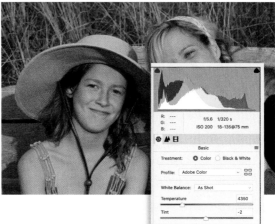

Working with the Temperature and Tint settings

▶ **Tip:** There are no hard and fast rules in color correction; there might be times when you choose to retain a slight color cast for aesthetic purposes. For example, although it's *technically* in need of correction, you might prefer the original, too-warm cast of our lesson image (caused by late afternoon sunlight) for its evocative, summery look. Although most often used for fine color correction, the white balance settings can also be applied creatively to achieve surprising and dramatic atmospheric effects.

The White Balance tool can accurately remove any color cast or tint from an image, but you may still want to tweak the Temperature and Tint settings. In this case, the color tint seems fine, but the skin tones still have a slightly orange look that can be corrected by fine-tuning the blue/yellow balance using the Temperature control.

1   Use the Zoom tool or the Zoom Level menu in the lower-left corner of the preview window to focus closely on the woman's face.

2   Test the Temperature slider by dragging it from one end of its range to the other. You'll see that the colors of the image become cooler or warmer as you move the slider. Reset the Temperature control a little below the edited value of 3700 (your value may differ, depending on where you clicked to set the white balance) either by dragging the slider or by typing the value **3400** into the text box.

3   Double-click the Hand tool or choose Fit In View from the Zoom Level menu. Now that the temperature has been adjusted toward blue, the automatically corrected tint of the image appears just a little pink.

4   Decrease the Tint setting to **−5** with the slider or type **−5** in the Tint text box. Press Ctrl+Z / Command+Z to toggle between the new Tint setting and the value set with the White Balance tool, comparing the effect.

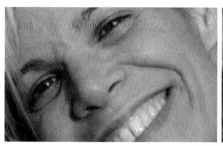 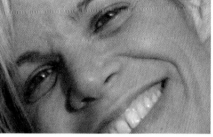

At the left, the skin tones produced by the White Balance tool still look a little too orange. On the right, the skin tones look more natural once the Temperature and Tint values have been reduced manually.

Using the tone controls on a raw image

Below the White Balance sliders on the Basic tab are sliders for improving a photo's tonal range and *presence*, or image definition.

Exposure adjusts the overall lightness or darkness of an image. Its effect is most apparent through the middle of the histogram; an increased Exposure setting will move the body of the curve to the right, compressing the highlights, if possible, rather than shifting them off the end of the curve. Tweak the Exposure to brighten a dull, underexposed photo or correct the flat, faded look of an overexposed image.

Contrast is the amount of difference between the lightest and darkest areas of an image. The Contrast control has the most effect at the ends of the histogram; an increased setting moves information outward from the center of the curve. Adjust Contrast to add definition to a flat image or to soften one that is too harsh or stark.

Highlights recovers detail from overexposed highlights and improves midtone definition by shifting image information from the far right of the curve inward.

Shadows recovers details from shadowed areas—something close to the inverse of the action of the Highlights control—and adds depth to the midtone range.

Whites specifies which input levels are mapped to pure white in the final image. Lowering the Whites value decreases clipping at the right end of the histogram. Clipping occurs when a pixel's color values are higher or lower than the range that can be represented in the image; over-bright values are clipped to output white, and over-dark values are clipped to output black.

Blacks specifies which input levels will be mapped to black in the final image. Raising the Blacks value decreases clipping at the left end of the histogram.

Clarity increases the *local* contrast between adjacent light and dark areas, sharpening detail without producing halo effects, and enhancing the midtone contrast.

Vibrance boosts color saturation selectively, having the most effect on the muted colors in an image, while avoiding over-saturation of bolder colors and skin tones.

Saturation is the purity, or strength, of a color. Increasing the Saturation reduces the amount of black or white mixed with the color, making it more vivid. Reducing the Saturation increases the amount of black or white, making it more muted.

> **Tip:** To quickly reset a single control to its original value, double-click its slider handle. If you want to start over without exiting the Camera Raw dialog box, hold Option / Alt and click the Reset button (which is normally the Cancel button without the modifier keys).

First you'll adjust the overall exposure and contrast; then, you'll set the white and black points to avoid clipping at the ends of the histogram before tweaking the highlights and shadows to bring out as much image detail as you can.

1   Keep an eye on the histogram as you drag the Exposure slider slowly all the way to the right; then, press the letter O on your keyboard to activate the white clipping warning. The red areas that appear in the preview warn you which parts of the image are being clipped to white.

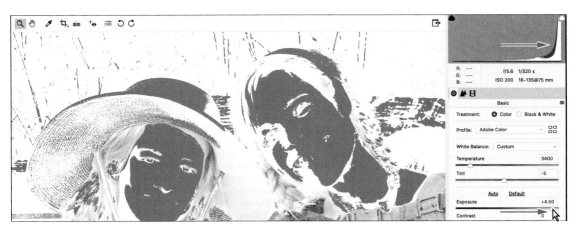

Note: The values at which clipping appears may differ slightly for you, depending on where you clicked with the White Balance tool.

2   Drag the slider to the left until all the red areas disappear—even from the woman's headband. The Exposure control doesn't cause white clipping until the setting is extreme; for now, set the Exposure value to +0.5.

3   Watch the histogram as you drag the Contrast slider through its full range, before setting it to a value of +50.

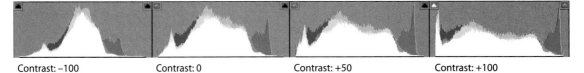

Contrast: –100   Contrast: 0   Contrast: +50   Contrast: +100

4   Put the Whites slider through its paces. White clipping is already beginning to appear when the setting reaches +15. Bring the Whites down to –50.

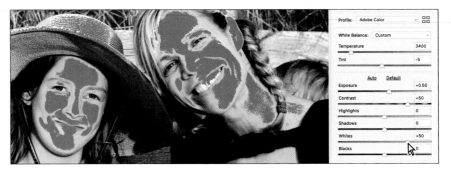

5 Press U on your keyboard to activate the black clipping warning, and then play with the Blacks slider. When you're done, set the Blacks to −10, the point below which the blue clipping warning appears in the darkest areas of the image.

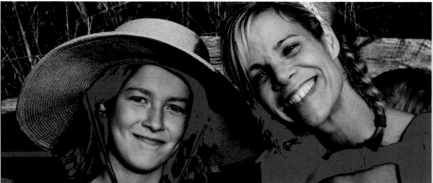

6 Move the Highlights slider all the way to the right. Although the effect on the image is quite extreme, there is no clipping now that you've set the white point. Watch the textural detail reappear in the sunlit wood as you reduce the Highlights setting to −50. Drag the Shadows slider to set a value of +50, watching as detail is retrieved from the darkest areas in the photo. Press the U and O keys on your keyboard to disable the clipping warnings.

7 Choose a magnification level of 100% from the Zoom menu at the lower left of the image window, or double-click the Zoom tool; then, use the Hand tool to center your view on the girl's face. Drag the Clarity slider to +30. Double-click the Hand tool to see the entire image, and then set the Vibrance value to +25.

8 To compare the adjusted photo to the raw image, toggle the Before And After Views button (Y) at the right of the bar immediately below the preview.

● **Note:** The Camera Raw plug-in, used by Photoshop Elements to open raw files, is updated as new cameras are added to the list of those supported. Check for updates and download the latest version of the plug-in at www.adobe.com.

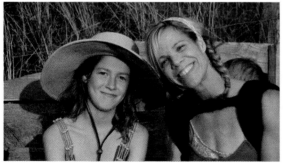
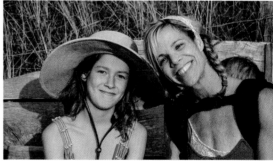

The photo originally looked somewhat dull, muddy, and indistinct, and a little too dark. It now shows a broader range of detail and is more vivid; the colors are brighter and the tones are more realistic. For the sake of clarity in our demonstration, however, some of the adjustments you made were quite extreme. If you wish, you can now tone down the corrections to balance the image to your taste.

Saving the image in the DNG format

Each camera manufacturer has its own proprietary raw format, and not every raw file can be read or edited by software other than that provided with the camera. There is also the possibility that manufacturers might not support every format indefinitely. To help alleviate these problems, Photoshop Elements gives you the option to save raw images in the DNG format, a publicly available archival format for raw images that provides an open standard for files created by different camera models, ensuring that you'll still be able to access your images in the future.

1 To convert and save the image, click the Save Image button at the lower left of the Camera Raw dialog box. Under Destination in the Save Options dialog box, click Select Folder. Navigate to and open your Lessons folder; then, highlight your My CIB Work folder and click Select.

2 Under File Naming, leave Document Name selected in the menu on the left. Click the menu on the right and select 1 Digit Serial Number. This will add the number 1 to the end of the file name.

● **Note:** The DNG file you create contains none of the edits you made; it's just like the original raw image, but saved in the DNG format.

3 Click Save. The file, together with all your current settings, will be saved in DNG format, which you can reprocess repeatedly without losing the original data.

4 Click the Open Image button in the lower-right corner of the Camera Raw dialog box. Your image will open in a regular image window in Photoshop Elements. Choose File > Save. Navigate to your My CIB Work folder, name the file **DSC_5683_Work**, and choose the Photoshop format. Make sure that the new file will be included in the Organizer but not in a version set.

5 Click Save, and then choose File > Close.

Congratulations! You've completed your first lesson on the Editor; take a look at all the images in the Media Browser to refresh your memory about how many new photo editing techniques you've learned.

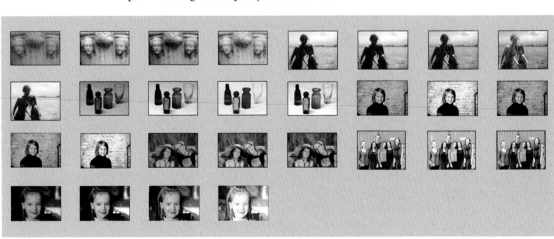

Review questions

1 What are the key differences between adjusting images in Expert mode, Quick Edit mode, and Guided Edit mode?

2 Can you apply automatic fixes when you are in Expert mode?

3 What is the purpose of the Photo Bin?

4 What is the Smart Brush tool?

5 What do the terms *temperature* and *tint* refer to in image editing?

Review answers

1 Expert mode provides the most flexible and powerful image-correction environment, with lighting and color-correction commands and tools for fixing image defects, making selections, adding text, and painting on your images. Quick Edit provides easy access to a range of basic image-editing controls for quickly making common adjustments and corrections. If you're new to digital photography, Guided Edit steps you through each procedure to help you get professional-looking results.

2 Yes; the Enhance menu in Expert mode contains commands that are equivalent to the Auto buttons in the Quick Edit adjustments panel: Auto Smart Fix, Auto Levels, Auto Contrast, Auto Color Correction, and Auto Red Eye Fix. The Enhance menu also provides an Adjust Smart Fix command, which opens a dialog in which you can specify settings for automatic adjustments.

3 The Photo Bin provides easy access to the photos you want to work with, without needing to leave the Editor workspace. You can set the Photo Bin to display all the photos that are currently selected in the Media Browser, just those images that are open in the Editor (helpful when some of the open images are hidden behind the front window), or the entire contents of any album in your catalog.

4 The Smart Brush is both a selection tool and an image-adjustment tool—it creates a selection based on similarities in color and texture, through which your choice of editing preset is applied. You can choose from close to 70 Smart Brush presets, each of which can be customized, applied repeatedly for a cumulative effect, or layered with other adjustment presets to produce an almost infinite variety of results.

5 If an image's color temperature is too warm or too cool, it will have either an orange-red or blue color cast. A yellow-green or magenta color cast is referred to as a tint.

5 WORKING WITH COLOR AND MAKING SELECTIONS

Lesson overview

Photoshop Elements delivers a broad selection of tools and controls for correcting, adjusting, and getting creative with color. Whether you want to make corrections to compensate for inadequate lighting conditions, brighten a smile, or paint the town red, you'll find a range of solutions, from one-click auto fixes to customizable tools that give you precise control of the adjustments you apply.

This lesson introduces you to a variety of tools and techniques for fixing color problems in your photos:

- Using automatic options to correct color
- Adjusting skin tones
- Whitening yellowed teeth
- Removing red-eye and "pet-eye" effects
- Making, saving, and loading selections
- Changing the color of a pictured object
- Replacing a color throughout an image
- Working with color management

This lesson will take about 90 minutes to complete. To get the lesson files used in this chapter, download them from the web page for this book at www.adobepress.com/PSECIB2020. For more information, see "Accessing the lesson files and Web Edition" in the Getting Started section at the beginning of this book.

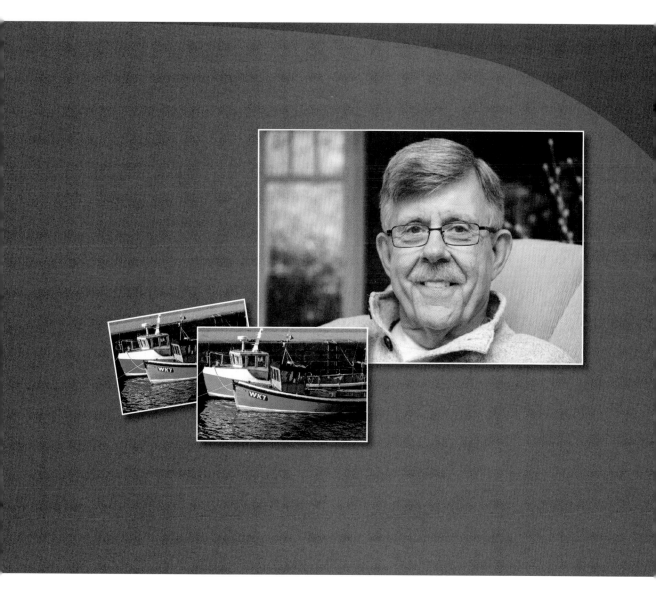

From one-step fixes to more specialized features and techniques, you'll find that the powerful and versatile color tools in Photoshop Elements are easy to master, giving you the control you need to quickly correct the color balance across an entire image, adjust just one area selectively, or let your creativity run wild.

Getting started

● **Note:** Before you start this lesson, make sure you've set up a folder for your lesson files and downloaded the Lesson 5 folder from your Account page at www.peachpit.com, as detailed in "Accessing the lesson files and Web Edition" and "Creating a work folder" in the "Getting Started" section at the beginning of this book. You should also have created a new work catalog (see "Creating a catalog for working with this book" in Lesson 1).

You'll begin by importing the sample images for this lesson to the CIB Catalog that you created at the beginning of Lesson 1.

1 Click the Import button at the upper left of the Organizer workspace, and choose From Files And Folders. In the Get Photos And Videos From Files And Folders dialog, navigate to and select your PSE2020CIB / Lessons / Lesson 5 folder. Disable any automatic options that are active; then, click Get Media.

2 In the Import Attached Keyword Tags dialog, click Select All; then, click OK.

Batch-processing the lesson files

Before you start working with the Lesson 5 images, batch-process them as you did in Lesson 4. At the end of each exercise in this lesson, you can compare the combined auto-fixes to the results that you achieve using various other techniques.

1 Click the Editor button ( ) in the taskbar to switch to the Editor. If necessary, click Expert in the mode picker to switch the Editor to Expert mode.

2 Choose File > Process Multiple Files. In the Process Multiple Files dialog box, click the check boxes to activate all four Quick Fix options. Browse to select the Lessons / Lesson 5 folder as the source for the images to be processed and your My CIB Work folder as the destination for the processed copies.

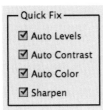

3 Activate Rename Files and set the options to add the appendix "_AutoFix" to the existing document names. If necessary, disable the resizing and file conversion options under Image Size and File Type, and then click OK.

4 Click the Organizer button ( ) in the taskbar. In the Organizer, click the Import button and choose From Files And Folders. Open your My CIB Work folder. Select the files with names that begin with "05," and then click Get Media.

5 In the Import Attached Keyword Tags dialog box, click Select All, then click OK.

Correcting color problems

▶ **Tip:** Even when a photo is technically perfect, you may still wish to adjust the color—either across the entire image or just for a particular area or object—to create an effect, such as adding some golden hue to a late afternoon sunset.

Artificial lighting, weather conditions, and mismatched camera settings can result in one of the most common image problems: a color cast that affects the entire image.

For some images your color problem may be more localized, such as red eyes in a photo taken with a flash, or a portrait spoiled by yellow-looking teeth.

You'll begin this lesson by revisiting and comparing some of the tools for making quick and easy image-wide adjustments in the Quick and Guided Edit modes. Later, you'll explore methods for fixing red eyes and yellow teeth, and learn how to use the selection tools—an essential skill for making localized edits in Expert mode.

Comparing methods of fixing color

The automatic correction features in Photoshop Elements do an excellent job of bringing out the best in most photographs, but each image—and each image problem—is unique; some photographs require a more hands-on approach.

Photoshop Elements offers a variety of tools and controls for adjusting color; the more techniques you master, the more likely it is that you'll be able to meet any challenge presented by a difficult photograph.

1   If you don't see the Lesson 5 images already isolated in the Media Browser, click the check box beside the imported Lesson 05 keyword tag.

2   Select the image 05_01.jpg in the Media Browser; then, click the Editor button (⬛) in the taskbar.

This photo exhibits the overly warm, yellow-orange cast common to many images taken in standard tungsten—or incandescent—lighting.

In the exercises in this section, you'll compare three different techniques for correcting the same color problem, so you'll create three copies of the original photo.

3   Click Quick in the mode picker to switch the Editor to Quick mode. Choose Window > Reset Panels. In the actions bar above the Edit pane, make sure that the View is set to After Only, and then choose View > Fit On Screen. If the Adjustments panel is not open at the right of the Quick Edit workspace, click the Adjustments button (⚏) at the right of the taskbar.

4   Show the Photo Bin, if necessary. Right-click the image in the Photo Bin and choose Duplicate from the context menu. In the Duplicate Image dialog box, click OK to accept the default name, 05_01 copy. Repeat the process to create two more duplicates, 05_01 copy 2 and 05_01 copy 3.

While you're in Quick Edit or Guided Edit mode, you won't see image window tabs displayed at the top of the Edit pane; in both these modes you can view only one image at a time in the work area. To see which photos are open in the Editor and which of them is currently active, and also to switch between them, you'll use the Photo Bin. The name of each image appears as a tooltip when you hold the pointer over its thumbnail in the Photo Bin. Alternatively, right-click anywhere inside the Photo Bin and choose Show Filenames from the context menu.

In the Photo Bin, a blue frame highlights the active image; that is, the photo that you see in the After Only view in the Edit pane.

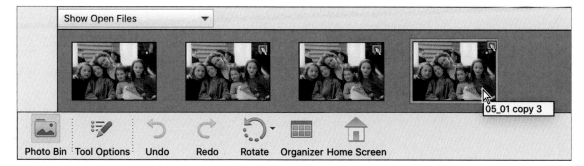

Correcting color automatically

For the batch processing at the start of this lesson, you applied all four automatic Quick Fix options together. In this exercise, you'll apply the automatic color adjust ment on its own so you can assess the result unaffected by other settings.

1 In the Photo Bin, click the second photo, 05_01 copy, to make it active; then, choose Before & After - Vertical from the View menu in the actions bar above the Edit pane. Use the Hand and Zoom tools to focus on the faces.

2 If the tool options pane replaces the Photo Bin when you select the Hand tool or the Zoom tool in the toolbar, click the small menu icon (▼☰) at the upper right of the tool options pane and disable Auto Show Tool Options; then, click the Photo Bin button (▣) in the taskbar to show the Photo Bin.

3 In the Adjustments panel, expand the Color pane and click the Auto button. Compare the Before and After views. There is a marked improvement; the Auto Color fix has corrected the worst of the orange color cast. Skin tones are slightly cooler and clothing colors a little brighter, but the tonal range is still somewhat flat.

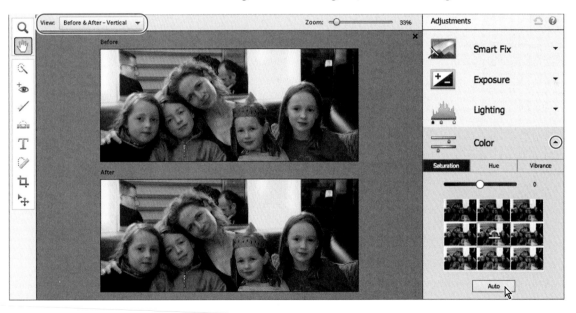

▶ **Tip:** If you can't find the My CIB Work folder, refer to "Creating a work folder" in the "Getting Started" section at the beginning of this book.

4 Choose File > Save. Name the file **05_01_AutoColor**, to be saved in JPEG format to your My CIB Work folder and included in the Organizer but not as part of a version set. Click Save; then, click OK in the JPEG Options dialog box.

Adjusting the results of an automatic fix manually

An automatic fix can serve as a good starting point for some manual fine-tuning.

1 In the Photo Bin, click the third photo, 05_01 copy 2, to make it the active image; then, expand the Color pane and click the Auto button.

2 Click the Saturation tab at the top of the Color pane; then, reduce the setting to −25 to give the color a more natural look. Click the Hue tab and reduce the value to −5 to shift the color away from yellow-green. Increase the Vibrance to a setting of 20 to re-saturate the color a little without affecting the skin tones.

▶ Tip: To type a new value for any setting, first click to select the number to the right of the adjustment slider.

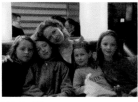 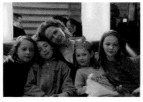 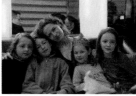 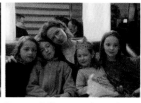

Original image   Auto color adjustment   Saturation reduced   Hue and Vibrance adjusted

3 Expand the Balance pane and click the Temperature tab. Reduce the Temperature setting to 40 and increase the Tint value to 15 to further reduce the color cast.

4 Expand the Exposure pane, and then increase the Exposure setting to 0.8. In the Lighting pane, set the Midtones value to 15.

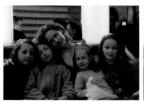 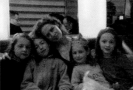 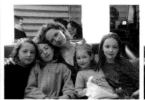 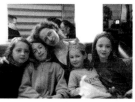

Temperature reduced   Tint increased   Exposure boosted   Midtones adjusted

The contrast has improved, the colors are brighter, and the skin tones have lost the "fake tan" look common in photos captured without a flash in tungsten lighting.

5 Choose File > Save. Name the file **05_01_AutoColorPlus**, to be saved in JPEG format to your My CIB Work folder and included in the Organizer but not as part of a version set. Click Save; then, click OK in the JPEG Options dialog box.

Tweaking an automatic fix using color curves

You can use commands from the top half of the Enhance menu to apply the same adjustments as the Auto buttons in the Adjustments panel; these Enhance menu commands are available in Quick and Expert modes, but not in Guided Edit mode.

Both the Quick and Expert Edit modes also offer other methods of enhancing color that give you finer control over the results. These are the commands in the lower half of the Enhance menu. In this exercise, you'll use one of these options to tweak the adjustments applied by the Auto Color fix button.

1 In the Photo Bin, click the image 05_01 copy 3 to make it active.

2 In the Color pane, click the Auto button to apply the automatic Quick Fix correction; then, choose Enhance > Adjust Color > Adjust Color Curves to open the Adjust Color Curves dialog box.

● **Note:** Why does the Exposure control use decimals instead of whole numbers, like other controls? Exposure in photography is measured in "stops" according to how much light comes through the lens. So when you increase the Exposure control to 1.0, you're doubling the amount of light in the scene—in this case digitally, not through a lens.

3 In the Select A Style menu at the lower left of the Adjust Color Curves dialog box, click each color curve preset in turn, noting the effect on the curve in the graph at the right as well as on the After image above it. Select Increase Midtones.

4 Drag the Adjust Highlights slider to a point about a third of the distance from the default central position to its limit at the right. Drag the Midtone Brightness and Midtone Contrast sliders about half as far to the right; then, click OK.

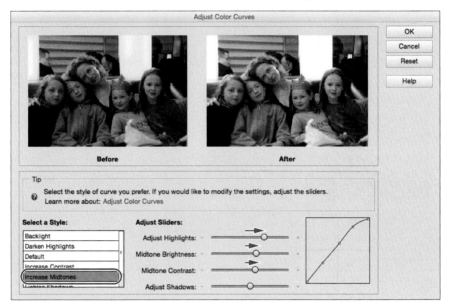

5 Choose File > Save. Name the file **05_01_ColorCurves**, and set up the usual work file settings. Click Save; then, click OK in the JPEG Options dialog box.

Comparing results

A glance at the Photo Bin will tell you that all three of your saved work files are still open in the Editor. Let's compare them to the batch-processed AutoFix file.

1 Right-click the image at the left of the Photo Bin—the original photo—and choose Close from the context menu.

2 Choose File > Open. Locate and open your My CIB Work folder; then, select the file 05_01_AutoFix and click Open. Click Expert at the top of the workspace to switch to Expert mode.

3 Choose Preferences > General from the Edit / Adobe Photoshop Elements Editor menu. Activate Allow Floating Documents In Expert Mode; then, click OK.

Floating document windows are now the default for Expert mode. Throughout the rest of this book, however, it will be assumed that you are working with image windows that are docked (consolidated) in the Edit pane. At the end of this exercise you'll disable floating windows so that you can follow the exercises as written.

4   Hide the Photo Bin, if necessary, by clicking the Photo Bin button (![]).
    Choose Window > Images > Float All In Windows, and then choose Window >
    Images > Tile. To synchronize the view across all four image windows, choose
    Match Zoom, and then Match Location, from the Window > Images menu.

5   Click the Zoom tool (Q) in the toolbar; then, click the Tool Options button (![])
    in the taskbar. In the tool options pane, activate the Zoom All Windows option
    below the Zoom slider. Click the Hand tool (![]) and activate Scroll All Windows;
    then, click the Tool Options button to hide the tool options pane. Use the Zoom
    and Hand tools to focus on the faces in any of the image windows.

Note: Depending on the resolution of your monitor, you may need to move one of the floating windows to view the tool options pane.

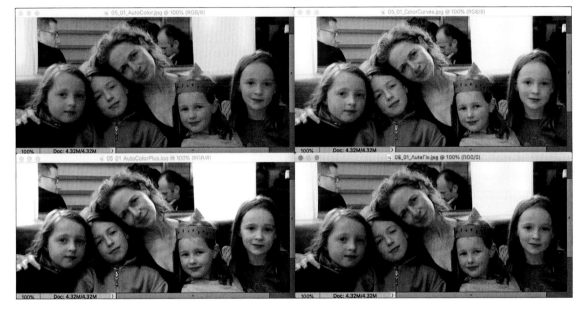

6   Drag your favorite version out of the tiled arrangement by its header bar,
    and float the image window in the center of the work area; then, double-
    click the Hand tool to fit it to the screen. Press Ctrl+Tab / Command+~ or
    Ctrl+Shift+Tab / Command+Shift+~ to cycle through all the open image
    windows, bringing each to the front in turn.

7   Choose Preferences > General from the Edit / Photoshop Elements Editor menu
    and disable floating documents; then, click OK. Choose File > Close All.

Note: Only one image window is active at any given time. The file name and image details are dimmed in the title bars of all but the currently active image window.

Adjusting skin tones

When your primary concern is the people in your photo, you can correct a color
cast across the entire image by concentrating on achieving natural, good-looking
skin tones. Photoshop Elements offers tools to do just that in all three Edit modes.

1   In the Organizer, select the image 05_01.jpg in the Media Browser, and then click
    the Editor button (![]) in the taskbar. Use the Zoom and Hand tools to focus on
    the faces of the mother and the two daughters sitting closest to her.

2 Choose Enhance > Adjust Color > Adjust Color For Skin Tone. In the Adjust Color For Skin Tone dialog box, make sure the Preview option is activated.

3 As you move the pointer over the image, the cursor changes to an eyedropper tool. With the eyedropper tool, click the lightly shaded area of skin to the right of center on the youngest sister's forehead. The color balance of the entire photo is adjusted using the sampled skin tone as a reference.

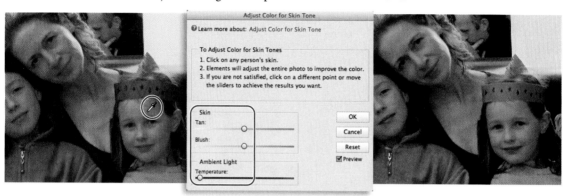

4 Move the Tan, Blush, and Temperature sliders to achieve the skin tones you want, and then click OK. Choose File > Save As. Name the file **05_01_Skin** and save it to your My CIB Work folder with the usual options. Choose File > Close.

Removing a color cast with one click

As you learned in Lesson 4, the Color Cast eyedropper tool provides yet another solution to difficult color balance problems. If you wish to try the Color Cast eyedropper on the photo you've been working with, you can do so in any of the three edit modes. In Quick Edit and Expert modes, choose Enhance > Adjust Color > Remove Color Cast. In Guided Edit mode, select Remove A Color Cast.

Use the Color Cast eyedropper to define a color that should appear temperature-neutral—neither warm nor cool; the color balance is recalculated around that tone. The best choice is a mid gray, though black or white can also work. Choosing the right color can take a little practice. In our sample photo, for example, the zippered sweater that appears to be a neutral gray in the Before image actually contains a lot of cool blue; instead, try sampling the brightest point on the lily in the foreground.

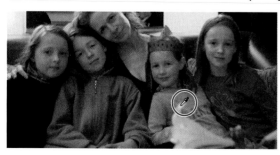
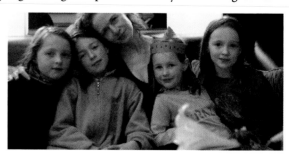

Working with red-eye

As you learned in Lesson 2, Photoshop Elements can apply an automatic red-eye fix during import so that your images are corrected before they reach the Organizer. However, the automatic solution is not effective for every photo; in this exercise, we'll look at the manual techniques you can use to deal with those difficult cases.

Note: The red-eye effect happens when the camera's flash is reflected off the retina at the back of the eye, causing the pupil at the center to appear bright red instead of black.

Using the automatic red-eye fix

1   If necessary, use the Tags panel or the My Folder list to isolate the Lesson 5 images. Select the images 05_02a.jpg and 05_02b.jpg, and then click the Editor button (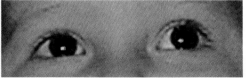) in the taskbar. Switch the Editor to Expert mode.

2   At the top of the work area, click the name tab for the image 05_02a.jpg to bring that photo to the front. Use the Zoom and Hand tools to focus as closely as possible on both of the girls' faces; then, choose Enhance > Auto Red Eye Fix.

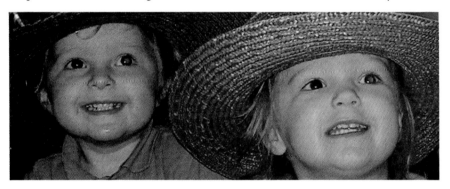

As you can see, the auto correction does a great job with two of the four red eyes. Unfortunately, they're not even on the same face! The Eye tool may fail to identify a pupil if your photo is out of focus, is poorly exposed, or has a color cast; if possible, try correcting those problems before tackling the red eyes.

3   Press Ctrl+Z / Command+Z to undo the Auto Red Eye Fix. Keep the file open.

Using the Eye tool to fix red eyes

For stubborn red-eye problems, you can use the Eye tool ( ), which you'll find in the toolbar in both Quick Edit and Expert modes.

1   Zoom and drag the photo to focus the view on the eyes of the girl at the left.

2   Select the Eye tool ( ); then, click the Tool Options button ( ) in the taskbar to open the tool options pane, if necessary. Choose Reset Tool from the options menu ( ) at the far right. Click once in each eye, close to center of the pupil.

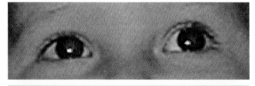

For this example, the Eye tool works perfectly. If you ever find that the red-eye correction is over-extended, blackening portions of the iris or spilling onto the skin around the eye, try clicking at a different point.

Tip: Once again, the Eye tool produces a good result easily. For difficult cases that don't improve no matter where you click or drag, undo and adjust the Pupil Radius and Darken sliders in the tool options pane before you try clicking or dragging again.

3   Zoom and drag the photo to focus the view on the eyes of the girl at the right.

4   This time, drag a marquee rectangle with the Eye tool around each eye in turn. Experiment with the size and placement of the rectangle to get the best results. If you're not satisfied, undo and try again. Hold the Alt / Option key to draw the rectangle from its center.

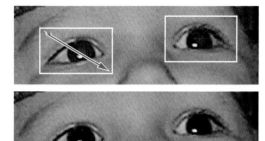

5   Choose File > Save As. Name the new file **05_02_RedEye**, to be saved to your My CIB Work folder in JPEG format and included in the Organizer but not in a version set. Click Save. Accept the JPEG settings and choose File > Close.

Eye treatments for furry friends

As every pet owner knows, animals' eyes also reflect light from a camera flash. Though the reflection from pets' eyes is sometimes red, it's more often blue, green, yellow, or white and will not respond well to the automatic red-eye fix; for these cases, you can switch the Eye tool to Pet Eye mode.

1   You should still have the image 05_02b.jpg open in Expert mode in the Editor. Select the Eye tool ( ); then, click the check box in the tool options pane to switch the tool to Pet Eye mode.

2   Try both of the techniques you practiced in the previous exercise in turn, undoing after each attempt. Experiment with the full range of the Pupil Radius and Darken sliders in the tool options pane until you're happy with the result.

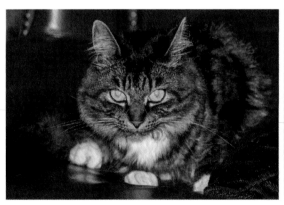
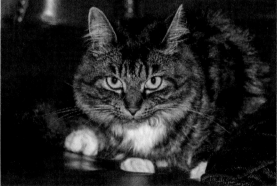

3   Choose File > Save As. Name the new file **05_02_PetEye** and save it to your My CIB Work folder with all the usual settings; then, choose File > Close.

Brightening a smile

Sometimes a photo can be spoiled by a color problem as simple as yellow-looking teeth. As with the red-eye effect, Photoshop Elements offers an easy solution that's available in all three Edit modes.

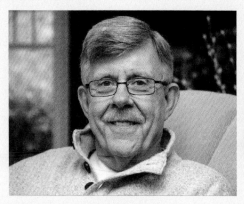 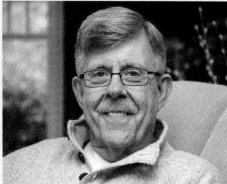

Located in the toolbar in Quick Edit mode and as part of the Perfect Portrait procedure in Guided Edit mode, the Whiten Teeth tool is a preset variant of the Expert mode's Smart Brush, which functions as both a selection tool and an image adjustment tool. You can use the Whiten Teeth tool (or the Smart Brush with the Whiten Teeth preset loaded) to select the yellowed teeth, exactly as you would with the Quick Selection tool, and the preset whitening adjustment is applied inside the selection.

The Whiten Teeth selection and adjustment is made on a new layer separate from the original image in the Background layer. The edit remains active on its own adjustment layer—so you can return to alter the selection area or the way the adjustment is applied at any time. You can use the tool more than once on the same area, building up multiple layers that you can then blend for a natural effect.

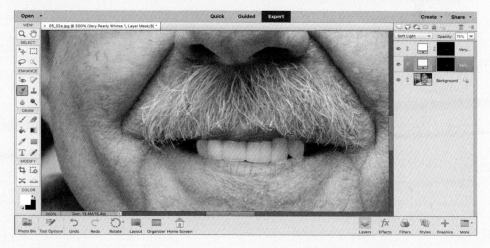

Why won't Photoshop Elements do what I tell it to do?

In some situations, the changes you try to apply to an image may not seem to work. You may hear an error sound, indicating that you're trying to do something that's not allowed. The following list offers explanations and solutions for common issues that might be blocking your progress.

Commit is required

Several tools, including the Type tool, the Crop tool, and the Move tool (when used to scale a selection), require you to click the green check mark Commit button on the bounding box surrounding your type, crop, or selection before you can move on to another task.

Cancel is required

The Undo command isn't available while you have uncommitted changes made with tools such as those listed above; to undo these edits, click the Cancel button rather than the Undo command.

Edits are restricted by an active selection

When you create a selection, you limit the active area of the image; edits will apply only within the selected area. If you try to make changes to an area outside the selection, nothing happens. To deactivate a selection so you can work on another part of the image, choose Select > Deselect.

Move tool is required

When you drag a selection with a selection tool pointer, the selection outline moves, rather than the selected part of the image. If you want to move a selected part of the image or an entire layer, first select the Move tool.

Background layer is selected

You can't erase, delete, or change the opacity of the Background layer, or change its level in the layer stack, unless you first unlock it for editing. To do this, double-click the Background layer in the Layers panel and rename it.

Active layer is hidden

In most cases, the edits you make apply only to the currently selected layer (highlighted in the Layers panel). An eye icon with a red bar beside a layer in the Layers panel shows that the layer is hidden and cannot be edited. Click the eye icon to make the layer visible.

If the image on the selected layer is hidden by an opaque area on an upper layer, your edit may actually be working, but the results are simply blocked from view in the image window.

Active layer is locked

If you lock a layer by selecting it and then clicking the Lock icon at the top of the Layers panel, the layer cannot be edited. To unlock the layer, select it and then click the Lock icon again.

Wrong layer is selected (for editing text)

If you want to make changes to text, be sure that the text layer is selected in the Layers panel before you start. If a non-text layer is selected when you click the Type tool in the image window, Photoshop Elements creates a new text layer instead of placing the cursor in the existing text.

Making selections

By default, adjustments you make are applied across the whole photo. If you wish to edit only a specific area or object, you first need to select it. An active selection is the only area of the image that can be edited; the rest of the photo is protected.

The boundaries of a selection are indicated by a *selection marquee*: a flashing border of black and white dashes. For selections with soft—or *feathered*—edges, the selection marquee extends as far as the center-line of the feathering; outside the marquee, the "hardness" of the selection is less than 50%.

You can save a selection and then reuse it or edit it later, saving you time when you're creating a complicated selection or when you need to isolate the same area again.

Using the Auto Selection tool

In Quick and Expert modes, the Editor offers a suite of selection tools, each helpful for a different situation or working style. We'll start by taking a look at the Auto Selection tool.

1 If necessary, use the Tags panel or the My Folder list to isolate the Lesson 5 images. Select the uncdited image 05_07.jpg; then, click the Editor button () in the taskbar. Switch the Editor to Expert mode.

2 Select the Quick Selection tool, or whichever variant is currently visible to the right of the Lasso tool in the toolbar. If necessary, click the Tool Options button () in the taskbar to open the options pane below the image preview.

3 In the tool options pane, select the Auto Selection tool ( ). Make sure the New button at the left is activated; then, choose the Rectangle selection style.

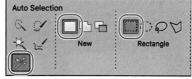

4 Click outside the image, just beyond the rock's right edge; then, drag upward and to the left to surround the mermaid and her rock with the marquee.

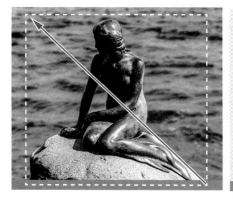
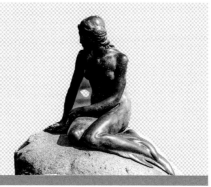

> **Tip:** Sometimes the most powerful features have the smallest footprints. If your photo has a prominent person or object in it, choose Select > Subject, or grab a selection tool and click the Select Subject button in the tool options pane. The Editor automatically discerns the subject and makes a selection, even faster than the Auto Selection tool! You'll likely need to do some cleanup of the edges, as described on the following pages, but it's a great first step.

Photoshop Elements looks for the object's outline and contracts the selection to fit. The Auto Selection tool can be used as a stand-alone tool, as in this exercise, but it is most effective in combination with the other tools in the group, making quick work of establishing a rough base selection that can then be further edited.

5   In the tool options, switch from New selection mode to Add To Selection, and change the selection style from Rectangle to Lasso. Zoom in and out by pressing the Control / Command key together with the plus or minus sign key as you work around the selection border, drawing small, rough selections around unselected areas you wish to add. Switch to Subtract From Selection mode and repeat the process to subtract unwanted background areas.

6   When you're done, choose Select > Inverse to select the water; then press the Delete key to see how well you did. Choose Edit > Undo Delete; then, choose Edit > Undo Select Inverse, and continue to tweak the selection.

7   When you're happy with the result, delete the background as you did in step 6; then choose File > Save As. Add _**AutoSelect** to the file name and save to your work folder in high-quality JPEG format, to be included in the Organizer but not in a version set. Choose File > Close.

Loading selections

If an image has been saved with layers or saved selections (*alpha channels*), you can load the alpha channel, or transparent areas of a layer, as an active selection.

Note: The lesson image has been saved in Photoshop file format, which can store layers and saved selections.

1   In the Organizer, select the unedited image 05_03.psd in the Media Browser; then, click the Editor button ( ) in the taskbar.

2   If necessary, switch to Expert edit mode. Hide the Panel Bin by deselecting its name in the Window menu; then, hide the Photo Bin by clicking the Photo Bin button ( ) in the taskbar. Choose View > Fit On Screen.

3   Choose Select > Load Selection. In the Load Selection dialog box, choose the saved selection "Bees" from the Source menu; then, click OK.

The saved selection is loaded. The four bees and the central crown of the water lily flower are now surrounded by a flashing selection marquee. The area inside the flashing border has become the active portion of the image; the rest of the photo is protected from the effects of any edits you may execute. In the exercises to follow, you'll select the flower together with the bees and then use the saved selection to help isolate the petals.

4   Choose Select > Deselect to clear the current selection.

Using the Selection Brush

Perhaps the most intuitive and controllable way to create a selection is to "paint" it directly onto the image, adding and erasing areas to correct the selection as you go. This exercise and the next focus on the use of two selection tools that let you do just that: the Selection Brush and the Quick Selection tool.

The Selection Brush tool has a Selection mode, in which you paint over the area you want to select for editing, and a Mask mode, which lets you brush a semi-opaque overlay onto the areas you want to protect from editing. The Selection Brush ( ) is grouped with the Quick Selection tool ( ), the Magic Wand tool ( ), the Refine Selection Brush ( ), and the Auto Selection tool ( ).

1 Select the Quick Selection tool—or whichever of its variants is currently visible to the right of the Lasso tool in the toolbar—then, click the Tool Options button ( ) in the taskbar to open the tool options pane at the bottom of the Edit window.

2 In the tool options pane, click the Selection Brush tool to activate it. In the Selection Brush tool options, make sure that the Add To Selection button at the left is activated (see below); then, choose Selection from the Mode menu, set the Size to 35 px (pixels), and set the Hardness value to 100%. Click the Tool Options button ( ) in the taskbar to hide the tool options pane.

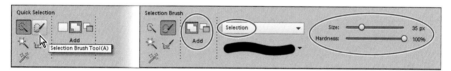

3 Drag with the Selection Brush to paint a live selection over four or five of the petals at the lower left. Don't try to paint all the way to the edges; you'll do that in the next step. You can paint over the bees to include them in the selection.

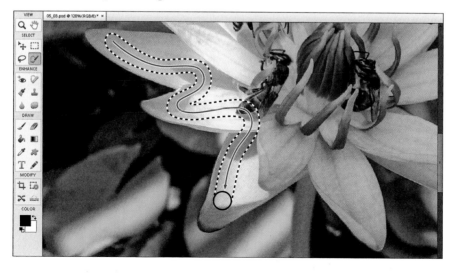

> **Tip:** While you paint your selection onto the image, release the mouse button every second or two so that you don't have to repeat too much work if you need to undo a stroke.

Now you need to reduce the brush size to paint around the edges of the petals, adding to your selection. You could open the tool options to change the brush size, but while you're working it's far more convenient to press the left bracket key ([) to reduce the brush size in increments and the right bracket key (]) to enlarge it.

Note: The bracket keys change the brush size in different pixel increments depending on the size of the brush. For a brush above 100, the increments are 25 pixels; from 50 to 99, the increment is 10 pixels; below 50, the brush adjusts in 5-pixel increments; when the brush is set smaller than 10, the increments are reduced to one pixel.

4 Press the left bracket key ([) five times to reduce the Selection Brush size to 10 pixels, and then paint your selection to the edges of the petals. If you go too far, simply hold down the Alt / Option key to switch the Selection Brush to Subtract From Selection mode, and paint out your mistakes. Use the bracket keys to change the brush size, as needed, until the selection outline completely surrounds the petals in the lower-left quadrant of the flower.

Using the Quick Selection tool

With the Quick Selection tool, all you need to do is click or "scribble" in the area you wish to select and Photoshop Elements will do most of the work. You don't need to be precise; the quick selection border automatically expands to find the edges of the area you're selecting by identifying similarities in color and texture.

1 Click the Selection Brush tool in the toolbar; then, open the tool options pane.

2 In the tool options pane at the bottom of the workspace, click the Quick Selection tool (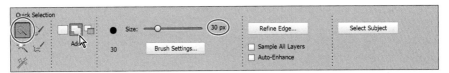); then, make sure the Add To Selection mode is activated. You can set the brush size with the slider and adjust other brush attributes by clicking Brush Settings. For the purposes of this exercise, you can use the default brush with a diameter of 30 px (pixels). Click the Tool Options button in the taskbar to hide the tool options pane.

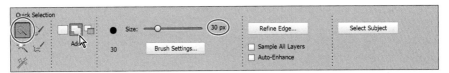

3 Starting from inside your active selection, scribble slowly inside the outline of the flower, making sure to draw through areas of different color and brightness—including the bees and the central stamens. Release the mouse button once or twice to see the result. As you draw, Photoshop Elements automatically expands the selection to any area adjacent to your stroke that has similarities in color and texture.

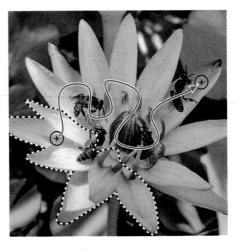

Selecting the flower directly was simple enough, but objects with more complex shapes and a lot of internal detail can sometimes be more difficult. In those cases, it can be more effective to use the Quick Selection tool to select everything *but* the object, and then invert the selection.

4 Press Ctrl+D / Command+D to deactivate the current selection; then, drag around the outside of the flower to select the leafy background. Once more, be sure to draw through areas of different brightness.

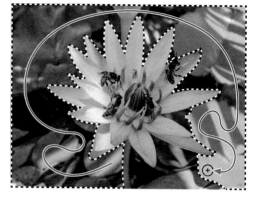

5 To turn the selection inside out, choose Select > Inverse. Check the tips of the petals and the angles where they meet; if you're missing a petal tip, paint it in with the Selection Brush tool. If fragments of background are selected between the petals, hold down the Alt / Option key and paint out the extraneous areas.

The background is now masked, and the water lily flower is selected—together with its furry friends—ready for the next exercise.

Working with saved selections

In this exercise you'll save your live selection and then modify it by loading the selection that was previously saved with the image file.

1 With your selection still active, choose Select > Save Selection.

2 In the Save Selection dialog box, name the selection **Flower**.

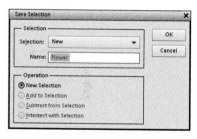

By default, the Selection menu is set to New; the selection will be saved in its own channel. At this setting the alternative Operation options are unavailable; you'll look at those a little later.

3 Click OK to close the Save Selection dialog box.

4 Without deactivating the selection, choose Select > Load Selection. In the Load Selection dialog box, click the Source Selection menu to see your Flower selection listed. Choose the saved selection Bees as the selection to be loaded.

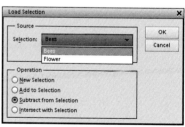

5 Under Operation, activate Subtract From Selection. This will deselect any areas where the selection you're loading and the currently active selection overlap. Click OK.

6 Choose Select > Save Selection. In the Save Selection dialog box, name the new selection **Petals**. Make sure that the Selection menu is set to New to save the selection in its own channel, rather than replacing one of the existing selections.

7 Click OK to close the Save Selection dialog box.

Next, you'll apply adjustments to the image through your new saved selections.

● **Note:** "Add To Selection" combines the saved and current selections. "Intersect With Selection" selects the areas where the two selections overlap.

Editing through selections

Now that you've saved different selections from the image, you can use them to do some selective editing, applying different treatments to separate areas of the photo.

1   Choose Select > Load Selection. In the Load Selection dialog box, choose the Flower selection from the Source Selection menu. Click the check box to activate the Invert option; this will select everything *but* the flower. Make sure the Operation option is set to New Selection, then click OK.

2   Choose Enhance > Adjust Lighting > Brightness/Contrast. Reduce the Brightness value to **–100**, increase the Contrast to **20**, and then click OK.

The adjustment to the background lighting has put the flower in the spotlight. As well as focusing attention on the flower, it has also given the photo a different feel, shifting it from mid-day to morning, and perhaps deeper into the forest.

3   Choose Select > Load Selection. This time, choose the saved Petals selection from the Source Selection menu in the Load Selection dialog box. Make sure that the Operation option is set to New Selection; then, click OK.

The petals look underexposed in some areas and burned-out in others as a result of the dappled light. Let's bring out some midtone detail and recover some color.

4   Choose Enhance > Adjust Lighting > Shadows/Highlights. Reduce the default Lighten Shadows value to **0**. Increase the Darken Highlights setting to **10**% and the Midtone Contrast to **20**%, and then click OK.

The petals now have much more color detail, and an improved tonal spread that helps to increase texture and definition.

5   Choose Enhance > Adjust Color > Adjust Hue/Saturation. Decrease the Hue value to **–50**. Leave the Saturation and Lightness values unchanged. Click OK.

Changing the color of the petals serves to narrow the focus even further to the bees and their business at the center of the flower.

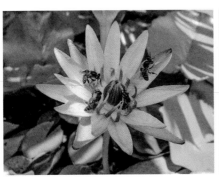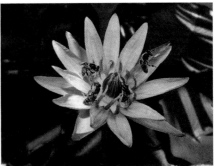

6   Choose File > Save As. Name the file **05_03_SavedSelections**, to be saved in Photoshop format with all the usual settings. Click Save, and then close the file.

Selecting fine edge detail

The Refine Selection Brush helps you make complex selections—even for difficult subjects like hair, fur, grass, and foliage. You can switch the Refine Selection Brush between four working modes to add to or subtract from a basic selection, to push a misaligned selection border into place, or to smooth jagged edges.

1 In the Editor, make sure you're in Expert mode. If necessary, hide the Panel Bin and click the Tool Options button (⛭) to show the tool options pane. Choose File > Open; then, locate and open the file 05_04.psd.

2 To save you time, we've provided the lesson image with a pre-saved base selection. Choose Select > Load Selection; then, click OK to load the saved base selection.

3 In the tool options pane, select the Refine Selection Brush (🖌); then, set the tool to Add mode. Set the brush size to 900 px, and the Snap Strength and Selection Edge values to their maximums. Reduce the opacity of the selection overlay to 70%.

● **Note:** Snap Strength affects how closely the selection will "adhere" to edge detail. The Selection Edge control increases or decreases the tool's sensitivity; a "soft" setting will detect finer edge detail.

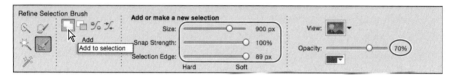

4 Position the cursor as shown below, so that the outer circle *just* includes the extremities of the feathers. The area under the gray circle will become "solidly" selected, so make sure the inner circle falls inside the edge detail and does not include any of the background. Press and hold until the selection stops growing (below, center); then, release the mouse button and move the cursor away.

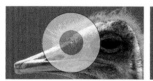
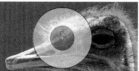
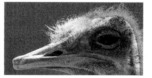

▶ **Tip:** The Push Selection and Smooth Selection cursor modes let you further refine the selection by nudging and smoothing the existing selection.

5 Repeat step 4 in the same position; then, work clockwise around the selection edge, treating each segment twice (or more, if you still see unselected areas). When you reach the area under the narrowing beak, reduce the brush to 500 px, but whenever you change the brush size, be sure to reset the Selection Edge control to its maximum value. If you find that you've selected parts of the background, switch the tool to Subtract mode and work the same way, from outside the selection.

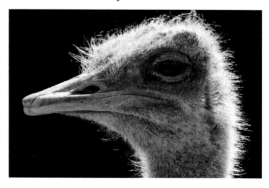

6 When you're done, click the View swatch in the tool options pane and switch the preview from Overlay to On Black mode. Choose Select > Save Selection, and save your work as a new selection. Save the file in PSD format, and then close it.

Changing the color of a pictured object

▶ **Tip:** The color replacement technique that will be most effective depends on the characteristics of the photo that you're working with and the extent of the changes that you wish to make.

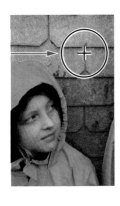

Photoshop Elements offers two very different methods for switching a specific color in an image: the Color Replacement tool and the Replace Color dialog box.

Using the Color Replacement tool

The Color Replacement tool enables you to replace a targeted color in an image by painting over it with another; it's equally effective for making localized color corrections or as a "magic brush" to enhance a photo creatively.

The cursor for the Color Replacement tool consists of crosshairs at the center of a circle that indicates the brush size. When you drag in the image, the color pinpointed by the crosshairs is sampled as the target color and the new color is then applied to any pixel inside the cursor circle that matches the targeted color, within the tolerance range set in the tool options bar.

What this means is that you can be quite relaxed as you paint; as long as you keep the crosshairs inside the area of color that you wish to replace, the circle can overlap the neighboring area without changing the color, making it easy to paint right up to the edge. The only pixels affected are those inside the cursor circle that match the targeted color under the crosshairs.

1 Use the Lesson 05 keyword tag, if necessary, to isolate the Lesson 5 images. Select the image 05_05.jpg; then, click the Editor button (⬛) in the taskbar.

2 If necessary, switch the Editor to Expert mode. Hide the Panel Bin by unchecking its name in the Window menu; then, hide the Photo Bin by clicking the Photo Bin button (⬛) in the taskbar. Choose View > Fit On Screen.

3 Click the foreground color swatch below the toolbar to open the Color Picker. Type in the text boxes to set the Hue (H), Saturation (S), and Brightness (B) to values of **200**, **80**, and **100**, respectively. Click OK to close the Color Picker.

4 Select the Brush tool (✎) (grouped in the toolbar with the Impressionist Brush and the Color Replacement tool); then, click the Tool Options button (▤✎) in the taskbar, if necessary, to access the tool settings. In the tool options pane, select the Color Replacement tool at the lower left; then, click the small menu icon (▾≡) at the far right and choose Reset Tool. Set the brush size to **200** px. Leave the rest of the settings unchanged and hide the tool options pane.

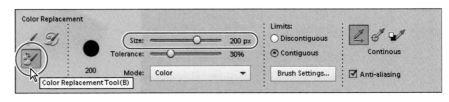

You'll use the new foreground color to repaint the boat behind the Rhea (WK7).

5 Click in the upper-left corner of the red paint at the boat's bow; then drag around the edges of the area bounded by the white paint at the top, the ropes to the right, and the stone wall at the left. Work carefully into the edges, always keeping the crosshairs within the outlines of the red paint. Reduce the brush size by pressing the left bracket key ([ ) and magnify the view as needed as you move toward the back of the boat, painting over all the red areas. Release the mouse button frequently so you can undo any over-painting without losing too much work.

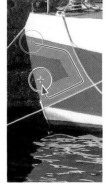 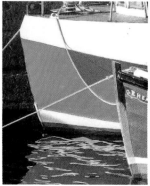

So far, so easy; the Color Replacement tool automatically adapts the new color for both lit and shaded areas. Now you need to deal with the reflections on the water. Obviously, it won't be possible to "keep inside the lines" to protect the areas reflecting white, so you'll change the way the Color Replacement tool operates.

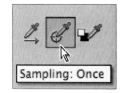

6 In the tool options pane, switch the sampling mode from Continuous to Once, increase the Tolerance setting to **40**%, and set the brush size to **100** pixels.

7 Zoom in so that you see only the area where the reflections are to be re-colored. Click inside one of the darker red patches close to the blue boat; then, without releasing the mouse button, "scrub" over all the reflections that should now be blue. Take your time, paying attention to any small areas still showing red.

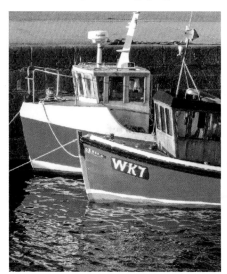 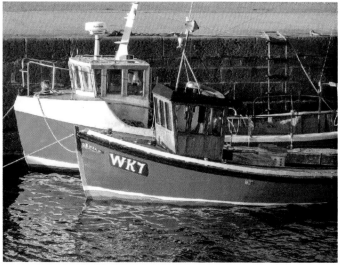

8 Choose File > Save. Name the file **05_05_BlueBoat**, to be saved as a JPEG file to your My CIB Work folder and included in the Organizer but not in a version set. Click Save; then, click OK in the JPEG Options dialog box. Close the file.

Replacing a color throughout an image

Using the Replace Color dialog box can be faster than painting with the Color Replacement tool, but it can be difficult to control—especially when the color of the object you want to change is also present in other parts of the photo. Even with difficult images, you can achieve a good result by using the Replace Color dialog box in conjunction with a selection.

In the following exercises, you'll switch the colors of two pictured objects, making your changes on a duplicate of the Background layer so that you can easily compare the finished project to the original picture. First, you'll work on the entire image, which will give you an indication of just where—and how much—the color change will affect the rest of the photo. In the second stage, you'll use a selection to constrain the changes.

1 In the Organizer, use the Lesson 05 keyword tag, if necessary, to isolate the Lesson 5 images. In the Media Browser, click to select the image 05_06.jpg, and then click the Editor button (⌂) in the taskbar.

2 In the Editor, switch to the Expert mode and choose Window > Reset Panels. Hide the Photo Bin, if necessary, by clicking the Photo Bin button (⌂) in the taskbar; then, double-click the Hand tool or choose View > Fit On Screen. If you don't see the Layers panel at the right of the workspace, click the Layers button (⌂) in the taskbar.

3 The layers panel shows that this image has only one layer, which is active (selected) by default. Choose Layer > Duplicate Layer and accept the default name. Alternatively, drag the Background layer to the New Layer button (⌂) at the upper left of the Layers panel. With a duplicate layer, you'll have an original to fall back on should you need it.

4 With the new Background Copy layer selected in the Layers panel, choose Enhance > Adjust Color > Replace Color.

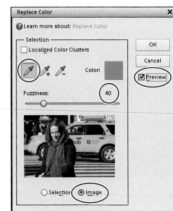

5 In the Replace Color dialog box, make sure that the left-most of the three eyedropper buttons is activated—as in the illustration at the right—and that Fuzziness is set to the default value of 40. Make sure that Preview is activated, and switch the selection preview thumbnail to the Image view option.

6 Move the pointer over the thumbnail preview in the Replace Color dialog box and click once with the eyedropper on the yellow taxi. Change the selection preview from Image to Selection so that you can see the extent of the color selection you just made highlighted in white on a black background.

7 Below the selection preview, either use the sliders or type in the text boxes to set the Hue, Saturation, and Lightness values to **90**, **100**, and **0**, respectively, a bright green that will be easily seen wherever it appears in the image.

8 To adjust the area of selected color—or color-application area—start by clicking the second of the three eyedropper buttons to switch the eyedropper tool to Add To Sample mode, as illustrated at the right, below; then, click in the main image window in a few areas where the paint on the car still appears yellow.

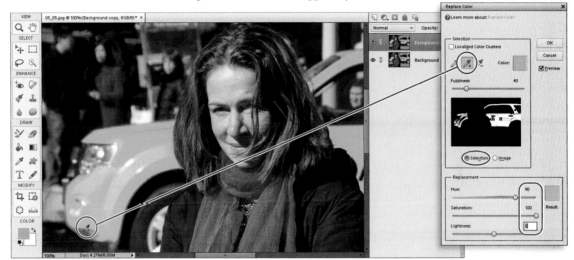

9 Use the Add To Sample eyedropper again, if necessary, and then drag the Fuzziness slider left and right until you have full coverage on the car. In both the Edit pane and the black and white selection preview, you can see that it's not possible to change the color of the car using this technique without affecting the woman's skin and hair, as well as various parts of the background. Click Cancel to close the Replace Color dialog box.

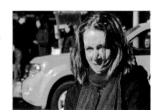

Replacing a color in a limited area of an image

In this exercise you'll limit the color change to a selected area of the photograph.

1 Make sure the layer Background Copy is still selected in the Layers panel. In the toolbar, switch to the Quick Selection tool (⟋). Press the left and right bracket keys ([,]) to set a workable brush size.

2 Use the Quick Selection tool to select all the yellow areas of the car. As much as possible, try to include the reddish halo that surrounds the yellow areas (clearly visible on the roof, at the front of the taxi, and around the wheel arches and signage). If you go too far and need to trim the selection, simply hold down the Alt / Option key as you work to switch the Quick Selection tool temporarily to Subtract From Selection mode.

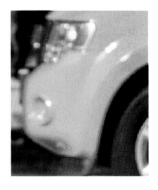

3 Choose Enhance > Adjust Color > Replace Color. Repeat steps 5 through 8 from the previous exercise. Be sure that you follow the steps in order; you need to sample the original yellow before setting Hue, Saturation, and Lightness to define the replacement color. This time, set the Hue, Saturation, and Lightness values to **−85**, **−30**, and **0**, respectively, a color that will match the woman's scarf.

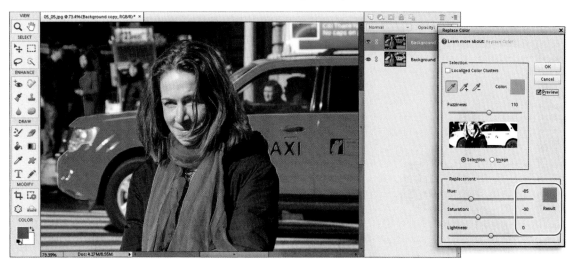

4 When you're satisfied with the results, click OK to close the Replace Color dialog box; then choose Select > Deselect, or press Ctrl+D / Command+D.

5 Repeat the process for the scarf. First, select it with the Quick Selection tool, taking particular care with the shaded areas in the deeper folds, and the areas adjacent to the woman's hair and under her chin. Then, choose Enhance > Adjust Color > Replace Color, sample the scarf thoroughly, and set the Hue, Saturation, and Lightness values to **70**, **60**, and **0**; a color that would have once matched the taxi.

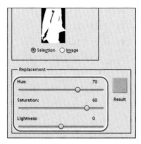

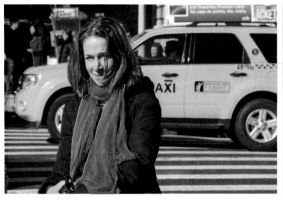

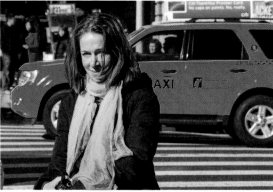

6   To compare the edited image to the original, toggle the visibility of the Background Copy layer by clicking the eye icon beside the layer thumbnail. Make the new layer visible again, and then right-click the Background Copy layer and choose Flatten Image from the menu. The image is flattened to a single layer; the layer you edited replaces the original Background layer.

7   Choose File > Save. Name the file **05_06_ColorSwitch**, to be saved to your My CIB Work folder, and included in the Organizer but not in a version set. Click Save; then, click OK in the JPEG Options dialog box. Close the file.

Colorizing a photo

Black and white photos have a special appeal, but occasionally don't you wish you could see them in color? The new Colorize Photos feature does a pretty good job of adding color where it didn't exist in the image before—great for giving life to old photos.

1   Open the file 05_08.jpg in the Editor and switch to the Expert mode, if necessary.

2   Choose Enhance > Colorize Photo. After analyzing the image, a colorization is chosen. Click between the four options to see the warm and cool options.

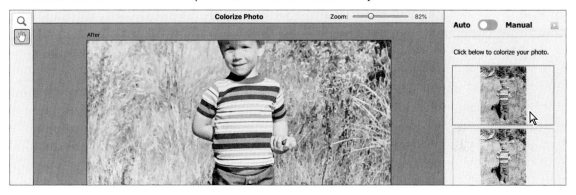

3   Move the switch at the top from Auto to Manual mode. Notice the boy's left hand didn't get the same skin-colored treatment as his other arm and face.

4   Click the Quick Selection tool (✎) in the sidebar and select that hand and arm.

5   Click the Droplet Tool button and click once within your selection to define the area to be colored manually.

6   Under Color Palette, click the eyedropper tool, and then click the boy's right arm.

7   Click the Before / After button to compare the results of your work, and then click OK to apply the effect.

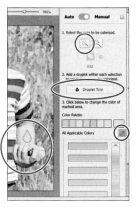

8   Choose File > Save. Name the file **05_08_Colorize**, to be saved to your My CIB Work folder, and included in the Organizer but not in a version set. Click Save; then, click OK in the JPEG Options dialog box. Close the file.

Working with color management

Moving a photo from your camera to your monitor and from there to a printer or other device can cause an apparent shift in the colors in the image. This shift occurs because every device has a different *color gamut*, or *color space*—the range of colors the device is capable of interpreting and reproducing.

To achieve consistent color between digital cameras, scanners, monitors, and printers, you need to use color management. The software acts as an interpreter, translating colors so that each device can reproduce them in the same way. Device-specific *color profiles*, mathematical descriptions of each device's color space, help you maintain consistent color. When you save a file, select Embed Color Profile in the Save As dialog box. In Photoshop Elements, you can access the color management controls from the Edit menu in both the Organizer and the Editor.

Setting up color management

1   Choose Edit > Color Settings; then, select one of these color management options in the Color Settings dialog:

- **No Color Management** uses your monitor profile as the working color space. This setting removes any embedded profiles when opening images and does not apply a profile when saving.

- **Always Optimize Colors for Computer Screens** uses sRGB as the working color space, preserves embedded profiles, and assigns sRGB when opening untagged files. Computer screens are capable of reproducing all of the colors in the sRGB range, so this setting will ensure an accurate display for any device that supports the sRGB color space.

- **Always Optimize for Printing** uses Adobe RGB as the working color space, preserves embedded profiles, and assigns Adobe RGB when opening untagged files. This setting will display your photos based on the colors within the AdobeRGB color space, commonly used for printing images.

- **Allow Me to Choose** lets you choose whether to assign sRGB (the default) or Adobe RGB when opening a file that has an unsupported color profile or no embedded profile at all.

2   Click OK to close the Color Settings dialog.

Further information on color management, including monitor calibration, can be found in a series of topics in Photoshop Elements Help.

Congratulations, you've completed another exercise. Now, take a minute to refresh your knowledge by reading through the review questions and answers on the following page.

Review questions

1 What makes selections so important for adjusting color?

2 Name at least two selection tools and describe how they work.

3 How does the Color Replacement tool work?

4 What is the difference between the Continuous and Once sampling modes for the Color Replacement tool, and how are they used?

Review answers

1 A selection defines an area as the only part of a layer that can be altered. The areas outside the selection are protected from change for as long as the selection is active. This enables you to make adjustments selectively, targeting specific areas or objects.

2 The first selection tool you used in this lesson is the Selection Brush tool, which works like a paintbrush. The Quick Selection tool is similar, but is in most cases a faster, more flexible option. There are more selection tools than are discussed in this lesson: The Magic Wand tool selects areas with the same color as that which you click. The Rectangular Marquee tool and the Elliptical Marquee tool make selections of a fixed geometric shape. The Lasso tool lets you draw free-form selections, and the Magnetic Lasso tool helps you draw complicated selections around even irregular object edges. The Polygonal Lasso tool is the tool of choice for selecting straight-sided objects.

3 The Color Replacement tool samples the color under the pointer and replaces it with any color that you choose. The cursor for the Color Replacement tool consists of crosshairs at the center of a circle, indicating the brush size. When you drag in the image, the color under the crosshairs is sampled, and the foreground color is applied to any pixel inside the circle that matches the sampled color, within the tolerance value specified in the tool options pane. As long as you keep the crosshairs inside the area of color that you wish to replace, you can overlap the adjacent area without changing the color, making it easy to paint right up to the edge.

4 In Continuous sampling mode, the Color Replacement tool continuously samples the pixels under the cursor crosshairs, updating the target color as you drag across your image. This is useful for recoloring an area that has varied tones, without increasing the tolerance. In the Once sampling mode, the target color is set with the first click. Use this mode for detailed areas where it's not easy to keep the crosshairs inside the lines.

6 FIXING LIGHTING AND EXPOSURE PROBLEMS

Lesson overview

Photoshop Elements makes it easy to fix images that are too dark or too light and to rescue photos that are dull, flat, or simply fading away.

Start with quick and guided edits, and work up to Expert mode as you learn how to use powerful, easy-to-use tools in all three editing modes to make the most of poorly exposed images, retrieve detail from photos that are too dark or pale and faded, and liven up images that look flat and washed out.

In this lesson, you'll be introduced to a variety of techniques for dealing with a range of common exposure problems:

- Brightening underexposed photographs
- Correcting parts of an image selectively
- Saving selection shapes to reuse in later sessions
- Working with adjustment layers and layer masks
- Using layer blending modes and opacity settings
- Adjusting lighting controls manually
- Enhancing overexposed, faded, and hazy photographs

This lesson will take about 60 minutes to complete. To get the lesson files used in this chapter, download them from the web page for this book at www.adobepress.com/PSECIB2020. For more information, see "Accessing the lesson files and Web Edition" in the Getting Started section at the beginning of this book.

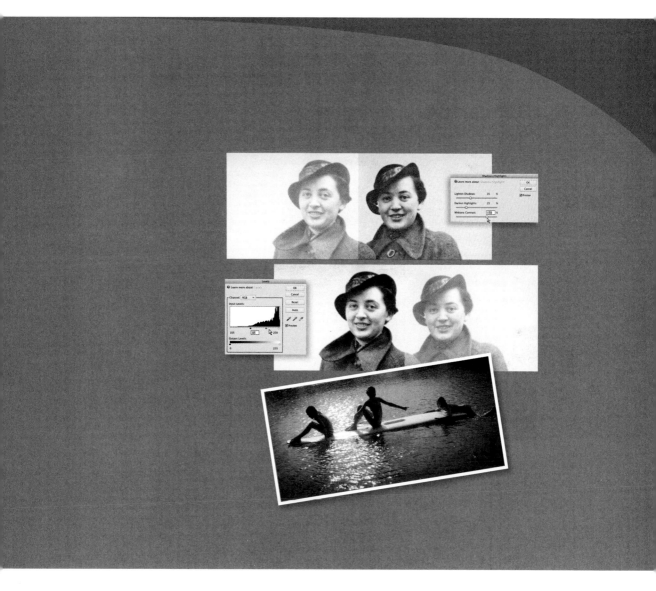

Learn how to make the most of images that were captured in unusual lighting conditions, retrieving detail from overly dark photos and putting the spark back into images that look dull or washed out. Find out how Photoshop Elements can help you save those faded memories, no matter what your level of experience.

Getting started

Note: Before you start this lesson, make sure you've set up a folder for your lesson files and downloaded the Lesson 6 folder from your Account page at www.peachpit.com, as detailed in "Accessing the lesson files and Web Edition" and "Creating a work folder" in the "Getting Started" section at the beginning of this book. You should also have created a new work catalog (see "Creating a catalog for working with this book" in Lesson 1).

To start, you'll import the sample images for this lesson to the CIB Catalog that you created at the beginning of Lesson 1.

1 Start Photoshop Elements and click Organizer in the Home screen.

2 In the Organizer, check the lower-right corner of the workspace to make sure the CIB Catalog is loaded—if not, choose File > Manage Catalogs and select it from the list.

3 Click the Import button at the upper left of the Organizer workspace and choose From Files And Folders from the drop-down menu. In the Get Photos And Videos From Files And Folders dialog box, locate and select your Lesson 6 folder. Disable the automatic processing options; then, click Get Media.

4 In the Import Attached Keyword Tags dialog box, click Select All; then, click OK.

Batch-processing the lesson files

As you've already seen, the batch-processing command lets you apply automatic adjustments to an entire folder of image files at once.

1 Before you start this lesson, set up automatic processing for all the Lesson 6 images by following the steps in the exercise "Batch-processing the lesson files" at the beginning of Lesson 5.

2 At the end of each exercise in this lesson, compare the automatic fixes to the results that you achieve using various other techniques.

Adjusting images for tonal balance

Most image problems fall into two basic categories: color and exposure. In some photos, the two issues can be interrelated, and there is also some overlap in the tools and techniques you'll use to correct them.

In the previous lesson, you gained experience recognizing and dealing with color deficiencies in your photos. This lesson will focus on exposure and lighting—issues that affect the *tonal balance* of your image.

Ideally, an image should have a good spread of tonal values from dark to light; any imbalance can result in a photo that is too dark or too light, has too little contrast or too much, or is lacking detail in the shadows, the midtones, or the highlights.

As with color correction, Photoshop Elements offers a range of tools for adjusting exposure, available in all three edit modes. In the exercises to follow, you'll look at a variety of ways to get the best from poorly exposed images, retrieve detail from photos that are too dark, and liven up images that look flat and washed out.

Brightening an underexposed image

Underexposed photographs look too dark or dull and flat, often across the entire image but sometimes in just part of it. While the lighting auto-fixes do a good job with many photos, this exercise will teach you techniques to give you more control for adjusting the exposure in problem images.

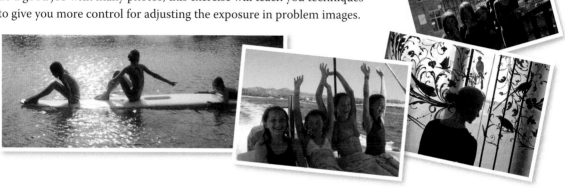

Applying Quick Edit lighting adjustments

Let's start by combining Exposure and Lighting adjustments in Quick Edit mode.

1 If necessary, click the check box beside the Lesson 06 tag to isolate the lesson images. Select the file TooDark.jpg; then, click the Editor button (⌨) in the taskbar. Click Quick in the mode picker to switch to Quick Edit mode.

2 Expand the Exposure pane and increase the Exposure setting to **2.0** to brighten everything.

3 Expand the Lighting pane and click the Shadows tab. Set the Shadows value to **25** to lighten them.

> ▶ **Tip:** Use the View menu above the Edit pane to switch between the After Only view and the Before & After views, which will help you assess the results of your adjustments as you work.

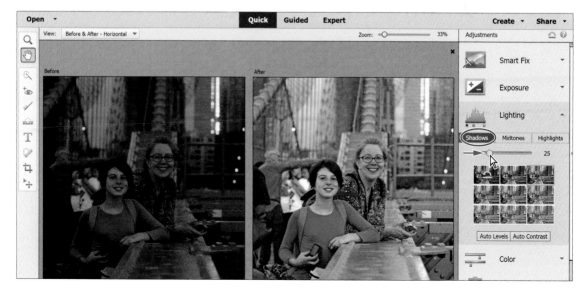

You've improved the image substantially with just a few clicks. However, though the skin tones have been lightened and have more definition, they're oversaturated.

4 Expand the Color pane. Click the Saturation tab and reduce the value to **–30**. Expand the Balance pane and set the Tint value to **–10**.

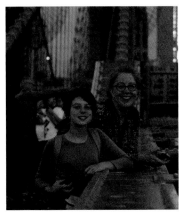
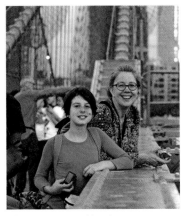
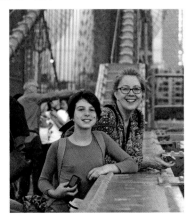

Original image   Adjust exposure and levels   Correct saturation and tint

5 Choose File > Save. Make sure that Include In The Elements Organizer is activated, and disable Save In Version Set With Original. Name the new file **TooDark_QuickEdit**, to be saved to your My CIB Work folder in JPEG format. Click Save. In the JPEG Options dialog box, use the slider to set the Quality to 9, and then click OK. Choose File > Close.

Adjusting exposure in Guided Edit mode

When you're not sure what adjustments a poorly exposed image needs, the Basics category in Guided Edit mode offers three procedures for correcting lighting and exposure: Brightness And Contrast, Levels, and Lighten And Darken—each with easy-to-follow prompts that make it simple for even a novice to get great results.

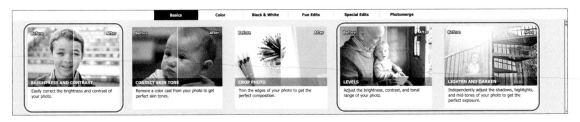

● **Note:** In the Guided Edit panel, numerical values for the settings are displayed in tooltips when you click or move the slider controls.

1 In the Organizer, select the image TooDark.jpg. Click the Editor button (⊡) in the taskbar; then, click Guided in the mode picker to switch the Editor to Guided Edit mode. Select the Basics category and click Brightness And Contrast. Drag the sliders to increase the Brightness to 80 and the Contrast to –50. Click Next below the Brightness And Contrast panel; then, click Done.

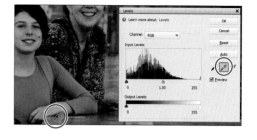

2 Click the Levels guided edit; then, click the Create Levels Adjustment button at the top of the Guided Edit panel. Click OK in the New Layer dialog box to accept the default name for the new adjustment layer. Select the second of the three eyedropper tools in the Levels panel and click to sample a mid-gray from the railing in the foreground. Click OK. Click Next below the Levels panel; then, click Done.

3 Launch the Lighten And Darken edit from the Basics pane. Set the Shadows, Highlights, and Midtones to **15**, **10**, and **25**, respectively, and then click Next.

Tip: You can click other sample areas until you get an adjustment you like. It's common to click a spot you think is gray but that wildly affects the tones and color.

4 Click the Save As button. Make sure that the new file will be saved to your work folder and included in the Organizer but not in a version set. Change the file format from Photoshop to JPEG; then, name the new file **TooDark_Guided**. Click Save; then, click OK to close the JPEG Options dialog box. Choose File > Close, and then click No / Don't Save to avoid saving the changes to the original file.

Once again, the adjusted image looks considerably better than the original; however, it would be ideal if we could treat the people in the foreground separately from the background so that they stand out more from the busy background.

Fixing exposure in Expert Edit mode

If your photo is a difficult case, more elaborate methods than those you've used in the Quick Edit and Guided Edit modes might be necessary to achieve the best results. In Expert Edit mode you can work with multiple layers and blending modes, and also make selections to isolate specific parts of an image for special treatment.

Using blending modes

In a multiple-layer image file, each layer has its own blending mode that defines the way it will interact with any layer below it in the stacking order. By default, a newly created layer uses the Normal blending mode: it will not blend with the layers below it except where it contains transparency or when the master opacity for the layer is set to less than 100%. A layer with the blending mode set to Darken or Lighten will blend with the layers below it only where the result will darken or lighten the lower layers. Other blending modes produce more complex results.

If a photo is too dark, applying the Screen blending mode to an overlaid duplicate of the Background layer may correct the problem. If your photo is overexposed, an overlaid duplicate with the Multiply blending mode can be a solution. You can adjust the master opacity of the overlaid layer to control the intensity of the effect.

Tip: For information on the effects produced by the different layer blending modes, please refer to Photoshop Elements Help.

1 In the Media Browser, right-click the image TooDark.jpg and choose Edit With Photoshop Elements Editor from the context menu, taking care not to confuse the original file with the edited copies.

2 Switch to Expert mode by clicking Expert in the mode picker at the top of the Editor workspace. Choose Window > Reset Panels, and then hide the Photo Bin by clicking the Photo Bin button (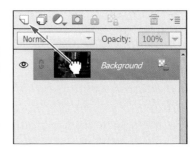) at the left of the taskbar. Choose View > Fit On Screen.

Tip: You can also duplicate a selected layer by choosing Duplicate Layer from the Layer menu or by right-clicking the layer and choosing from the layer's context menu.

3 In the Layers panel you can see that the image has only one layer: Background. Duplicate the Background layer by dragging it onto the New Layer button (⬇) at the left of the Layers panel's header.

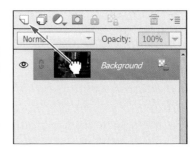

In the Layers panel, the new Background Copy layer is highlighted to indicate that it is the currently selected—or active—layer.

Tip: If the layer blending mode menu is disabled, make sure the copy layer—not the original Background layer—is selected in the Layers panel.

4 With the Background Copy layer selected, choose Screen from the blending mode menu at the top of the Layers panel. The image becomes much brighter overall, but the people are still darker than we'd like. Reduce the opacity of the Background Copy layer to 75%. Duplicate the layer Background Copy with its Screen blending mode by dragging it onto the New Layer button. At the top of the Layers panel, set the second duplicate layer's opacity to 50%.

5 Choose File > Save. Name the new file **TooDark_Blend**, to be saved to your My CIB Work folder and included in the Organizer but not as part of a version set. To preserve the layers you created, save the image in the Photoshop (PSD) file format and make sure the Layers option is activated, and then click Save.

6 To quickly compare the adjusted image to the original, toggle the visibility of the Background Copy layers by clicking the eye icon (👁, ⬚) beside each layer's thumbnail. When you're done, close the file without saving.

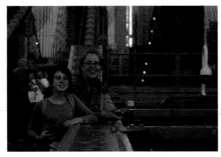 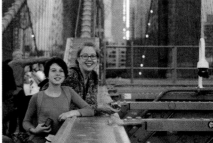

In this exercise you've seen how you can use a blending mode to brighten a dull image. For many photos, however, applying a blending mode over the entire image in this way can adversely affect areas that were okay to begin with.

In our example, the sky in the background is now overly bright and has lost almost all color and midtone detail. The resultant high-contrast glare of the blended background dominates the less well-lit subjects in the foreground.

About adjustment layers

An adjustment layer affects the underlying layers like an overlay or lens filter, perhaps darkening the photo, perhaps making it appear pale and faded or intensifying its hues—but remaining separate from the image itself. Effects applied on an adjustment layer can be easily revised, or even removed, because the pixels of the image layers are not permanently modified. You can even copy an adjustment layer from one photo and paste it on top of the image layers in another—a real time-saver when you wish to apply the same treatment to several similar images.

Using adjustment layers to correct lighting

In this exercise you'll try some different techniques to correct and enhance the same underexposed photo that you used for the last series of exercises.

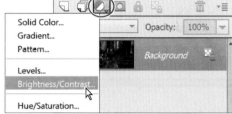

Note: A new adjustment layer is always created immediately above the selected layer.

1 In the Organizer, select the image TooDark.jpg in the Media Browser; then, click the Editor button (⌨) in the taskbar.

2 Click the Create New Fill Or Adjustment Layer button (⬤) in the header of the Layers panel and choose Brightness/Contrast from the menu. In the Brightness/Contrast panel, drag the sliders or type in the text boxes to set Brightness and Contrast values of **100** and **–50**, respectively.

3 Click the Create New Fill Or Adjustment Layer button again, this time choosing Levels from the menu. Notice the new Levels 1 adjustment layer in the Layers panel. The Adjustments panel is updated to present the Levels controls.

4 Select the lower of the three eyedropper tools at the right of the Levels controls and click the white shirt on the person in the background. The white point eyedropper improves the tonal range and also corrects the cool color cast, adding some life to the skin tones. Drag the gray midtones stop under the center of the histogram to the left to set a new value of 1.1.

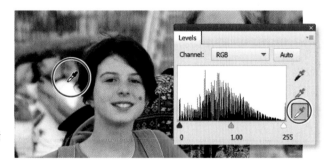

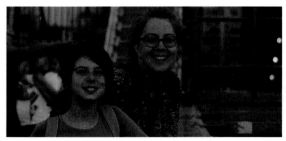
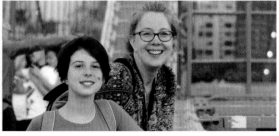

5   Choose File > Save. Name the new file **TooDark_AdjustLayers**, to be saved to your My CIB Work folder and included in the Organizer but not as part of a version set. To preserve the layers, save the image in the Photoshop (PSD) file format and make sure the Layers option is activated, and then click Save.

6   To quickly assess the effect of the adjustment layers, toggle the visibility of each layer by clicking the eye icon beside its thumbnail in the Layers panel. When you're done, close the file without saving.

As long as you save the file in the Photoshop format, preserving the layers, you can return to adjust your settings at any time. Even after you close the file, the adjustment layers retain the values you set, and remain live; if necessary, you could even revert to the original image by either hiding or deleting the adjustment layers.

Correcting parts of an image selectively

Our adjustment layers brought out color and image detail from the overly dark original photo, but the background is now lacking in tonal depth. So far in this lesson, all the corrections you've made have been applied to the entire image; in the next set of exercises you'll selectively adjust just part of the photo.

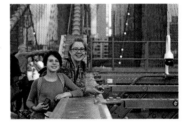

Creating a selection

In this exercise you'll isolate our subjects in the foreground from the busy background so you can treat the areas separately and help focus the viewer's attention. To start, you'll select the combined silhouette of the girls and save that selection.

You've already explored some of the many ways to make a selection, in Lesson 5. We'll start by revisiting the Quick Selection tool, which automatically determines selection borders based on similarity in color and texture.

1   Open the original image file TooDark.jpg once again.

▶ **Tip:** In the tool options pane, you can also click the Select Subject button to let the Editor have a crack at making the selection. It does a pretty good job! That said, choose Select > Deselect and follow the remaining steps in this exercise so you understand how to refine the selection.

2   In the toolbar, click the Quick Selection tool ( ) or whichever of its variants is currently visible at the right of the Lasso tool; then, click the Tool Options button ( ) in the taskbar to access the tool settings. In the tool options pane, make sure that the New Selection mode is activated for the Quick Selection tool. Set a brush diameter of around 100 px (pixels) and activate Auto-Enhance.

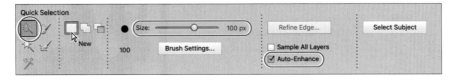

3 Place the cursor just inside the hairline above the woman's forehead and drag a line down the face and body of the girl in front of her. The active selection automatically expands to surround the combined silhouette of our subjects; not bad for a quick first pass.

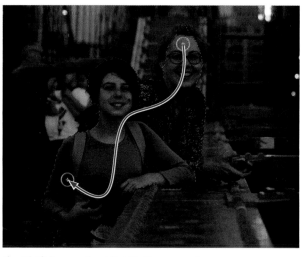

Next, you need to refine the border to capture the silhouette as closely as possible and grab areas outside the initial selection. You'll need to include the woman's hair, hand, and backpack, paying attention to the hair and highlight areas. You also want the railing that extends into the foreground and the first cross beam.

To refine your selection, you can hold down either the Shift key or the Alt / Option key as you work to alternate between the Add To Selection and Subtract From Selection modes of the Quick Selection tool.

▶ **Tip:** Use the left and right bracket keys ([,]) to reduce or increase the brush size as you work, without stopping to open the tool options.

4 Keeping the Quick Selection tool selected, hold the Ctrl / Command key and press the plus sign (+) to zoom in. Hold the spacebar and drag the image to focus your view on the woman's face.

5 Press the left bracket key ([ ) on your keyboard repeatedly to reduce the brush size to 70 px. Drag to select her hair, which will probably also select some of the bridge behind her. To deselect that portion, hold the Alt / Option key to operate the Quick Selection tool in Subtract From Selection mode and drag in it. The selection contracts to exclude the extraneous area. Use a combination of clicks and very short strokes, pressing the Alt / Option key as needed, to refine the selection border around the deselected area.

6 Without being overly fussy, use the same techniques as you continue to refine the selection around the woman's hand and phone. Your work will be much simpler if you use the keyboard shortcuts detailed in step 5 and in the margin Tip to navigate in the image and adjust the tool settings.

7 Finally, add the other foreground element—the railing and the closest support beam—to the selection, taking care to exclude the background areas.

8 To smooth and soften the edges of the selection, choose Select > Refine Edge. Alternatively, you could show the tool options pane and click the Refine Edge button. In the Refine Edge dialog box, activate the Smart Radius option for the Edge Detection control and set the Radius to **3** px. Under Adjust Edge, set the Smooth value to **3**, and the Feather amount to **1** px. Under Output, make sure the Output To option is set to Selection.

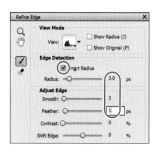

▶ **Tip:** Take a moment to move the pointer over each control in the Refine Edge dialog box in turn to see a description of its action displayed in a tooltip.

9   While you're working on refining your selection, you can preview the results against a variety of backgrounds, each helpful in different circumstances. Under View Mode, click the View button. Move the pointer over each of the seven preview options to see a tooltip description, then click each in turn to see the result in the Edit window.

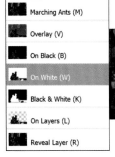

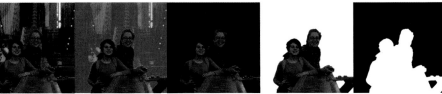

10 Click OK to apply your edge refinement settings to the selection; then, choose Select > Save Selection. In the Save Selection dialog box, choose New from the Selection menu, type **Girls** for the selection name, and then click OK. Once a selection is saved, you can always reuse it—after assessing your adjustments you can reload the selection to modify them. Choose Select > Deselect.

Using layer masks to isolate parts of an image

Now that you've created a selection including only the figures in the foreground, you can adjust the exposure and lighting for the subjects and the background independently. You could use your selection (even at a later date, now that you've saved it) to temporarily isolate part of the image for editing. Instead you'll use the saved selection to create separate layer masks for the different areas in the image.

A layer mask can be permanently linked to a particular layer in an image, so any modification made to that layer will be applied only through the mask. The parts of the layer protected by the layer mask are hidden from view when it's blended with the other layers in your image. Layer masks can be edited by painting and erasing, so you can add to or subtract from a layer mask (and thereby add to or subtract from the area that will be modified by an editing operation) without affecting the image pixels on the layer to which the mask is attached.

1   Duplicate the Background layer by dragging it onto the New Layer button (⧉) at the left of the Layers panel's header.

2   Click the menu icon (▼≡) at the far right of the Layers panel's header to open the Layers panel Options menu; then, choose Panel Options. In the Layers Panel Options dialog box, select either large or medium thumbnails—seeing the layer thumbnails can help you visualize the layers you're working with. Click OK. If necessary, choose View > Fit On Screen so that you can see the entire image.

3   Choose Select > Load Selection. Choose the saved selection Girls from the Source Selection menu, click the check box to activate the Invert option, and choose New Selection under Operation; then click OK.

4 Make sure the layer Background Copy is still selected, and then click the Add Layer Mask button (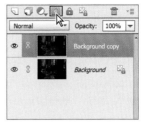) at the top of the Layers panel.

A mask thumbnail appears on the Background Copy layer, showing that your active selection in the image window has been converted to a layer mask on that layer. The blue frame around the mask thumbnail indicates that the mask is currently selected—any change you make right now will modify the mask, not the image pixels on this layer.

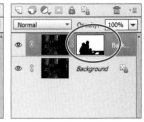

5 Alt-click / Option-click the layer mask thumbnail to make the mask visible in the Edit window. With the mask selected, as it is now, you can edit it using painting and selection tools—or even the Text tool. Alt-click / Option-click the layer mask thumbnail again to hide the mask. Choose Select > Deselect Layers.

6 Click to select the image thumbnail on the masked layer; then, click the eye icon on the original Background layer to make the layer temporarily invisible. You can see that the protected areas of the masked layer are actually hidden from view. Make the Background layer visible again.

▶ **Tip:** Edits made on a masked layer will be applied at full strength through the white parts of the mask; black areas in the mask represent the parts of your image that are completely protected. A gray area will allow a modification to be applied at a strength equivalent to the percentage of white present; a layer mask containing a gradient from white to black can be a great way to fade one image into another.

While this layer mask is active, any change made to the original Background layer will be visible only in the figures in the foreground; any change you make to the masked layer will be applied only to the backdrop around them.

7 Make another copy of the original Background layer by dragging it onto the New Layer button (⧉) at the left of the Layers panel's header bar. Choose Select > Load Selection. Select your saved selection, Girls, as the Source Selection, but this time, leave the Invert option disabled. Under Operation, choose New Selection; then click OK.

8 Make sure the new layer, Background Copy 2, is still selected, and then click the Add Layer Mask button (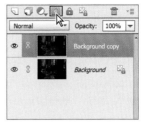) at the top of the Layers panel. Repeat steps 5 and 6 for the new mask layer.

If you keep the layer masks linked to the Background Copy layers as they are now, they will remain editable. For the purposes of this exercise, however, we've already refined our selection and we have no other reason to keep the mask active.

9 Right-click each black and white layer mask thumbnail in turn and choose Apply Layer Mask from the context menu.

The layer masks can no longer be edited; they have been permanently applied to their respective layers. The layer mask thumbnails have now disappeared and the image thumbnails show areas of transparency, indicating protected areas on those layers.

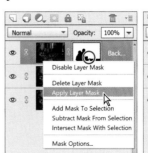
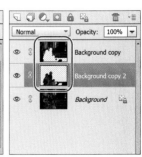

10 You'll find it much easier to deal with layers—especially when you're working with many of them—if you give your layers descriptive names in the Layers panel. Double-click the name text of Background Copy 2 and type **Girls** as the new name for the layer. Change the name of Background Copy to **Bridge**.

Correcting underexposed areas

We can now apply the most effective brightening technique from the earlier exercises to the subjects of our photo selectively.

1 In the Layers panel, make sure that the Background layer is visible; then, select the layer Girls and choose Screen from the blending menu.

2 Duplicate the Girls layer and set the opacity for the new copy to 25%. The figures are brighter and clearer, while the Bridge layer remains unchanged.

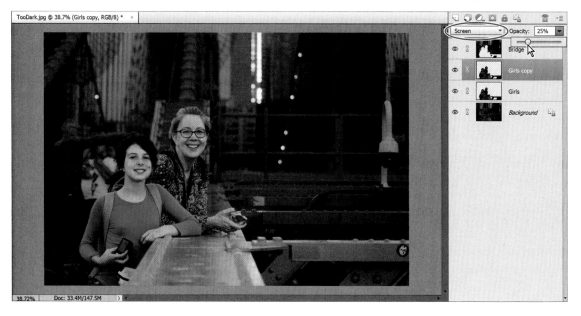

Adding more intensity

Now that the figures in the foreground look so much better, the structure behind them needs to be adjusted to appear less dull and murky.

With the foreground and background isolated on separate masked layers, you're free to apply whatever modifications you choose. There are no hard-and-fast rules; you might decide to emphasize the figures by making the background bright and pale (along the lines of the effect you achieved with TooDark_Blend.psd) or by making it even darker and more dramatic. For the purposes of this exercise, we'll simply boost the contrast to increase the clarity of the architectural detail without really interfering with the lighting dynamics of the original image.

1 In the Layers panel, select the layer Bridge. Choose Enhance > Adjust Lighting > Brightness/Contrast. Set the Brightness setting to **20**, and increase the Contrast setting to a value of **50**. Click OK. The bridge looks more dramatic and the other people are minimized, while the figures in the foreground are emphasized.

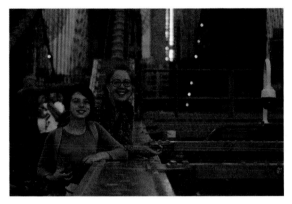 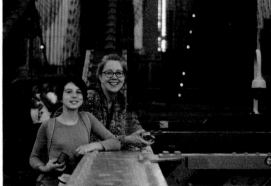

With these few adjustments to the separate layers, the photograph now looks far more lively. There are still possibilities for improving the separated areas of the image; for example, you could apply a Gaussian blur to the background to create a depth-of-field effect. There's also more you could do with blending modes and layer opacity—you'll learn more of those techniques as you work through this book.

2 Choose File > Save. Make sure that the Include In The Elements Organizer option is activated and that Save In Version Set With Original is disabled. Name the new file **TooDark_LayerMasks** and choose the Photoshop (PSD) format. Make sure the Layers option is activated, and then click Save. If the Format Options dialog box appears, activate Maximize Compatibility and click OK. Close the file.

3 In Lesson 5 you learned how to tile the image windows to best compare the results of different correction methods. Use that technique now to compare the six adjusted and saved versions of this photograph before moving on.

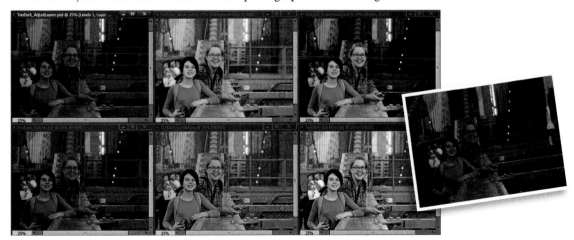

Improving faded or overexposed images

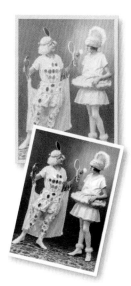

In this section, you'll work with the scan of a family keepsake in need of restoration. This badly faded photo has problems similar to those found in overexposed images and will respond to the same correction techniques.

The automatic fixes applied to a copy at the beginning of this lesson (see "Batch-processing the image files") improved the image markedly but also removed the characteristic sepia tint, treating it as a color cast. In this project, you'll try to do even better using other correction techniques, while preserving the evocative antique look.

1 In the Organizer, isolate the Lesson 6 images, if necessary. In the Media Browser, select the file TooLight.jpg; then, click the Editor button (⟳) in the taskbar.

2 If the Editor is not already in Expert mode, click Expert in the mode picker.

3 If you don't see the Photo Bin, show it by clicking the Photo Bin button (▦) at the left of the taskbar. If you don't see the file name beneath the thumbnail in the Photo Bin, right-click the thumbnail and choose Show Filenames. Choose Window > Reset Panels, and then View > Fit On Screen.

Creating a set of duplicate files

You'll compare a variety of editing techniques during the course of this project. You can begin by creating a separate file to test each method, named for the technique it will demonstrate.

1 Right-click the thumbnail image in the Photo Bin and choose Duplicate from the context menu. Name the file **TooLight_Shad-High** in the Duplicate Image dialog box; then, click OK. Repeat the process to create two more copies, with the names **TooLight_Bright-Cont** and **TooLight_Levels**.

2 In the Photo Bin, click the thumbnail TooLight.jpg to make that image active and bring its image window to the front. If you can't see the whole file name under a thumbnail in the Photo Bin, hold the pointer over the thumbnail; the name of the file is displayed as a tooltip.

3 Choose File > Save As. Select your My CIB Work folder as the destination for the new file, then activate Include In The Elements Organizer and disable the option Save In Version Set With Original. Type **TooLight_Blend-Modes** as the new file name and select Photoshop (PSD) from the Format menu. Click Save. Leave all four images open for the rest of this project.

Using blending modes to fix a faded image

The blending mode applied to a layer can make it interact with the layers beneath it in a variety of ways. The Multiply mode intensifies or darkens pixels in an image. The Overlay mode tends to brighten the image while preserving its tonal range.

1 Make sure that TooLight_Blend-Modes.psd is still the active image. If necessary, click its thumbnail in the Photo Bin to make it active. In the Layers panel, right-click the Background layer and choose Duplicate Layer from the context menu. Click OK in the Duplicate Layer dialog box to accept the default name, "Background Copy."

2 In the Layers panel, choose Multiply from the layer blending mode menu. Note the effect in the image window. Drag the Background Copy layer with its Multiply blend mode onto the New Layer button (⬍) at the top of the Layers panel to create a copy of the Background Copy layer.

3 Change the blending mode for the layer Background Copy 2 from Multiply to Overlay, watching the effect on the image. Set the layer's Opacity value to 50%, either by dragging the Opacity slider or by typing the new value in the text field.

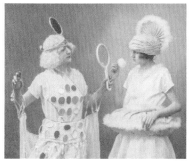
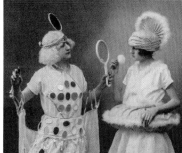
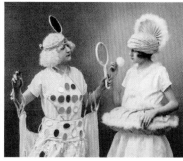

Original image · + Second layer: Multiply mode, 100% · + Third layer: Overlay mode, 50%

Adding a layer with the Multiply blending mode made the image bolder, and then the third layer in Overlay mode brightened it considerably and improved definition. Taken together, your changes have made the photo clearer, but the contrast in parts of the image, particularly in the lighter clothing, is still unimpressive.

4 Choose File > Save to save the file in your My CIB Work folder, leaving the image open. If a message appears about maximizing compatibility, click OK to close it, or follow the instructions in the message to prevent it from appearing again.

Adjusting shadows and highlights manually

Although both the auto-fix and blending modes do a good job of correcting many fading images, some of your own photos may be more challenging. You'll try three more techniques in the exercises to follow. The first involves manually adjusting the shadows, highlights, and midtone contrast of the image.

1 In the Photo Bin, click TooLight_Shad-High to make it the active image.

2 Choose Enhance > Adjust Lighting > Shadows/Highlights. If necessary, move the Shadows/Highlights dialog box so it doesn't obscure the image window. Make sure the Preview option is activated.

▶ **Tip:** If you can't see the whole file name in the Project Bin, hold the pointer over the thumbnail; the name of the file is displayed as a tooltip.

By default, the Lighten Shadows setting is 35%. You can see the effect on the image by toggling the Preview option on and off in the Shadows/Highlights dialog box.

3   In the Shadows/Highlights dialog box, set the Lighten Shadows value to **5%**, the Darken Highlights value to **25%**, and the Midtone Contrast value to **+75%**.

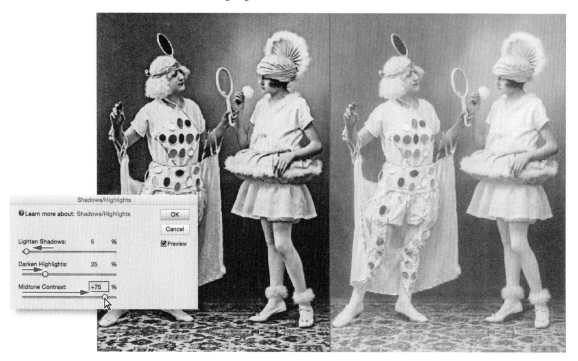

▶ **Tip:** The controls
you are using to make
the adjustments for
this technique are also
available in the Lighting
panel in the Quick Edit
mode.

4   Adjust the three settings as needed until you think the image is as good as it can be. When you're done, click OK to close the Shadows/Highlights dialog box.

5   Choose File > Save and save the file to your My CIB Work folder, in JPEG format. Make sure that the image will be included in the Organizer but not in a version set. Click Save, and then click OK in the JPEG Options dialog box and leave the file open.

Adjusting brightness and contrast manually

The next approach you'll take to fixing an exposure problem makes use of another option from the Enhance > Adjust Lighting menu.

1   In the Photo Bin, click the image TooLight_Bright-Cont to make it active. If necessary, choose View > Fit On Screen or double-click the Hand tool.

2   Choose Enhance > Adjust Lighting > Brightness/Contrast. If necessary, drag the Brightness/Contrast dialog box to one side so that it doesn't block your view of the image. Make sure the Preview option is activated so you can see the effects of your adjustments on the photo as you make them.

3 Drag the Brightness slider to –70, or type **–70** in the text field, being careful to include the minus sign when you type. Increase the Contrast to **100**.

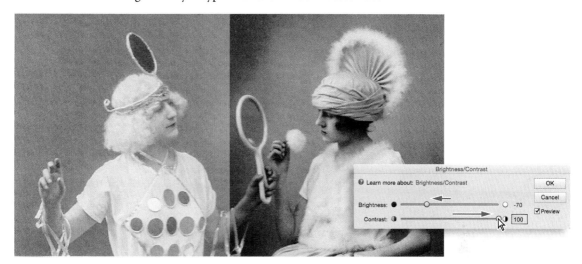

4 Adjust the Brightness and Contrast settings until you are happy with the look of the image. Click OK to close the Brightness/Contrast dialog box.

5 Choose File > Save and save the file to your My CIB Work folder, in JPEG format. Make sure the image will be included in the Organizer but not in a version set; then, click Save. Click OK in the JPEG Options dialog box, but keep the file open.

Adjusting levels

The Levels controls affect the distribution of tonal values in an image—the range of tones from dark to light, regardless of color. In this exercise, you'll enhance the image by shifting the reference points that define the spread of those tonal values.

1 In the Photo Bin, click the image TooLight_Levels to make it active.

2 Choose Enhance > Adjust Lighting > Levels. Activate the Preview option in the Levels dialog box, if it is not already active. If necessary, drag the Levels dialog box aside so that you can also see most of the image window.

The Levels graph represents the distribution of tonal values across all the pixels in the image, from darkest at the left to lightest at the right. A trough (or gap) in the curve indicates that there are few (or no) pixels mapped to that part of the range; a peak shows the opposite.

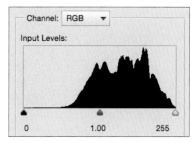

As you can see from the graph, this image has no black pixels, and very few tones of less than 40% brightness; most of the image information is clustered at the light end of the scale.

3 In the Levels dialog box, drag the black triangle below the left end of the graph to the right; the value in the first Input Levels box should be approximately 80. Drag the white marker from the right side of the graph until the value in the third Input Levels box is approximately 245. Drag the gray marker to set the midtones value to approximately 0.75. Click OK to close the Levels dialog box.

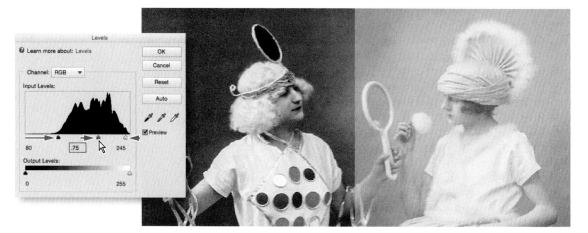

4 Choose File > Save and save the file to your My CIB Work folder in JPEG format as TooLight_Levels. Make sure that the image will be included in the Organizer but not in a version set. Click Save; then, click OK in the JPEG Options dialog box and leave the file open.

Comparing results

You can now compare the six versions of the image: the original file, the four files you edited, and the image that was fixed automatically at the start of this lesson.

1 Choose File > Open. Locate and open the file TooLight_Autofix.jpg from the My CIB Work folder; then repeat the process for the original file from your Lesson 6 folder, TooLight.jpg. The Photo Bin should show six open files.

2 Click the Photo Bin button in the taskbar to hide the Photo Bin; then, hide the Panel Bin by unchecking its name in the Window menu.

3 Choose Preferences > General from the Edit / Adobe Photoshop Elements Editor menu. Activate Allow Floating Documents In Expert Mode; then, click OK.

4 Choose Window > Images > Tile. Use the Zoom and Hand tools to position the photo in any of the image windows so that you can see enough of the image to enable you to make a comparison of the different treatments; then, choose Window > Images > Match Zoom and Window > Images > Match Location.

5 Choose File > Close All. Save any changes to your CIB Work folder if you're prompted to do so. On the General tab in the Editor's preferences dialog, disable Allow Floating Documents In Expert Mode; then, click OK.

More guided lighting solutions

Let's try a few more guided edits on an image with different lighting problems.

1   In the Organizer, select the image DSC_0347.jpg; then, click the Editor button. Switch to Guided Edit mode and select the Color category.

Fluorescent lighting behind the translucent surface on which the bottles are standing has caused a combination of problems in this photo. The image not only has a dull, yellow-green color cast, but like many backlit photos, it's also underexposed—in auto-exposure mode, the camera has reduced the exposure in order to compensate for the brightness of the background.

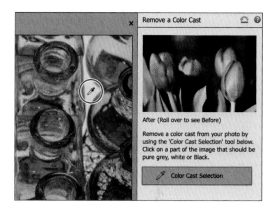

2   Click to launch the Remove A Color Cast adjustment. Move the eyedropper over the image and click the translucent background between the bottles to reset the white point. Click Next, and then click Done.

3   Switch to the Basics category and launch the Brightness And Contrast adjustment. Click the Auto Fix button. Click the Next button, and then click Done.

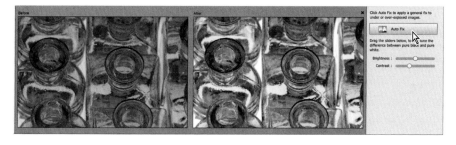

4   Launch the Sharpen guided edit from the Basics pane. Drag the Zoom slider to 100%, or choose View > Actual Pixels; working at 1:1 zoom level will help you see the effect of the sharpening operation clearly. Drag the Sharpen slider to set a value of 230. Click the Next button; then, click Save As. Save the new file as **DSC_0347_Guided**, in JPEG format, with the usual settings, and then close it.

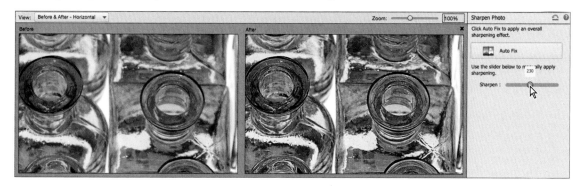

Removing haze and fog

Strictly speaking, our last photo for this lesson does not have an exposure problem, but it does exhibit some of the same deficiencies found in an overexposed image. Distance haze, caused by water vapor suspended in the atmosphere, makes distant objects appear paler and less distinct than those closer to the viewer. For some photos, this can be perfectly acceptable, imparting a sense of scale and grandeur or adding steamy atmosphere. In other cases, haze or fog may detract from an image by reducing contrast and clarity, and obscuring detail. The Haze Removal tool offers both automatic and manual modes that make it easy to correct the problem.

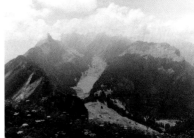

1 In the Organizer, select the image DSC_4567.jpg. Switch to the Editor in either Quick or Expert mode; the Haze Removal tool is available in both edit modes.

2 Choose Enhance > Haze Removal (not Auto Haze Removal). The Haze Removal dialog opens, with haze reduction already applied at the level that would have been implemented for the Auto Haze Removal adjustment.

▶ **Tip:** Cloudy skies are particularly prone to dehazing artifacts; for some photos you may need to reduce the automatic settings.

3 Move both the Haze Reduction slider and the Sensitivity slider to the right to apply the maximum effect. You'll notice a marked improvement in the clarity and overall contrast of the image, though it also takes on an artificial look. Pull back the sliders for a more natural look. Toggle the Before / After switch to assess the result; then, click OK.

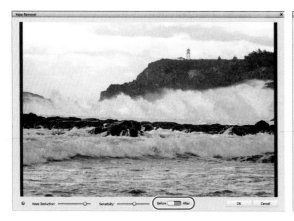
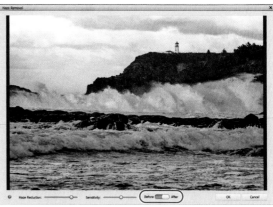

4 (Optional) Choose Edit > Undo Haze Removal; then, use the Quick Selection tool to select the sky. Choose Select > Inverse, and then repeat steps 2 and 3.

5 Choose File > Save As. Name the file **DSC_4567_Dehazed**, and save it to your My CIB Work folder in JPEG format, to be included in the Organizer but not in a version set. Choose File > Close.

Review questions

1 How can you create an exact copy of an existing layer?

2 Where can you find the controls for adjusting the lighting in a photograph?

3 How can you arrange multiple image windows in the work area automatically?

4 What is an adjustment layer and what are its unique advantages?

Review answers

1 You must be in Expert mode to copy a layer. Select a layer in the Layers panel, and choose Layer > Duplicate Layer. You can access the same command in the Layers panel Options menu or by right-clicking the layer in the Layers panel. Alternatively, drag the layer to the New Layer button. Whichever method you use, you get two layers identical in all but their names, stacked one above the other.

2 You can adjust the lighting for a photo in Expert, Guided Edit, and Quick Edit modes. In Expert mode, you can use the Enhance > Adjust Lighting menu to open various dialogs that contain the controls. Alternatively, you can choose Enhance > Auto Levels, Enhance > Auto Contrast, or Enhance > Adjust Color > Adjust Color Curves. In Guided Edit mode, choose the Brightness And Contrast, Levels, or Lighten And Darken operations from the Basics category. In Quick Edit mode, you can use the Exposure and Lighting panes in the Quick Fix panel.

3 You cannot rearrange image windows in Quick Edit and Guided Edit modes, which display only one photograph at a time. In the Expert workspace, there are several ways you can arrange them. Choose Window > Images, and select one of the choices listed there—you can access some of the same options, and several more, by clicking the Layout button in the taskbar. Some of the options require that you enable floating windows in Expert mode, which can be done in the Preferences dialog.

4 An adjustment layer does not contain an image; instead, it modifies some quality of all the layers below it in the Layers panel. For example, a Brightness/Contrast layer will alter the brightness and contrast of any underlying layers. One advantage of using an adjustment layer instead of adjusting an existing layer directly is that adjustment layers can be easily modified or even removed. Toggle the eye icon for the adjustment layer to remove or restore the edit instantly. You can change a setting in an adjustment layer at any time—even after the file has been saved. An adjustment layer can also be copied and pasted into another image to apply the same settings there.

7 REFRAMING, RETOUCHING, AND RECOMPOSING IMAGES

Lesson overview

Some photos have image flaws other than color or lighting problems; a picture that was taken hurriedly might be spoiled by being tilted or poorly composed, and even a technically perfect exposure can be diminished by dust or water spots on the lens, blemishes on a portrait subject's skin, or an extraneous object cluttering the composition.

In this lesson, you'll learn a range of techniques for cropping, retouching, and rearranging the composition of such images:

- Using the Straighten and Crop tools to reframe an image
- Correcting perspective distortion
- Creating a photo border
- Improving the impact of an image with the Recompose tool
- Enhancing composition by repositioning objects in the frame
- Retouching skin with the Healing Brush tool
- Removing unwanted objects with content-aware healing
- Reinventing an image with creative effects

 This lesson will take about 90 minutes to complete. To get the lesson files used in this chapter, download them from the web page for this book at www.adobepress.com/PSECIB2020. For more information, see "Accessing the lesson files and Web Edition" in the Getting Started section at the beginning of this book.

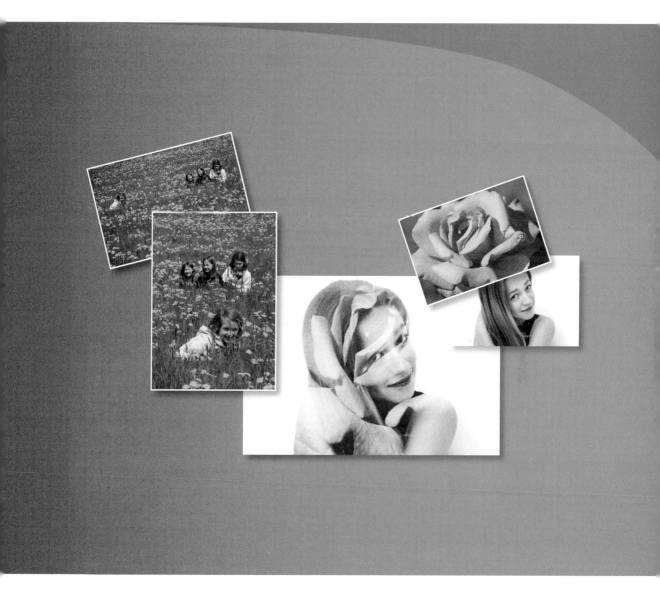

Photoshop Elements delivers a range of tools to help you bring out the potential in a photo, despite its flaws. The same tricks and techniques that enable you to remove or reposition an inconveniently placed object, retouch spots and blemishes in a portrait, or restore a treasured keepsake by repairing creases and tears can also be used creatively to manipulate reality in order to produce exactly the image you want.

Getting started

● **Note:** Before you start this lesson, make sure you've set up a folder for your lesson files and downloaded the Lesson 7 folder from your Account page at www.peachpit.com, as detailed in "Accessing the lesson files and Web Edition" and "Creating a work folder" in the "Getting Started" section at the beginning of this book. You should also have created a new work catalog (see "Creating a catalog for working with this book" in Lesson 1).

Begin by importing the sample images for this lesson to your CIB Catalog.

1 Start Photoshop Elements and click Organizer in the Home screen. Check the lower-right corner of the Organizer workspace to make sure the CIB Catalog is loaded—if not, choose File > Manage Catalogs and select it from the list.

2 Click the Import button at the upper left of the Organizer workspace and choose From Files And Folders from the drop-down menu. In the Get Photos And Videos From Files And Folders dialog box, locate and select your Lesson 7 folder. Disable the option Get Photos From Subfolders and the automatic processing options; then, click Get Media.

3 In the Import Attached Keyword Tags dialog box, click Select All; then, click OK.

Improving the composition of a photo

When you're hurried, distracted by movement, or shooting in awkward conditions, the result is often a photo that *could* have been great—if only it had been framed better. The Crop tool and the Straighten tool in the Expert Edit mode toolbar will help you turn the shot you got into the photo you *should* have captured.

Sometimes you're just too busy fitting everything you want into frame to notice a crooked horizon. The Straighten tool makes it easy to quickly correct a tilted image. The Crop tool can be customized, by choosing from a range of preset aspect ratios and cropping overlays, to help you bring out the visual potential of your image.

Using the Straighten tool

You can use the Straighten tool to designate a feature in your crooked photo that should be either horizontal or vertical; then, Photoshop Elements will rotate the image to straighten it in relation to your reference line.

1 Select the image 07_01.jpg in the Media Browser, and then click the Editor button (🖼️)—not the arrow beside it—in the taskbar. Alternatively, you could select the file and choose Edit > Edit With Photoshop Elements Editor. If the Editor doesn't open to Expert mode, click Expert in the mode picker.

2 Choose Window > Reset Panels; then use the Window menu again to hide the Panel Bin. If either the Photo Bin or the tool options pane is currently open, click the corresponding button at the left of the taskbar to hide it; then, choose View > Fit On Screen, or double-click the Hand tool to see the entire image at the highest magnification possible. Hold down the Ctrl / Command key and press the minus sign (–) key once to zoom out just enough to see a little of the blank artboard (colored gray by default) surrounding the photo in the Edit pane.

3 Select the Straighten tool (⌗) in the toolbar; then, click the Tool Options button (📝) in the taskbar, if necessary, to open the tool options pane. Make sure the Straighten tool is set to Grow Or Shrink Canvas To Fit mode and the Autofill Edges option is disabled; then, hide the tool options pane.

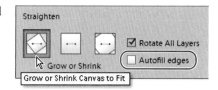

This photo features a sea horizon—the most reliable of reference levels. In the absence of a natural horizon, you can often use a horizontal architectural feature.

4 Drag a long line along the horizon in the left half of the photo (at the right the horizon is hidden by the land in the middle distance). When you release the mouse button, Photoshop Elements straightens the image relative to the line you drew. Note the newly enlarged canvas surrounding the rotated image.

> **Tip:** Choose Grow Or Shrink Canvas To Fit when you wish to crop the rotated image manually; the other options will trim it automatically.

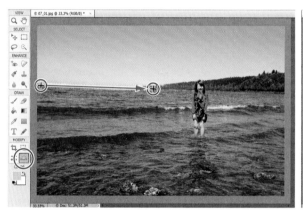
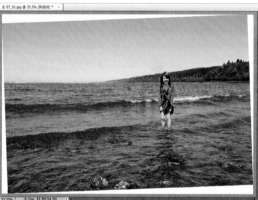

You could crop the straightened image manually to trim away the angled edges, but for the purposes of this exercise, you'll look at a couple of alternative options.

5 Press Ctrl+Z / Command+Z to undo the Straighten tool. Show the tool options pane and click the second of the three icons at the left to activate the Remove Background mode; then, use the Straighten tool to trace the horizon again. Photoshop Elements crops the largest area possible within the angled edges. Hide the tool options pane to examine the results.

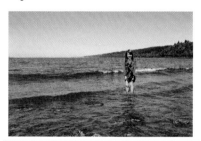

6 Undo the operation; then, reset the Straighten tool to the Grow Or Shrink mode and activate the Autofill Edges option. Trace the horizon, and then inspect the results; rather than trimming the angled edges, Photoshop Elements has used content-aware image analysis to fill the white extended canvas that you saw in step 4 with detail that matches the image.

As you can see in the illustration at the right, this method has preserved all the detail of the original photo.

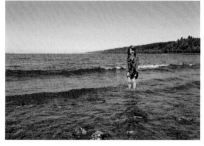

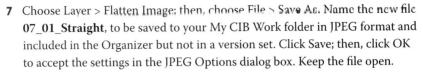

7 Choose Layer > Flatten Image; then, choose File > Save As. Name the new file **07_01_Straight**, to be saved to your My CIB Work folder in JPEG format and included in the Organizer but not in a version set. Click Save; then, click OK to accept the settings in the JPEG Options dialog box. Keep the file open.

8 Staying in the Editor, choose File > Open; then, navigate to your Lesson 7 folder, select the file 07_02.jpg, and click Open.

In many photos it's difficult to identify a reliable horizontal reference; in these cases, you can look for a vertical feature such as a signpost or any structural element that isn't too obviously affected by perspective or lens distortion. For this image, where the horizon is not visible and almost every man-made horizontal is pictured in perspective, the tower provides the strongest reference.

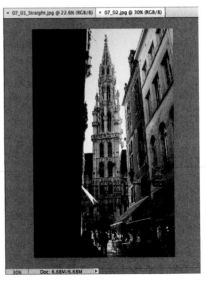

9 With the Straighten tool (⌷) selected, open the tool options pane. Click the second of the three icons at the left to activate the Remove Background mode.

In Remove Background mode, the Autofill Edges option is disabled; for our lesson photo, Autofill Edges is likely to produce unwanted artifacts, especially in the cluttered detail of the lower-right corner. The composition is unlikely to be diminished by trimming away the tilted edges after rotation, as the tower is the primary focus.

10 Starting at the tip of the tower, drag a line down through the center of the structure. As the tower is stepped in toward the top and pictured in slight perspective, the bottom of your reference line should pass through the entrance arch a little to the right of center. When you're done, release the mouse button.

Tip: The Straighten tool is also available in Quick Edit mode, with a simplified set of controls in the tool options pane. When you've completed this exercise, try straightening the same images in Quick Edit mode to see which you prefer.

Note: For some tilted images, you can achieve good results by choosing either Straighten Image or Straighten And Crop Image from the Image > Rotate menu. Both of these commands perform straightening functions automatically.

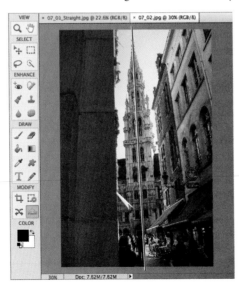

11 Choose File > Save As. Name the file **07_02_Straight.jpg**, to be saved to your My CIB Work folder in JPEG format and included in the Organizer but not in a version set. Click Save; then, click OK to accept the settings in the JPEG Options dialog box. Choose File > Close.

Reframing a photo with the Crop tool

Composing your photo well can make the difference between an ordinary snapshot and a striking, memorable image; framing too much irrelevant detail can detract from your intended focus, and an awkward arrangement of forms within the frame can make your picture appear unbalanced.

In practice, sometimes there isn't enough time while you're shooting to frame a photo carefully; fortunately, you can use the Crop tool to improve the composition once you get home.

1 With the image 07_01_Straight.jpg open in the Editor, select the Crop tool (🔳).

2 Inspect the settings in the tool options pane.

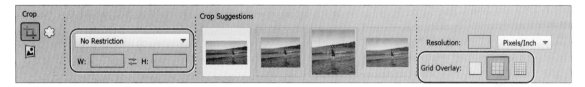

By default, the aspect ratio is set to No Restriction, which means that you're free to change the proportions of the crop, and Grid Overlay is set to Rule Of Thirds, a layout guide based on the principle that a composition looks balanced when its elements are aligned with the lines and intersections of a grid that divides the image into three equal parts on both axes.

Photoshop Elements offers cropping suggestions to help you make a start. You may see a different set of suggested crops from those in the illustration above.

▶ **Tip:** Remember that you can use cropping not only to trim an image or change its aspect ratio, but also as a way to draw attention to your subject or improve the balance of your composition.

3 Hover the pointer over each crop suggestion in turn to see the effect.

4 Change the crop aspect ratio from No Restriction to Use Photo Ratio. Drag the corner handles of the cropping rectangle to set up a crop with the upper horizontal guide aligned with the horizon, the lower guide aligned with the girl's knees, and the vertical guide at her shoulder to the right. Click the Commit button (✅) to execute the crop.

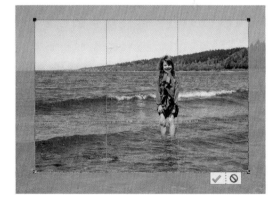

5 Choose File > Save As. Make sure that the new file will be included in the Organizer but not in a version set. Name the file **07_01_Cropped.jpg**, to be saved to your My CIB Work folder in JPEG format. Click Save; then, set the highest quality in the JPEG Options dialog box and click OK. Keep the saved file open for the next exercise.

Working with the image canvas

Think of the image canvas as the equivalent of the paper on which a photo is printed. While you're working with a digital photo, image data may temporarily lie outside the canvas space, but it will be clipped to the canvas boundary as soon as the image is flattened. To extend our limited analogy just a little further, think of the layer data as the image projected by a photographic enlarger in the darkroom. Although the projected image may be offset or enlarged so that it falls outside the borders of the paper, the data still exists; you can continue to work with it right up until the moment that the photographic paper is exposed.

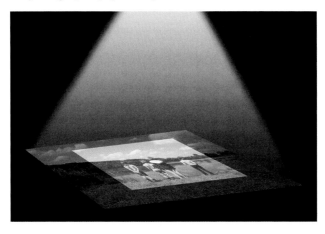

Adding a border to a photo

By default, the canvas is the same size as the image and is therefore not visible. If you increase the size of the image file, the canvas is enlarged automatically; however, you can also choose to enlarge the canvas independently of the image size, effectively adding a border around your photo—just as if you had printed a photo on a sheet of paper larger than the image.

By default, the extended canvas, and therefore the border, takes on the Background color as set in the color swatches at the bottom of the toolbar.

1   With the image 07_01_Cropped.jpg still open and the Editor in Expert mode, double-click the Hand tool (🖑) or choose View > Fit On Screen. Use the Window menu to hide the Panel Bin, if necessary; then, hide the tool options pane by clicking the Tool Options button (🖉) at the left of the taskbar.

2   If you don't see a reasonable amount of the blank gray background surrounding the image, hold down the Ctrl / Command key and press the minus key (–) on your keyboard, or choose View > Zoom Out.

3   Choose Image > Resize > Canvas Size. If necessary, move the Canvas Size dialog box aside so that you can see at least the left half of the image.

4 Set the Canvas Size dialog box as shown in the illustration at the right. Activate the Relative option; then, set the units menus to Inches, if necessary, and type a new value of **1** for both Width and Height. Leave the Anchor control at the default centered setting. Choose Black from the Canvas Extension Color menu, and then click OK.

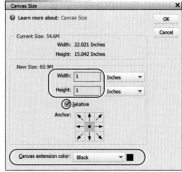

The new black border appears around the photo in the image window. For the purposes of this exercise, we'll take it one step further and extend the canvas again to turn the border into an asymmetrical frame.

5 Choose Image > Resize > Canvas Size. In the Canvas Size dialog box, confirm that the Relative check box is still activated. Leave the Width value at 0 and set the Height value to **2** inches. In the Anchor control grid diagram, click the central arrow in the top row. With this Anchor setting, the one-inch increase to the height of the canvas will be applied at the bottom edge of the image only. Leave the Canvas Extension Color setting unchanged and click OK.

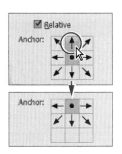

6 If you can't see the entire border framing the image, double-click the Hand tool or choose View > Fit On Screen.

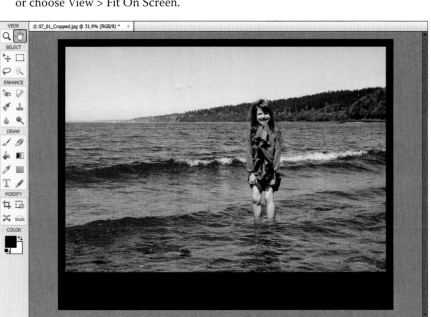

The extended border gives you space to add text to the image, making it an easy and effective way to create a postcard, a stylish cover page for a printed document, or a title screen for a slideshow presentation.

Working with text

Whether you wish to fit an image to a specific purpose or simply add a message, the Photoshop Elements type tools make it easy to create good-looking text.

▶ **Tip:** You can open the tool options pane by clicking the Tool Options button (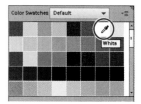) in the taskbar or by clicking a tool in the toolbar.

1 In the toolbar, click to select the Horizontal Type tool (T). In the tool options pane, choose Adobe Garamond Pro Bold from the Font menu. Type **110** pt in the Font Size box; then, press Enter / Return. Choose Center Text (≣) from the text alignment options.

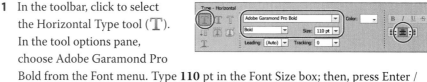

2 In the tool options bar, click the text color swatch to the right of the font menus. As you move the pointer over the Color Swatches picker, it becomes an eyedropper cursor. Use the eyedropper cursor to select the white swatch in the top row; then, press the Esc key to close the Color Swatches picker.

3 With the Type tool, click below the center of the black space beneath the photo and type **GREETINGS FROM SEATTLE**. Swipe over the text to select it. Click the foreground color swatch (now white) below the tools in the toolbar to open the Color Picker. Move the pointer over the image window; the cursor becomes an eyedropper.

4 Move the eyedropper over the light blue portion of the shirt; refer to the illustration at the right. Click to sample the blue and then click OK in the Color Picker to close it.

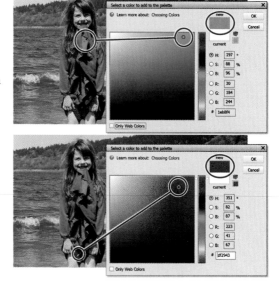

5 Swipe over the word SEATTLE to select it; then, click the foreground color swatch and use the eyedropper to sample a pinkish-red from the girl's shorts near her hand. Click OK in the Color Picker to close it.

6 Click the green Commit button (✔) at the lower-right corner of the new text. Drag the text with the Move tool to center it. Use the handles on the text bounding box to resize it slightly if necessary; then commit the changes.

7 Choose File > Save As. Name the file **07_01_Seattle** and save it to your My CIB Work folder in Photoshop format with Layers activated, to be included in the Organizer but not in a version set. Choose File > Close.

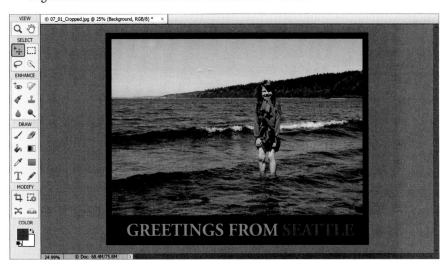

Adding a quick border

When precision isn't an issue, you can quickly add a border to an image by using the Crop tool, rather than increasing the size of the canvas.

1 Zoom out far enough so that you can see some of the blank artboard surrounding the image in the edit window.

2 Use the Crop tool to drag a cropping rectangle right around the image.

3 Drag the corner handles of the crop marquee outside the image area onto the artboard to define the size and shape of border that you wish to create.

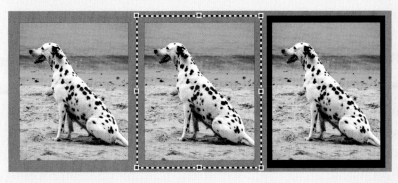

4 When you're satisfied, click the Commit button in the lower-right corner of the image. The canvas expands to fill the cropping rectangle, taking on the background color set in the color swatch at the bottom of the toolbar.

Recomposing an image within its frame

▶ **Tip:** Like the healing brushes and the Clone Stamp tool (covered later in this chapter), and the Photomerge tools that you'll use in Lesson 8, the Recompose tool is a lot of fun to use creatively, enabling you to manipulate reality in order to produce the image you want.

Do you have a group shot in which you wish the group had stood closer together? The Recompose tool enables you to crop your photo from the *inside* rather than at the edges. Whether you want to bring people closer together, fit a horizontal image to a vertical space, or remove extraneous elements that spoil the composition, the Recompose tool puts image editing magic at your fingertips. In this exercise, you'll use the Recompose tool to tighten the arrangement of a group photo and reframe the landscape format to create a square composition.

1   If you're still in the Editor, click the Organizer button (▦) in the taskbar. If necessary, click the check box beside the Lesson 07 tag in the Tags panel to isolate the images for this lesson. Right-click the image 07_03.jpg and choose Edit With Photoshop Elements Editor.

2   Make sure the Editor is in Expert mode; then, choose Window > Reset Panels. Hide the Panel Bin and the tool options pane, if it's visible. Double-click the Hand tool, or choose View > Fit On Screen; then, press Ctrl / Command together with the minus sign (–) key to zoom out just enough to see a little empty gray space around the photo in the Edit window.

3   Click the Recompose tool (⌗) in the toolbar. If necessary, click the Tool Options button (✎) in the taskbar to open the tool options pane.

A live bounding box now surrounds the image, with control handles at the corners and at the mid-point of each side. For simple recomposing operations, all you need to do is drag the handles; the Recompose tool makes use of content-aware scaling technology that distinguishes people and other featured objects and attempts to prevent them from being distorted as the background is compressed around them. For this exercise, however, we'll use the special Recompose brushes instead. For more complex images, this generally produces better results.

● **Note:** The Threshold control lets you adjust the degree to which content-aware scaling is applied as the image is "squeezed." At 100%, protected areas will be completely free of distortion when the photo is scaled. At a Threshold of 0%, the Content-Aware feature is turned off; scaling on one axis will "squash" pictured objects.

4   Select the Mark For Protection brush—the brush with a plus sign (+)—at the left of the tool options pane. Either type in the brush size text box or use the slider to increase the brush size to about **300** px. Make sure that Threshold and the aspect ratio are set to the default 100% and No Restriction, respectively.

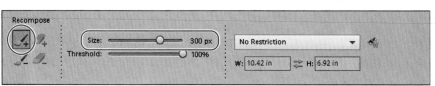

As its name suggests, you can use the Mark For Protection brush to define those areas in the image that you want shielded from any scaling operation.

5 Click the Tool Options button (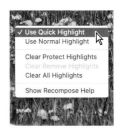) in the taskbar to hide the tool options pane.

6 Paint over the girl at the left of the photo. Extend your strokes to the left edge of the image, as shown at the right; the girl is very close to the edge of the frame and unless this "buffer" area is protected it will be compressed during the recompose operation. If you find you've over-painted, use the eraser with the plus sign, beside the protection brush in the tool options pane, to modify your strokes. Use the left and right bracket keys ([,]) to decrease or increase the size of the eraser as you work.

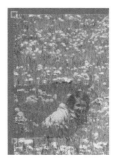

Note: The green protection-brush overlay is difficult to see against the grassy field in our lesson photo. For the sake of clarity, the surrounding image has been dimmed in these illustrations.

7 Right-click the image and change the brush mode from the default Use Normal Highlight to Use Quick Highlight. In Quick Highlight mode you can mark an area for protection by simply drawing a line around it. Show the tool options pane for a moment to set the brush size to **50** px. Draw an outline to surround the three girls at the right, including the space between the group and the right edge of the photo. When you're done, release the mouse button; Photoshop Elements fills the area inside the outline automatically.

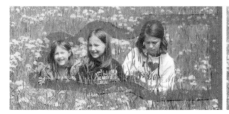
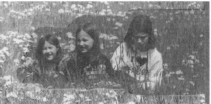

8 Right-click the image and reset the Recompose tool to the Use Normal Highlight mode. Show the tool options pane and select the Mark For Removal brush (the brush with a minus sign). Set the brush size to **100** px. Scribble through the space between the girl at the left and her sisters to mark the area for removal—rather than compression—during the scaling process.

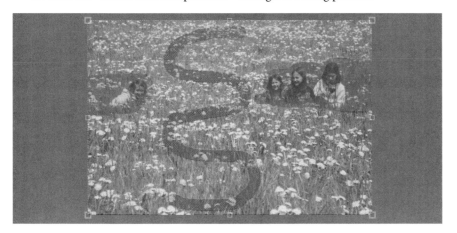

▶ **Tip:** If necessary, you can modify your Mark For Removal brush strokes with the associated eraser. Use the left and right bracket keys ([,]) to reduce or increase the brush size as you work.

9 Now for the fun part! Move the pointer over the handle on the left side of the bounding box and, when the double-arrow cursor appears, drag the handle slowly in toward the center of the photo. Watch the photo as you drag; some areas of the image are removed while others are compressed and merged with their surroundings. As the proportions of the image become closer to a square, keep an eye on the Width (W) and Height (H) values in the tool options pane; stop dragging and release the mouse button when the two values are equal.

▶ **Tip:** As this was a rather extreme editing operation, you may find some image artifacts, especially near the seam between areas that were removed or protected. If these are noticeable enough to worry you, a few strokes with the Clone Stamp or the Healing Brush will fix the problem. You'll learn more about those tools later in this lesson. Zoom in to inspect the seam. Try recomposing the image differently, marking a smaller area for removal, or limiting your strokes to the patch separating the sisters rather than to the larger vertical strip.

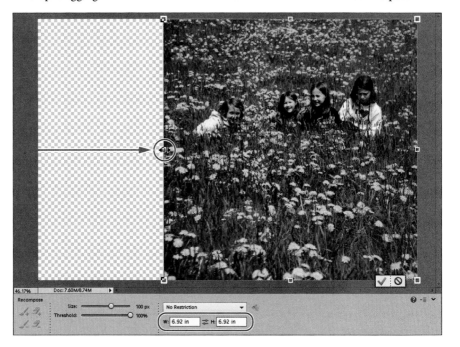

10 Click the green Commit button (✔) at the lower right of the recomposed photo or press Enter / Return to accept and render the new composition.

11 Choose Image > Crop. A cropping box appears on the image; drag the handles to crop the file to the new square format, trimming away the transparent area. The edges of the cropping box snap to the edges of the image to make the operation very easy. Click the green Commit button (✔) or press Enter / Return.

12 Choose File > Save As. Name the image **07_03_Recomposed**, to be saved to your My CIB Work folder and included in the Organizer but not as part of a version set. Change the file format to JPEG. Click Save; then click OK to accept the JPEG quality settings. The recomposed image is saved as a copy. Choose Edit > Revert to restore the original photo, keeping it open for the next exercise.

The Recompose tool is as easy to use as it is powerful—with creative possibilities that are virtually limitless. Play with as many pictures as you can; you'll learn how content-aware scaling works and what to expect from different types of images as you have fun finding creative new ways to make the most of your photos.

Moving objects to enhance a composition

The Content-Aware Move tool lets you reposition an object within the frame, and then uses content-aware photo magic to cover your tracks, blending the object with its new surroundings and patching the hole it left.

The Content-Aware Move tool is perfect for dealing with objects that are too close to the edge of a photo or separated from the main action, enabling you to improve an unbalanced composition and turn a bystander into a star. In the first part of this exercise, you'll use the Content-Aware Move tool on the image from the previous project—this time, reuniting the sisters without altering the photo's proportions.

1   With the image 07_03.jpg still open in Expert mode in the Editor, double-click the Hand tool, if needed, to see the whole photo as large as possible; then, select the Content-Aware Move tool ( ), beside the Straighten tool in the toolbar.

2   Open the tool options pane and make sure the tool is set to Move mode, rather than Extend, and the Healing slider is set to the middle stop. Draw loosely around thc girl at thc lcft. Include some of her surroundings in your selection, but draw the line closer at the right of the girl's form.

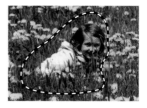

3   Press and hold inside the selection; then, hold the Shift key and drag the girl close to her sisters. The Shift key will constrain the movement horizontally, maintaining the girl's distance from the viewpoint. Release the mouse button, and then release the Shift key. Click the green check mark to commit the operation; the girl is blended into her new position and the hole she left is filled with detail to match the surroundings. Click outside the selected area to deselect it.

4   Draw around the four girls. Include a reasonable amount of the surrounding detail, except at the right, where your line should follow the older girl's form closely. Press and hold inside the selection; then, hold the Shift key as you drag the sisters to the left to center them horizontally in the frame. Release the mouse button, then the Shift key. Commit the operation; then, deselect the group.

> **Tip:** If the area from which the girls were moved is filled without any flowers at all, undo and vary the shape and size of your selection.

5   Choose File > Save As. Name the new image **07_03_Move-1**, to be saved to your My CIB Work folder with all the usual settings. Activate the option Save > As A Copy; then, click Save. Click OK to accept the JPEG quality settings, and then choose Edit > Revert to restore the original photo, keeping it open for the next part of the exercise.

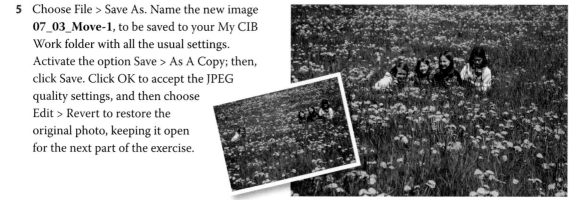

6 Draw around the girl at the left of the photo with the Content-Aware Move tool, just as you did in step 2, except that this time you can include the same amount of the surrounding area all of the way around her form.

7 Drag the selection on a downward diagonal to the right. Position the girl about half as far from her sisters and the bottom edge of the photo as her original position.

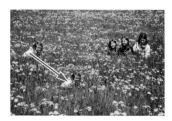

8 Hold down the Alt / Option key as you drag a corner handle of the selection's bounding box to scale the selection up from its center. Watch the Width and Height values in the tool options pane and stop when they are close to 200%. Press and hold inside the selection; then, hold the Shift key as you drag to center the girl below her three sisters. Click the green check mark to commit the transformation; then, click outside the selected area to deselect it.

9 Choose Image > Crop. In the tool options pane, set the cropping ratio to No Restriction. Starting outside the upper-right corner of the photo, drag downward and to the left to produce a balanced, portrait-format crop of the same height as the original image; then, commit the operation.

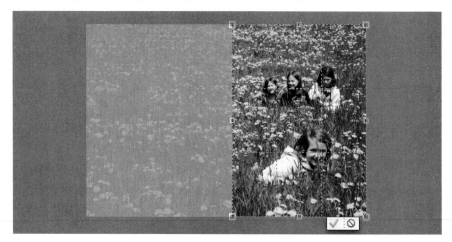

10 Choose File > Save As. Name the new image **07_03_Move-2**, to be saved with all the usual settings. There is no need to save the image as a copy. Click Save; then, click OK to accept the JPEG settings and choose File > Close.

Experiment on your own photos with the Content-Aware Move tool to get a feel for its capabilities. Switch from Move to Extend mode to copy your selection rather than merely move it. Tweak the Healing slider to improve a blend that is too obvious or produces artifacts; move the slider to the right to prioritize the selected content in the blend, or to the left to introduce more detail from the surroundings.

Changing the perspective in a photograph

The distortion caused by perspective can sometimes detract from the impact of a composition, especially when circumstances have made it impossible to capture the subject "head on."

The Perspective Crop tool makes it easy to correct perspective distortion and improve your composition by putting the subject front and center.

1 Select the image 07_10.jpg in the Media Browser, and then click the Editor button (⬛)—not the arrow beside it—in the taskbar. If the Editor is not already in Expert mode, click Expert in the mode picker. Hide the Panel Bin, if necessary, and then choose View > Fit On Screen.

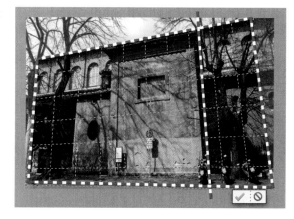

Perspective Crop

2 Select the Crop tool (⬛), and then select the Perspective Crop mode in the tool options pane. Click outside the upper-left corner of the photo, and then drag the crop rectangle to cover the entire image.

3 Hold down the Shift key and drag the upper-right handle of the crop rectangle to the left until the angle of the guides at the right matches that of the right edge of the sunlit wall. Drag the upper-left handle, without the Shift key, so that the upper guide is aligned as closely as possible with the edge of the roof, and the angle of the left guide is consistent with the perspective in the pillar at the far left of the photo. Hold down the Shift key again as you drag the lower-left handle up slightly to match the angle of the lines where the pavement meets the building.

4 Click the Commit button (✓); then, choose View > Fit On Screen. The areas outside the crop rectangle are trimmed away as the perspective is corrected.

5 Choose File > Save As. Name the new image **07_10_Perspective**, to be saved with all the usual settings. There is no need to save the image as a copy. Click Save; then, click OK to accept the JPEG settings and choose File > Close.

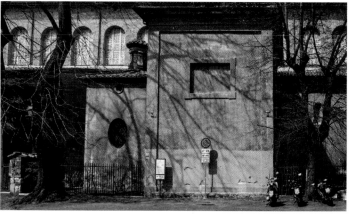

Removing wrinkles and spots

Retouching skin to improve a portrait photograph can be a real art, but fortunately Photoshop Elements provides several tools that make it easy to smooth out lines and wrinkles, remove blemishes, and blend skin tones—even for a novice.

1   If you're still in the Editor, click the Organizer button (▦) in the taskbar. If necessary, click the check box beside the Lesson 07 tag in the Tags panel to isolate the images for this lesson. Right-click the image 07_04.jpg and choose Edit With Photoshop Elements Editor.

2   Make sure that the Editor is in Expert mode. Choose Window > Reset Panels. Click the Layers button in the sidebar. Hide the Photo Bin or tool options pane, and then choose View > Fit On Screen.

This photo is quite a challenging candidate for retouching; the harsh flash lighting has caused strong reflections on the skin that only serve to accentuate the wrinkles.

Using the Smooth Skin tool

Sometimes a portrait can be improved by just subtly smoothing the subject's skin. The new Smooth Skin feature automatically recognizes facial features and applies a smoothing process that minimizes wrinkles and blemishes. It's the easiest method, and a good first step to see how it affects the image.

1   Choose Enhance > Smooth Skin. In the dialog, set the zoom level to 100% or 200% so you can see the skin texture well.

2   Drag the Smoothness slider three-quarters to the right. Click the Before/After toggle to see how the control affected the skin.

3   Since this photo still includes some prominent lines below the eyes, click Cancel. For those adjustments, you'll turn to the Healing Brush tool.

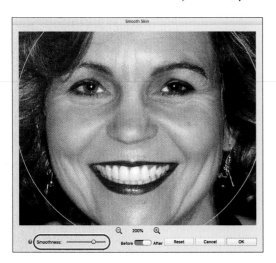 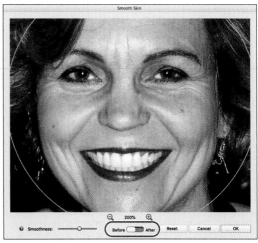

Using the Healing Brush tool

The Healing Brush tool's targeted corrections give you much more control over smoothing and fixing repairing skin.

1 Drag the Background layer to the New Layer button (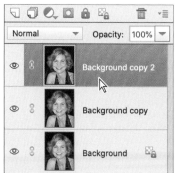) at the top of the Layers panel to create a duplicate layer. Repeat the process, dragging the new layer to create a third layer. Use the Zoom tool (Q) to zoom in on the upper half of the photo, as you'll be retouching the skin around the woman's eyes first.

2 Click to select the Healing Brush tool ( ) or its variant, the Spot Healing Brush tool ( )—whichever is currently visible beside the Red Eye Removal tool in the toolbar. If necessary, open the tool options pane at the bottom of the workspace.

3 Make sure that the tool is in Healing Brush mode, and then set the brush size to **20** px. Set the Source option to Sampled and the Mode to Normal. Make sure that the Aligned and Sample All Layers options are both disabled.

4 Make sure that the top layer, Background Copy 2, is still active. First, define the area in the image that will be sampled as a reference texture for the Healing Brush operation: Alt-click / Option-click a smooth area on the left cheek. If you were to switch to another tool and then back to the Healing Brush, you would need to repeat this step.

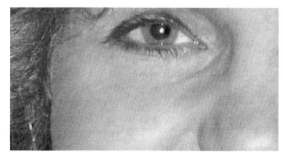

5 Draw a short horizontal stroke under the left eye. As you drag, it may appear that the brush is creating a strange effect, but when you release the mouse button, the color will blend and natural skin tones will fill the area.

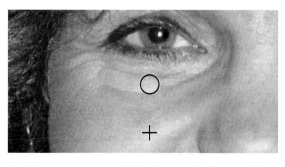

6 Continue to smooth the skin on the face with the Healing Brush. Avoid areas very close to the eyes, shadowed areas, and the hairline. You can also reduce the worst of the shine caused by the harsh flash. As you work, re-establish the reference area occasionally by Alt-clicking / Option-clicking in new areas of the face to sample appropriate skin tone and texture. Press the left and right bracket keys ([,]) to decrease or increase the brush size as you work. Be sure to remove the moles on the woman's right cheek and the spots on her left cheek and just below the lower lip. You can use the same techniques on the neck.

Long strokes may produce unacceptable results—especially near shaded areas where the darker tones may spread. If that happens, choose Edit > Undo Healing Brush. Try setting the brush to a smaller size or reversing the direction of your strokes. If the problem is related to the shadowed areas beside the nose or at the sides of the face, try stroking toward the shadows rather than away from them, or temporarily changing the mode for the Healing Brush tool from Normal to Lighten in the tool options pane.

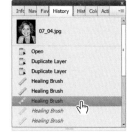

7 Choose Window > History. In the History Panel, every action you perform is recorded in chronological order, from the earliest at the top to the most recent at the bottom of the list. You can use the History panel to quickly undo a series of steps or to assess the success of your edits. To restore the file to an earlier state, simply select an earlier (higher) action in the History list.

Until you make further changes to the file, you can still return the image to a more recent state by selecting a step lower in the list. Once you've used the History panel to restore a photo to an earlier state, any change you make to the image will replace all the actions in the more recent history.

Refining the Healing Brush results

The Healing Brush tool copies *texture* from the source area, not color. It samples the colors in the target area—the area that you're brushing—and arranges those colors according to the texture sampled from the reference area. Consequently, the Healing Brush tool appears to be smoothing the skin. So far, however, the results are not convincingly realistic.

In this exercise, you'll make your retouching work look a little more natural by altering the opacity of the layer you've been working on, and then use another of the texture tools to refine the resulting blend.

1 Click the Navigator tab in the floating panel group. In the Navigator panel, use the zoom slider and drag the red frame in the preview to focus the view in the image window on the area around the woman's eyes and mouth.

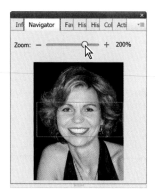

Extensive retouching can leave skin looking artificially smooth, looking a little like molded plastic. Reducing the opacity of the retouched layer will give the skin a more realistic look by allowing some of the wrinkles on the unedited Background layer to show through.

2 In the Layers panel, change the Opacity of the layer Background Copy 2 to about 50%, using your own judgment to set the exact percentage.

We opted for quite a low setting, intending a fairly natural look for this photo of a friend, but the Opacity value you set will depend on the extent of your retouching and the purpose for which the edited image is intended.

The opacity change restores some realism, but three noticeable blemishes have also made a reappearance—one on each cheek and one just below the lower lip.

3   In the Layers panel, select the layer Background Copy to make it active.

4   Set the brush size for the Healing Brush tool to **20** px and click once or twice on each blemish. Gone!

5   In the toolbar, select the Blur tool (⬤). In the tool options pane, set the brush size to approximately **13** px, the Mode to Normal, and the Strength to **50**%.

6   With the layer Background Copy still active, drag the Blur tool over some of the deeper lines around the eyes and brow. Use the Navigator panel to change the zoom level and shift the focus as needed. Reduce the Blur tool brush diameter to **7** px and smooth the lips a little, avoiding the edges.

Tip: To remove spots and small blemishes in your photo, try the Spot Healing Brush in Proximity Match mode as an alternative to the Healing Brush. With the Spot Healing Brush, you can either click or drag to smooth away imperfections without needing to set a reference point.

Compare your results to those below—the original, the version retouched with the Healing Brush, and final refined version. Toggle the visibility of your retouched layers to compare the original image in your Background layer with the edited results.

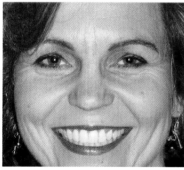
Original

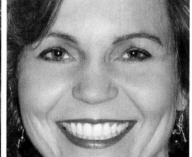
Healing Brush 100% Opacity

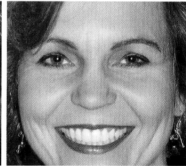
Healing Brush 50% Opacity over Blur tool

7   Choose File > Save As. Make sure that the new file will be included in the Organizer but not in a version set. Name the edited image **07_04_Retouch**, to be saved to your My CIB Work folder in Photoshop (PSD) format.

8   Make sure that the Layers option is activated, and then click Save.

9   Choose File > Close.

In this exercise, you've learned how to set an appropriate source reference for the Healing Brush tool, and then how to sample the texture of the source area to repair flaws in another part of the photograph. You also used the Blur tool to smooth textures, and made an opacity change to achieve a more realistic look. You've also gained a little experience in working with both the History and Navigator panels.

Tip: For a quick and easy solution to portrait retouching, try the improved Perfect Portrait procedure listed under Special Edits in the Guided Edit mode, where you're stepped through smoothing skin, removing spots, fixing red-eye, increasing definition in facial features, whitening teeth, and even slimming your subject!

Removing unwanted objects from images

In the modern world, it's often difficult to photograph even a remote landscape without capturing a fence, power lines, satellite dishes, or litter—mundane clutter that can reduce the drama of an otherwise perfect shot.

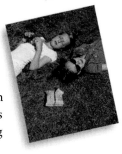

Photoshop Elements offers several tools to help you improve an image by getting rid of extraneous detail. In this set of exercises you'll use the Object Removal guided edit and the Spot Healing Brush tool to remove an object *without* altering the overall composition.

Using the Object Removal guided edit

The healing tools are quite useful, but let's start with something easy: the new Object Removal guided edit.

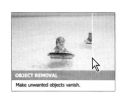

1 If you're still in the Editor, switch to the Organizer by clicking the Organizer button (▦) in the taskbar at the bottom of the workspace. Select the photos 07_01.jpg and 07_05.jpg and click the Editor button (🖉)—not the arrow beside it—in the taskbar.

2 Click the Photo Bin button (🖼) and select the image 07_01.jpg to make it the active document. Switch to the Guided mode and make sure you're viewing the Basics collection. Click the Object Removal guided edit.

3 Choose the Auto selection tool in the side panel, and drag a rectangular marquee around the girl and her reflection in the water. The tool creates a selection around her; if you need to refine it, click either the Add or Subtract button below the tools and make additional marquees.

4 Click the Remove Object button. If necessary, click the Spot Healing Brush or Clone Stamp Tool buttons and clean up any areas that look awry.

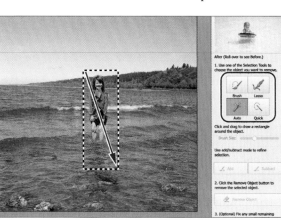

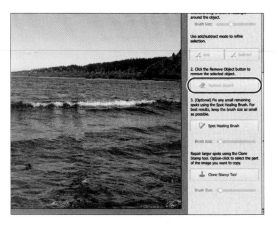

5   Click Next. Then, click Done.

6   Switch to the Expert mode and notice that the edited version has been saved to a new Background Copy layer.

7   Choose File > Save As. Name the new file **07_01_Removed**, to be saved to your My CIB Work folder in JPEG format and included in the Organizer but not in a version set. Click Save. Click OK to accept the JPEG Options settings; then, close the file.

Using the Content-Aware Healing feature

In the last project, you may have used the Spot Healing Brush in Proximity Match mode to help smooth skin blemishes in a portrait photo. In this exercise you'll set the Spot Healing Brush to Content-Aware mode. In this mode, the tool compares nearby image content to fill the area under the pointer, seamlessly matching details such as shadows, object edges, and even patterns like wooden decking shot in perspective, as shown in the illustration at right.

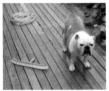
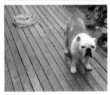

1   Make sure the Editor is in Expert mode; then, choose Window > Reset Panels. Click the Photo Bin button () and select the image 07_05.jpg to make it the active document. Select the Healing Brush tool (✎) or its variant, the Spot Healing Brush tool (✎)—whichever is currently visible in the toolbar. If necessary, click the Tool Options button (✎) in the taskbar to open the tool options pane.

2   In the tool options pane, check the header and buttons at the left to make sure the Spot Healing Brush tool (✎) is the active variant, and see that the tool is set to Content-Aware mode. Set the brush size to **100** pixels.

Note: Depending on your operating system and whether you have a graphics tablet, your brush shape may differ from that illustrated.

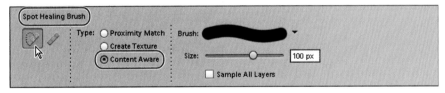

3   Press the Z key to switch to the Zoom tool, and then drag a zoom marquee to zoom in on the signpost and a little of the sky above it. Press the J key to reactivate the Spot Healing Brush. Center the circular cursor over the top of the signpost and drag downward, stopping just before you reach the yellow sign.

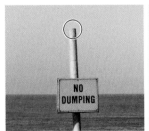
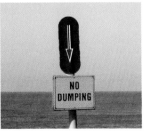
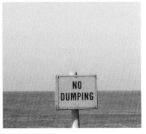

4 Press the right bracket key (]) six times to increase the brush size to 300 pixels. Center the cursor over the yellow sign (the horizon should bisect the circle) and click once; then, center the cursor over the smaller sign and click again.

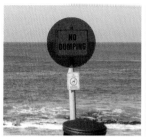 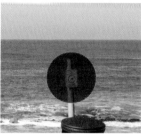 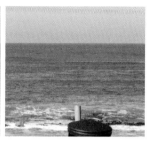

5 Press the left bracket key ([) six times to reduce the brush size to 100 pixels; then, make a short downward stroke to remove the remnants of the signpost, stopping just before you reach the top of the litter bin.

▶ **Tip:** Try to limit yourself to as few of these repairs as possible; two or three should suffice. The more you interfere, the more likely you are to introduce problems.

6 Use the Zoom and Hand tools to focus on the area previously occupied by the late signpost. If you see any noticeable artifacts, such as blurring or misaligned texture, press the J key to reactivate the Spot Healing Brush and click or make very short strokes to remove them. If a stroke fails, or makes things worse, undo and try again, resizing the brush and varying the stroke direction as needed.

7 In the tool options pane, make sure the brush size is 100 pixels. Focus your view on the shadow of the litter bin. Starting at the right, make a series of overlapping clicks, keeping the brush on the grass. Don't be concerned about a little repeated detail, but undo and try again if you introduce any of the rocky foreshore.

⬤ **Note:** It may take more than the six spot healing clicks illustrated here to clear the litter bin's shadow smoothly; we used 10 overlapping clicks to achieve a satisfactory result. In some cases, you may get better results with short strokes in addition to spot-clicks.

8 If your overlapping spots have produced noticeable smears or obvious repetition of detail, reduce the brush size to around 50 pixels and remove them; very short strokes should do the trick, if single clicks are not enough. You can remove the scraps of white litter at the roadside while you're at it, if you don't mind.

9 In the tool options pane, set the brush size to **350** pixels. Drag down over the litter bin, starting below the crest of the wave behind it and ending your stroke before you reach the gold band near the base, as shown in the first pane on the next page.

10 Make a short horizontal stroke with a 250-pixel brush to remove the base of the bin; then break up any misplaced detail using a few clicks with a smaller brush.

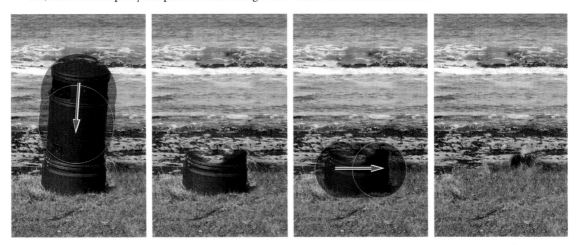

As you've just discovered, the Spot Healing Brush in Content-Aware mode enables you to remove even a very prominent, irregularly shaped, shadowed object from a complex background quickly and easily, without the need to make fussy selections.

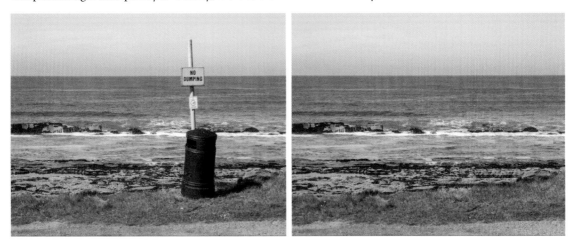

11 When you're done, choose View > Fit On Screen. Choose File > Save As. Name the new file **07_05_DumpingOK**, to be saved to your My CIB Work folder in JPEG format, and included in the Organizer but not in a version set. Click Save. Click OK to accept the JPEG Options settings; then, close the file.

Creative fun with guided edits

The Guided Edit mode offers far more than just correction, adjustment, and retouching tasks. In the Fun Edits and Special Edits categories you'll find guided procedures that let you experiment with a range of striking and unusual creative treatments for your photos—all presented with step-by-step instructions.

Changing the depth of field

The Depth Of Field guided edit adds a soft background blur that helps draw attention to the subject.

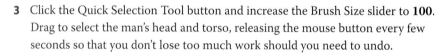

1 In the Organizer, select the image 07_12.jpg; then, click the Editor button (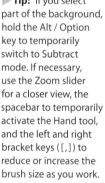). Switch to the Guided Edit mode and click the Special Edits tab.

2 Click the Depth Of Field effect—the second-last guided project on the Fun Edits tab. In the panel at the right, click the Custom button.

Tip: If you select part of the background, hold the Alt / Option key to temporarily switch to Subtract mode. If necessary, use the Zoom slider for a closer view, the spacebar to temporarily activate the Hand tool, and the left and right bracket keys ([,]) to reduce or increase the brush size as you work.

3 Click the Quick Selection Tool button and increase the Brush Size slider to **100**. Drag to select the man's head and torso, releasing the mouse button every few seconds so that you don't lose too much work should you need to undo.

4 Click the Add Blur button. Increase the Blur setting to **15**.

5 Click Next at the bottom of the panel; then, click the Save As button. Name the file **07_12_Depth**, and save it to your My CIB Work folder in Photoshop (PSD) format, with the Layers option enabled. Include the new image in the Organizer but not in a version set. Choose File > Close, or click the Close button (X) at the upper right of the Guided Edit preview pane.

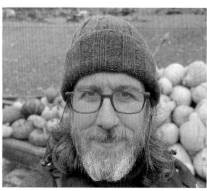

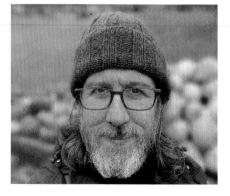

Combining photos for a double exposure effect

For another type of artistic treatment, the Double Exposure guided edit enables you to merge two images in a variety of striking ways to create atmospheric, evocative picture-stories or surreal, dream-like effects.

1 In the Organizer, select the image 07_11.jpg; then, click the Editor button (⌨). If you're not already in Guided Edit mode, switch modes now. Click the preview for the Double Exposure effect in the Fun Edits category to start the project.

The first two steps in this guided edit are not strictly essential; once you are familiar with the process you may choose to skip them, depending on the images you're working with and the effect you wish to achieve. Step 1 asks you to use the Crop tool to center your subject; in step 2, you select the subject, either by dragging a selection rectangle with the Auto Selection tool or by painting a selection onto the photo with the Quick Selection tool. The effect is as you see in the before and after previews; the background around the selected subject is replaced by white and the overlaid image is visible only inside the selection.

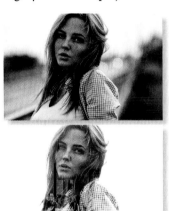

Note: The superimposed image will not show through any part of the base photo that is pure white; it will appear most clearly against the darkest areas. In these before and after preview images, you can see that the overlaid image is excluded from the composite, not only by the white background around the woman but also by her white shirt.

For our lesson image, neither of these steps would have any effect; the subject of our studio portrait is already centered and surrounded by a white background. We'll start with the third step: choosing a second photo to create the effect.

2 In the Double Exposure pane, click each of the three preset images (Forest, City, and Cloud) to see how well they work with our base photo; use the Intensity slider to control the way the photos are merged.

3 Click the Import A Photo button; then, locate and open the folder Extras inside your Lesson 7 folder. Select the image DSC_0229.jpg, and then click Place.

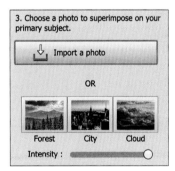

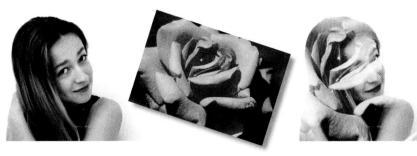

The two lesson images work quite well together, but the superimposed rose is obscuring too much of the girl's face; we'll try altering the blend intensity and use the Move tool to adjust the alignment.

4 Use the slider below the preset thumbnails to reduce the intensity of the super-imposed image to 92%; the numerical value is displayed in a tooltip as you drag.

5 Choose View > Zoom Out. Click the Move tool provided in the Double Exposure pane. Drag the center handle on the top edge of the bounding box upward until the tooltip displays a Height (H) value of 7.4 inches. Drag the center handle on the lower edge of the bounding box down to set a Height (H) value of 8.2 inches.

6 Click the image, and then hold Shift as you press the right arrow key four times to nudge the image to the right. Drag the center handle on the left edge of the bounding box to the right to set a Width (W) value of 9.8 inches. Click the green check mark (✔) at the lower right of the preview to commit the changes.

▶ **Tip:** If you wish to try the other effects, be sure to clear each before applying the next. To do this, click the No Effect thumbnail at the upper left of the Effects palette.

7 Click the Effects button; then click the thumbnail at the upper right.

The images are better aligned, but the girl's nose is still obscured. We'll switch to Expert mode, where we can correct the problem in the Layers panel.

8 Click Next at the lower right of the workspace; then, under Continue Editing, choose In Expert. If necessary, choose Window > Layers. In the Layers panel, click the layer Screen Mode—the higher of the two layers with the rose image.

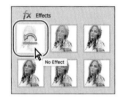

9 Select the Eraser tool in the toolbox. In the tool options pane, choose a soft-edged brush such as "Soft Round 5 pixels," the seventh brush from the top of the list. Set the size of the brush to 220 pixels and its opacity to 75%; then, make three or four passes across the girl's cheeks and nose. Reduce the brush size to 60 pixels and its opacity to 60%; then, use three or four clicks or short strokes in each eye to reveal a little more of the girl's pupils and lashes.

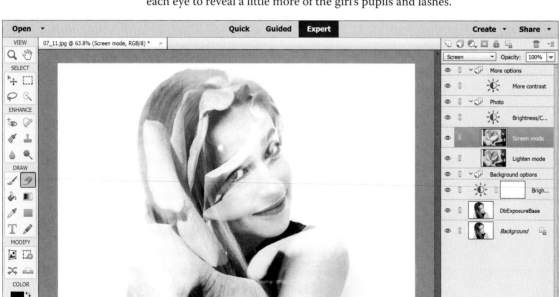

10 Choose File > Save As. Save the file with all its layers in Photoshop format, with an appropriate name and all the usual settings; then, choose File > Close.

Creating effects with filters

The guided edits in the Fun Edits and Special Edits categories give an image a completely new look by applying several adjustments and filters in combination. You can have a lot of fun devising your own special effects and sophisticated photo treatments in the Filter Gallery, where you can combine multiple filters and tweak the way they work together to create unique new custom effects.

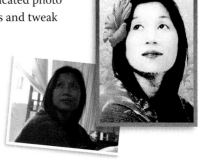

Use the Filter Gallery to reinterpret an image and present it in an entirely new light. This can be a great way to redeem a technically inferior photo, enabling you to turn even a flawed or uninteresting image into a work of art. The possibilities are limitless!

Before exploring the Filter Gallery, set up a work file with some extra layers for working copies of the image.

1   In the Organizer, isolate the images for this lesson, if necessary, by clicking either the Lesson 7 folder in the left panel's Folders list or the check box beside the Lesson 07 keyword in the Tags panel. Right-click the image 07_09.jpg in the Media Browser and choose Edit With Photoshop Elements Editor from the context menu. Make sure that the Editor is in Expert mode, and then choose Window > Reset Panels.

2   Many filters make use of the foreground and background colors set in the toolbar to create effects, so start by resetting them to the default black and white. Click the Default Foreground And Background Colors button beside the overlapping swatches at the bottom of the toolbox; then, click the arrows to switch the foreground and background colors.

3   Drag the Background layer to the New Layer button (⧉) at the left of the Layers panel's header to create a second layer. Drag the Background Copy layer to the New Layer button to create a third layer. Click the eye icon (👁) beside the top layer, Background Copy 2, to hide it from view in the image window. Click the middle layer, Background Copy, to make it active for editing.

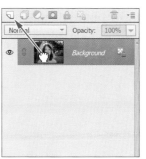
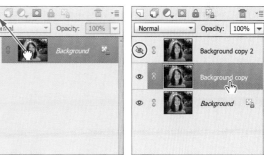

4   If you don't see the Quick Selection tool (🖌) at the right of the Lasso tool in the toolbar's Select category, Alt-click / Option click whichever tool is currently active to cycle through the variants until the Quick Selection tool is foremost.

5   With the Quick Selection tool, select the girl's lips and shirt. Use the left and right square bracket keys ([,]) to decrease or increase the brush size as you work. Hold down the Alt / Option key as you paint to subtract from your selection.

6 When the selection is complete, choose Select > Refine Edge or click the Refine Edge button in the tool options bar. In the Refine Edge dialog box, set both the Smooth and Contrast values to **0**, the Feather amount to **1** px, and the Shift Edge value to **1**%. These settings will soften the edges of the selection without reducing its effective area. Click OK.

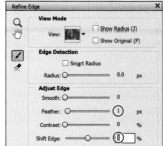

7 Choose Select > Save Selection. Name the new selection **color details**. Under Operation, activate New Selection; then, click OK. Choose Select > Deselect.

8 Choose File > Save As. Name the file **07_09_Work**, to be saved to your My CIB Work folder in Photoshop format, with layers intact. Make sure the image will be included in the Organizer but not as part of a version set; then, click Save.

Using the Filter Gallery

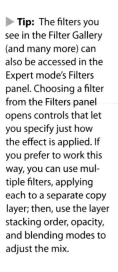

▶ **Tip:** The most reliable way to assess the effects of the filters as you work is to set the zoom level to 100%.

1 Choose Filter > **Filter Gallery**. If necessary, use the menu at the lower left of the Filter Gallery window to set the magnification to 100%. If you can't see the whole photo, drag in the preview pane so that most of the girl's face is visible.

2 If you don't see the center pane with its list of filter categories, click the arrow beside the OK button at the upper right.

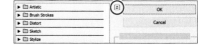

3 If you see more than one filter listed in the right pane, select the top filter and click the Trash icon to delete it. In the center pane, expand the Artistic category and choose the Watercolor filter. Experiment with the full range of the sliders. Set the Brush Detail to **5**, the Shadow Intensity to **1**, and the Texture to **1**.

▶ **Tip:** The filters you see in the Filter Gallery (and many more) can also be accessed in the Expert mode's Filters panel. Choosing a filter from the Filters panel opens controls that let you specify just how the effect is applied. If you prefer to work this way, you can use multiple filters, applying each to a separate copy layer; then, use the layer stacking order, opacity, and blending modes to adjust the mix.

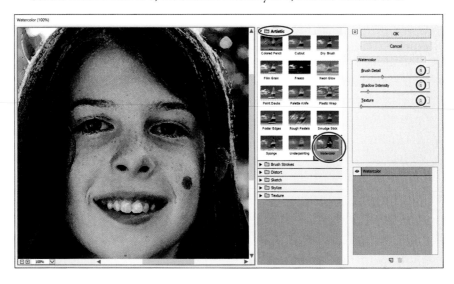

4 Click the New Effect Layer button (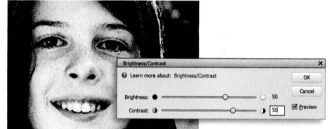) below the right pane in the Filter Gallery dialog box. Collapse the Artistic category; then, expand the Texture category and choose the Texturizer filter. The Watercolor and Texturizer filters are applied simultaneously. Choose Canvas from the Texture menu; then, set the Scaling value to **200%** and the Relief to **4**. From the Light menu, choose Top Left.

Tip: In the Filter Gallery, you can combine as many filters as you wish, building up your own complex custom effects.

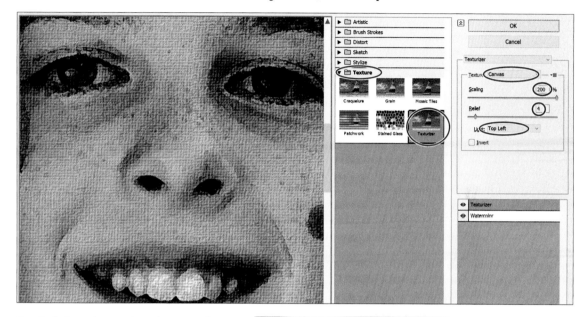

5 Click OK. The combined Watercolor and Texturizer filters are applied to the layer Background Copy. From the Enhance menu, choose Adjust Color > Remove Color; then, choose Adjust Lighting > Brightness/Contrast. Set the values for both Brightness and Contrast to **50**, and then click OK.

Layering filters and effects

Although the Filter Gallery offers endless possibilities for combining filters, you can achieve even more sophisticated results by using it in tandem with the Layers panel—applying combinations of filters to multiple duplicate layers, and then blending the layers using partial transparency, blending modes, or masks.

1 Click the eye icon beside the layer Background Copy 2 to make it visible; then, click the layer thumbnail to make it active. Reverse the swatches at the bottom of the toolbar so that the background color is white. Choose Filter > Filter Gallery. Be careful to choose the second listing for the Filter Gallery—the first listing simply applies the previous settings without opening the Filter Gallery.

Tip: If you've set up an effect that looks great in the background but makes the faces of your subjects unrecognizable, use layer masks to separate the subjects from the background, and then apply the same set of filters to each part of the image at different settings.

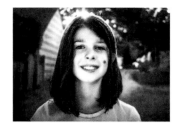

Note: The stacking order of filters in the list in the Filter Gallery will alter the way they interact, though this may be more noticeable with some filters than others. You can change the order of the filters by simply dragging them in the list.

2 The Filter Gallery window opens with your previous filters, and all their settings, exactly as you left them. Click the New Effect Layer button again. Expand the Distort category and choose the Diffuse Glow filter. Set the Graininess and Glow Amount values to **10**, and the Clear Amount to **15**. Click OK.

3 In the Layers panel, select the layer Background Copy. At the top of the panel, decrease the layer's opacity to **70**%. Select the top layer, Background Copy 2. Choose Overlay from the Blending Mode menu and then set the opacity to **30**%.

4 Right-click the layer Background Copy 2 and choose Duplicate Layer from the context menu. In the Duplicate Layer dialog box, type **Color Details** as the name for the new layer, and then click OK. Change the new layer's blending mode to Multiply, and its opacity to **70**%.

5 Choose Select > Load Selection. In the Load Selection dialog box, choose your saved selection, Color Details, from the Selection menu under Source. Make sure the New Selection option is activated under Operation, and then click OK. With the top layer selected in the Layers panel, click the Add Layer Mask button (🔘) at the top of the panel. The selection is converted to a layer mask.

In the Layers panel, a layer mask icon is added to the top layer, Color Details, which is now masked so that only the girl's lips and shirt remain visible.

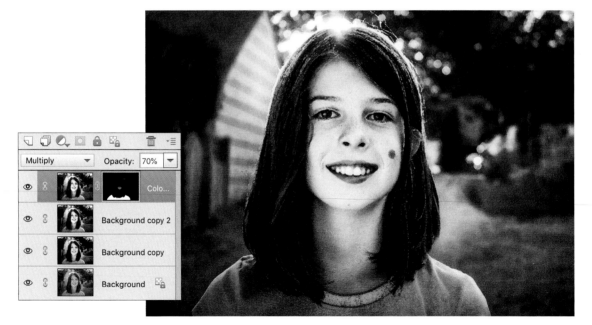

6 Toggle the visibility of each layer in turn, watching the effect in the Edit window. Choose File > Save, and then close the file.

Review questions

1 Dragging in a tilted image with the Straighten tool designates a reference in relation to which your photo will be rotated. What are the best references to look for?

2 What is the purpose of the grid overlays offered in the tool options pane when you select the Crop tool?

3 How do you use the different brushes and erasers that appear in the tool options pane when you select the Recompose tool?

4 How can you quickly undo a whole series of edit steps at once?

5 What are the similarities and differences between the Healing Brush tool and the Spot Healing Brush tool for retouching photos?

Review answers

1 The most reliable reference for straightening a tilted photo is a sea horizon line. In the absence of a natural horizon, you can often use either horizontal or vertical architectural features—or structural elements such as signposts and flag poles—as long as they are not pictured in perspective or too obviously affected by lens distortion.

2 The Crop tool's grid overlays can guide you in framing a balanced composition. The Rule Of Thirds overlay divides the image horizontally and vertically into three equal parts; according to this rule, objects look more balanced when aligned with the lines and intersections of the grid.

3 Use the Mark For Protection brush to define areas in the image that you wish to protect from a scaling operation. Use the Mark For Removal brush to define any areas that you want removed from the image; the Recompose tool will cut those areas before compressing others. Each of the Recompose brushes has an associated eraser.

4 The History panel lists every action performed in chronological order. To restore the file to an earlier state, select an action higher in the list. Until you make further changes, you can restore the image to a later state by selecting a step lower in the list.

5 Both healing tools blend pixels from one part of an image into another. Although the Spot Healing Brush tool enables you to remove blemishes more quickly than is possible with the Healing Brush, the Healing Brush can be customized and enables you to specify the source reference area, giving you more control.

8 COMBINING IMAGES

Lesson overview

Although you can do a lot to improve a photo with tonal adjustments, color corrections, and retouching, sometimes the best way to produce the perfect image is simply to fake it! Photoshop Elements delivers powerful tools that enable you to do just that by combining images.

Merge ordinary scenic photos into a stunning panorama that truly recaptures the feel of the location—or blend differently exposed pictures to conquer difficult lighting conditions. Move objects from one image to another—or combine a series of shots to produce the perfect group photo, where everybody is smiling with open eyes.

In this lesson, you'll learn some of the tricks you'll need for combining images to put together the perfect shot that you didn't actually get:

- Merging a series of photos into a panorama

- Assembling the perfect group shot

- Removing unwanted elements

- Blending differently exposed photographs

- Combining images using layers, selections, and masks

 This lesson will take about 90 minutes to complete. To get the lesson files used in this chapter, download them from the web page for this book at www.adobepress.com/PSECIB2020. For more information, see "Accessing the lesson files and Web Edition" in the Getting Started section at the beginning of this book.

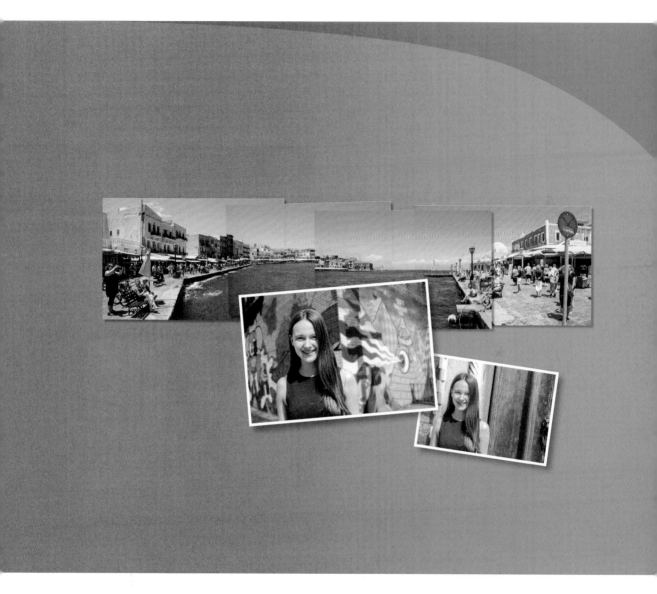

If you're ready to go beyond fixing pictures in conventional ways, this lesson is for you. Why settle for that scenic photo that just doesn't capture the way it really looked? Or that group portrait where Dad is looking away and Mom's eyes are closed? Combine images to produce the perfect shot. Merge photos to make a stunning panorama, remove obstructions from the view, and even get little Jimmy to stop making faces.

Getting started

● **Note:** Before you start this lesson, make sure you've set up a folder for your lesson files and downloaded the Lesson 8 folder from your Account page at www.peachpit.com, as detailed in "Accessing the lesson files and Web Edition" and "Creating a work folder" in the "Getting Started" section at the beginning of this book. You should also have created a new work catalog (see "Creating a catalog for working with this book" in Lesson 1).

Begin by importing the sample images for this lesson to your CIB Catalog.

1 Start Photoshop Elements, and click Organizer in the Home screen.

2 Click the Import button at the upper left of the Organizer and choose From Files And Folders from the drop-down menu. In the Get Photos And Videos From Files And Folders dialog box, locate and select your Lesson 8 folder. Disable the option Get Photos From Subfolders and the automatic processing options; then, click Get Media.

3 In the Import Attached Keyword Tags dialog, click Select All; then, click OK.

Combining images automatically

The Photomerge tools offer a variety of ways to combine photos. These tools not only deliver effective solutions to some tricky photographic problems, but are also great fun to use creatively, enabling you to produce striking and unusual images.

In this lesson, you'll use the Photomerge Exposure tool to combine exposures made in difficult lighting conditions into a composite image that would have been virtually impossible to capture in a single shot. You'll compose a group photo from two single-subject images with the Photomerge Group Shot tool, and combine a number of photos from a busy scene to produce an unobstructed view using the Photomerge Scene Cleaner. Let's start by blending a series of scenic photographs into a dramatic panorama using the Photomerge Panorama tool.

Merging photos into a panorama

A common problem for many of us when taking photos at a scenic location is that standard lenses don't have a wide enough angle to capture the entire scene. The Photomerge Panorama tool provides the solution: You can capture a series of overlapping shots, and then merge them to create a panorama. In the following pages, you'll learn how to have Photoshop Elements do most of the work for you.

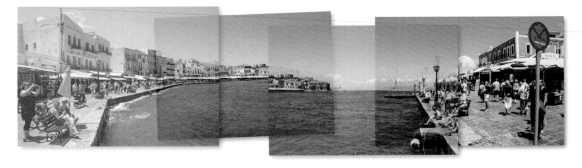

You could start the Photomerge Panorama process from the Organizer by choosing Photomerge > Photomerge Panorama from the Edit menu, but for this exercise, you'll switch to the Editor and launch the operation from the Guided Edit mode.

1   In the Organizer, Ctrl-click / Command-click to select the images 08_01a.jpg through 08_01d.jpg in the Media Browser; then, right-click any of the selected thumbnails, and choose Edit With Photoshop Elements Editor.

▶ **Tip:** If you don't see file names displayed below the thumbnails in the Media Browser, make sure that the Details and File Names options are selected in the View menu.

2   If necessary, switch the Editor to Guided mode by clicking Guided in the picker at the top of the workspace. Click the Photomerge tab above the preview pane.

3   Shift-click to select all four photos in the Photo Bin, and then click the Photomerge Panorama preview to launch the process.

Setting up Photomerge Panorama options

The Photomerge dialog offers a choice of layout methods that will affect the way the source images are aligned and stitched together to create your panorama.

1   In the Photomerge Panorama pane at the right, click the arrow to the right of the projection preview diagram under Panorama Settings, and then select Cylindrical from the layout options.

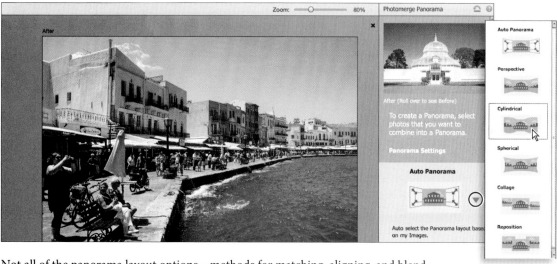

Not all of the panorama layout options—methods for matching, aligning, and blending your source images—will work well for every series of photos. Experiment with your own photos to get a feel for the differences between the layout options and for which will work best for a given set of source images.

2   Expand the Settings options and make sure Blend Images Together is activated.

With the Blend Images Together option activated, Photoshop Elements will color match the source photos, align overlapping detail, and automatically create layer masks to define the areas from each image that will contribute to the panorama.

▶ **Tip:** You might disable the Blend Images Together option if you want to control precisely which part of each photo is to be included in the panorama, by creating the layer masks manually.

3 Click the Create Panorama button at the right of the taskbar; then watch the Layers panel while Photoshop Elements creates a new file for the panorama and places each source image on its own layer. Photomerge calculates the overlaps, masks each image layer accordingly, and then color matches adjacent images as it blends the seams.

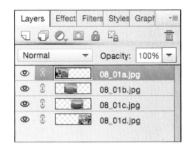

The Clean Edges dialog appears, asking if you'd like to automatically fill in the edges of your panorama. If you were to click No, Photoshop Elements would automatically crop away any areas of transparency surrounding the composite image. These transparent areas, as indicated by a checkerboard pattern in the illustration below, result from the process of aligning the separate source images.

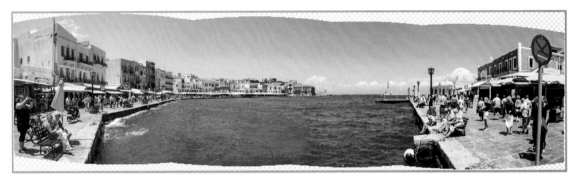

For this combination of photos, cropping away the transparent areas would not remove any significant detail; however, substantial slices of the image would be lost, making the composition somewhat cramped. Instead, Photoshop Elements can help you solve this problem by using content-aware healing to fill in the missing areas.

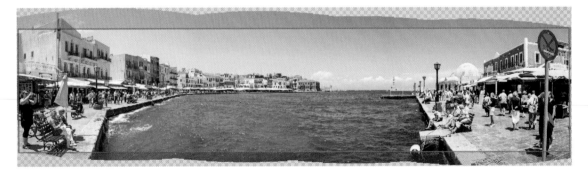

4 In the Clean Edges dialog, click Yes.

The content-aware fill usually does a great job with nonspecific or organic content such as clouds, water, or foliage, and even with regular patterns like brickwork, but can't deal with too much man-made detail. Let's check over the results.

5   In the Photomerge Panorama pane, under Continue Editing, select In Expert.

6   In Expert mode, you can use the Zoom and Hand tools ($\mathbf{Q}$, $\sqrt[3]{y}$) to examine the extended image; the active "marching ants" selection border will help you look in the right places to spot any anomalies.

The results at the top of the photo are very good, but the content-aware fill has produced artifacts in the lower corners of the merged image. You may see different results than those pictured in the illustration below; the content-aware fill operates with a degree of randomness in selecting areas for sampling in its attempt to avoid repetition of image detail.

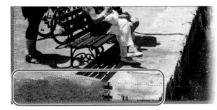 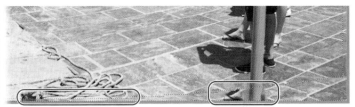

7   (Optional) If you wish to see if Photomerge will produce a better result on its second attempt, choose Edit > Undo Fill, and then choose Edit > Fill Selection. In the Fill Layer dialog, choose Content-Aware from the Use menu; then, click OK. If you wish, you can retouch the unwelcome blend artifacts using the Spot Healing Brush and the Clone Stamp tool before moving on.

8   When you're done, press Ctrl+D / Command+D, or choose Select > Deselect.

Now let's have a closer look at how well Photoshop Elements matched the areas where the source images are overlapped.

9   In the Layers panel, click the eye icon ($\bigodot$) for the layer with the merged panorama to hide it. Hold Alt+Shift / Option+Shift, and click the black-and-white layer mask thumbnail for the third layer. In the Edit window, the mask associated with the layer appears as a semitransparent red overlay, enabling you to see which part of the image 08_01b.jpg has contributed to the panorama. The unused portions are hidden by the layer mask.

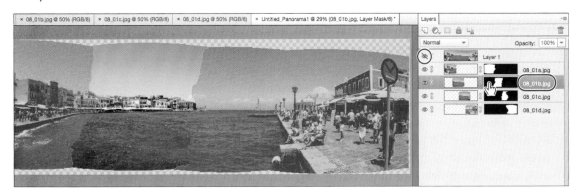

Note: For our lesson images, you probably won't find noticeable blend problems, but some source photos can produce misaligned edges or displaced, floating details along the blended seams.

10 Use the Zoom and Hand tools to focus on the area where the blend border passes through the waterfront buildings. Hold Alt+Shift / Option+Shift, and click the layer mask thumbnail to toggle the overlay as you inspect the seams. Hide the red mask overlay.

11 Alt-click / Option-click the black-and-white layer mask thumbnail. The layer mask is displayed in opaque black and white. Black represents the masked portions of the layer; white represents the areas that have contributed to the blend.

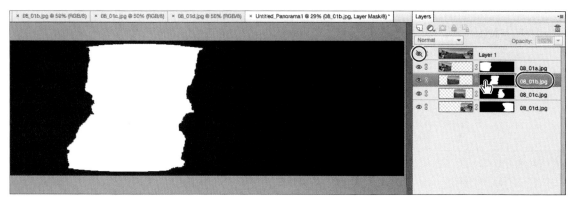

Tip: If you do find artifacts along seams in a panorama, try recombining the source images using a different layout method. Alternatively, you can adjust the placement of the seams by retouching the layer blending masks manually.

If you wished to edit any portion of a seam between images, you could alternate between the opaque and semitransparent views of the layer mask, and adjust the blend by painting (or erasing) directly onto the mask. If your panorama is extended by content-aware fill, you'll need to erase the corresponding area of the top layer, creating a "window" so that your changes to the lower layers are visible.

12 Use the same technique to inspect the blended seams between the other source layers. When you're done, make the merged panorama layer visible once more.

13 Choose View > Fit On Screen. If you didn't repair the content-aware fill in step 7, choose Image > Crop. Drag the handles of the cropping rectangle to make it as large as possible without including the blurred image artifacts in the lower corners of the photo; then, click the Commit button (✓) at the lower right to commit the crop.

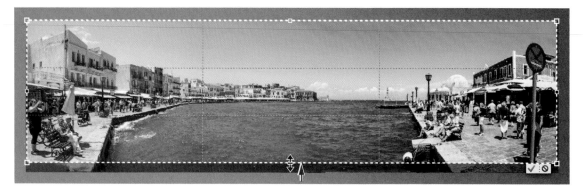

The finished composite panorama presents a well-composed, natural-looking view, with no more distortion than is apparent at the outside edges of the source series.

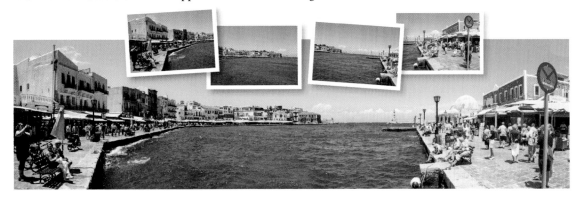

14 Choose File > Save. Name the merged image **08_01_Panorama**, to be saved to your My CIB Work folder in Photoshop format with Layers activated. Saving your file in Photoshop format enables you to preserve the layers so that you can always return to adjust them if necessary. If you saved in JPEG format, the image would be flattened, and layer information lost. Make sure that the file will be included in the Organizer. Click Save; then, choose File > Close All.

Not every set of images will perform the same way in a Photomerge panorama. Different sets of source images can produce very different results, even with the same layout option settings. The way a given series of photos will combine to form a panorama depends on many factors, from lighting that varies markedly across the series to issues of perspective, foreshortening, and lens distortion.

Our sample photos feature even lighting and few foreground elements, but a series of images taken close to a building or other large object—like photos shot indoors or in a confined urban space—would present different challenges. Try creating panoramas in a variety of locations; the results can be both striking and surprising.

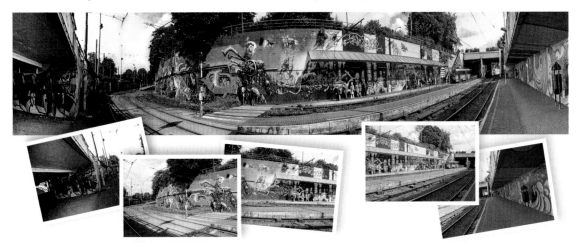

Creating a composite group shot

Shooting the perfect group photo is a difficult task, especially if you have a large family of squirmy kids. Fortunately, Photoshop Elements offers a solution: a powerful photo-blending tool called Photomerge Group Shot.

No longer do you need to put up with family photos where someone has turned away, frowned, or closed their eyes at the wrong moment. Photomerge Group Shot lets you merge the best parts of several images to create the perfect group photo.

Photomerge Group Shot also makes a great solution to another common group photo problem: It lets you put the person behind the camera back in the frame.

1 If you're still in the Editor, click the Organizer button (🎞) in the taskbar.

2 If necessary, use the Lesson 08 tag in the Tags panel to isolate the images for this lesson, and then Ctrl-click / Command-click to select the images 08_02a.jpg and 08_02b.jpg in the Media Browser.

3 Choose Edit > Photomerge > Photomerge Group Shot. Open the Photo Bin.

The Photomerge Group Shot panel opens at the right, with tools and tips for merging photos; the toolbox now offers only the Zoom and Hand tools. By default, Photoshop Elements has designated the first photo in the Photo Bin as the *source* image and placed it in the Source pane on the left. The Photomerge tools will let you extract the figure from the Source image and blend it into the Final image.

Tip: If you don't see checkerboard transparency around the default source image, as shown in the illustration at the right, click Cancel, close both images without saving, and quit the Editor; then, start again from step 2.

Note: Photoshop Elements begins the Photomerge process by finding matching detail; the checkerboard areas, and any skewing in either image, show what has been done to align the two photos.

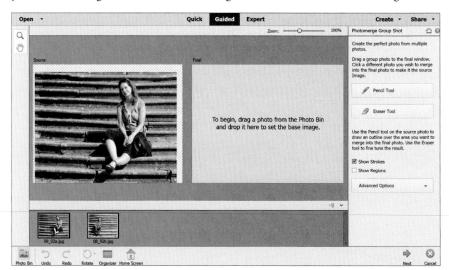

Before you begin merging photos for a composite group shot, you need to consider your choice for the Final image—the "target" image into which the figures from your source images will be blended. You may choose the image with the most balanced composition, a photo with more background detail than the others, or the image with the most room for the additions you're planning.

4 Click the second thumbnail in the Photo Bin to replace the default source photo with the image 08_02b.jpg. Drag the first thumbnail (08_02a.jpg) from the Photo Bin into the Final image pane on the right.

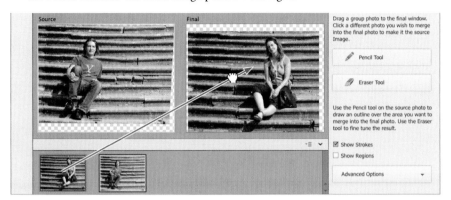

For this demonstration, with only two images in the operation, we chose the image 08_02a.jpg as the Final image (the base for the composite) because the exposure and composition are better, with more clearance at the subjects' feet. Also, you'll notice that the other shot has been skewed slightly in the alignment process.

5 In the Photomerge Group Shot panel at the right, select the Pencil tool (✐), if it's not already active. Click the Size slider to see a numerical value displayed; if necessary, reset the Pencil tool to its default size of 13 pixels. Make sure that the Show Strokes option is activated and Show Regions is disabled.

6 In the Source image, start at the top of the man's head, and draw an uninterrupted line as shown in the illustration below, passing through his face, looping across the chest, and then tracing the outside line of his leg as closely as possible from the knee down, making sure that you stay just inside the edge of his jeans. If you go off track, press Ctrl+Z / Command+Z and start again.

▶ **Tip:** Try to copy the yellow line in the illustration as closely as you can so that you'll see results very similar to those described in this exercise. In normal circumstances, you can be much more casual with your pencil stroke.

When you release the mouse button, the figure of the man is copied into the Final image, together with a patch of the stone stairs that hides parts of the woman's right forearm and leg, as well as her shadow. Some of the hair at the right of the man's face has been left behind. Note that the color and contrast of the area copied from the Source image have been adjusted to match the Final image.

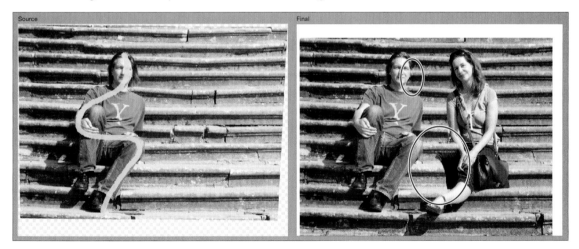

With a practiced stroke, it's actually possible to merge the man to the Final image without the unwelcome extras and missing detail; however, one objective of this exercise is to demonstrate techniques that will help you combine more complex source images, where it can be challenging to make the perfect selection.

Whenever you have difficulty defining the element you wish to copy from the Source image, it's preferable to make a stroke that picks up extra detail from the background, rather than one that leaves portions of the subject behind. The missing hair will be easy to deal with, but where objects touch or overlap, it's much easier to remove extraneous elements than it is to add missing detail.

7   With the Pencil tool, click once in the Source image to pick up the area of hair that was not merged to the Final image.

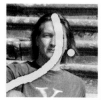

8   Press Ctrl / Command together with the plus sign key (+) to zoom in; then hold the spacebar and drag the Source image to center your view on the man's left leg. Make sure you have a clear view from the knee to the foot.

9   Press the left bracket key ([ ) twice to reduce the default brush (or pencil) size; then, draw a short stroke just a little outside the line of the knee, as shown in the illustration at the right.

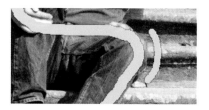

10 In the Photomerge Group Shot panel, select the Eraser tool ( ) (you may need to click twice); then, press the left bracket key ([ ) twice to reduce the brush size. Carefully erase the short line, taking care to keep the Eraser tool cursor clear of the edge of the blue jeans. The original line will protect the edge of the man's jeans while the extraneous detail is removed, revealing the woman's leg and its shadow, and reinstating the hidden part of her right forearm.

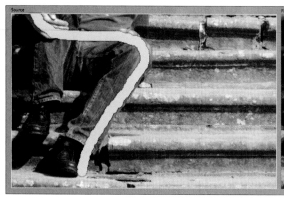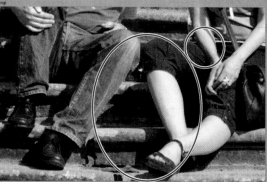

When you're working with an object that's particularly difficult to isolate, try varying your strokes with the Pencil and Eraser tools. Use a combination of long lines, short strokes, and clicks. Both the brush size and the stroke direction can also make a difference to the area that will be affected by either tool.

The Advanced Options button in the Photomerge Group Shot panel gives you access to controls that let you edit a blended composite by adjusting the way the images are aligned. You'll look at the Show Regions option in the next exercise.

11 Click the Next button at the right of the taskbar; then, under Continue Editing, click In Expert. The merged image needs cropping; choose Image > Crop, and then drag the handles of the cropping rectangle to trim off the empty areas. Click the green check mark icon at the lower right to commit the crop.

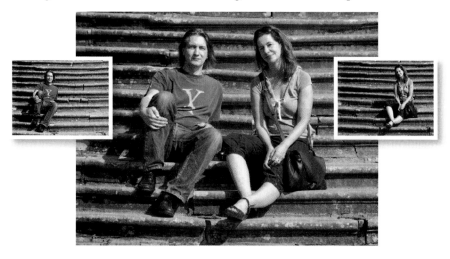

12 Choose File > Save. Name the merged image **08_02_GroupMerge**, to be saved to your My CIB Work folder in Photoshop (PSD) format with Layers activated, and included in the Organizer. Click Save; then, choose File > Close All.

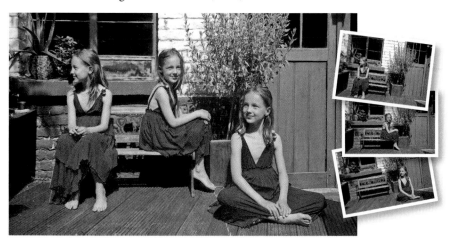

Like all the Photomerge tools, Group Shot not only provides useful solutions to a variety of photographic problems, but can also be a lot of fun to use creatively— making it easy to add a touch of humor and fancy to your shots with a little photo magic.

Removing unwelcome intruders

The Photomerge Scene Cleaner enables you to combine the unobstructed areas from several photos of the same scene to produce a clear view—without the tourists, traffic, or uninvited extras that can draw attention away from your subject.

Tip: Sequences shot with burst mode are ideal for use with the Scene Cleaner tool.

When you're sightseeing, it's a great idea to take extra shots of any busy scene so that you can use the Scene Cleaner to put together an uncluttered image later. It's not necessary to use a tripod; as long as all your photos were shot from roughly the same viewpoint, Photoshop Elements will align the static content in the images.

You can use up to 10 images in a single Scene Cleaner operation; the more source images, the more chance that you'll produce a perfect result. In this exercise, you'll clear a busy scene completely by combining just four photos.

1 Select the images 08_03a.jpg, 08_03b.jpg, 08_03c.jpg, and 08_03d.jpg in the Media Browser; then, choose Edit > Photomerge > Photomerge Scene Cleaner.

2 If necessary, open the Photo Bin; then, double-click the Hand tool to re-fit the previews to the work area. By default, 08_03a.jpg (framed in blue) is loaded as the Source image. Click the thumbnail framed in yellow (08_03b.jpg) to replace it; then drag the thumbnail with the blue frame to the Final pane. This is the photo you will "clean"—the base image for your composite. In the Photomerge Scene Cleaner panel, make sure that Show Strokes is activated.

Tip: If what you see onscreen differs from the illustration at the right, click Cancel, close the images, quit the Editor, and then start again from step 1.

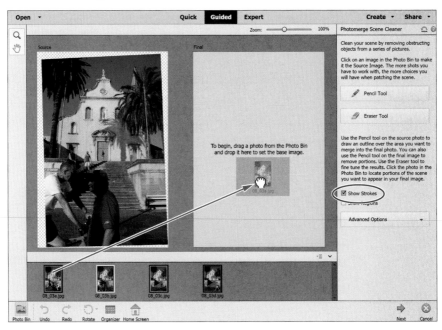

The tools and options in the right panel are very similar to those in the Photomerge Group Shot panel. The principal difference is that in the Scene Cleaner, the Pencil and Eraser tools can be used in both the Source image and the Final image.

3 Compare the photos in the Source and Final panes. Use the Zoom and Hand tools to focus on the lower-right quadrant of the image. Note that the Source image (08_03a) has several clear areas where the Final image has obstructions. Select the Pencil tool (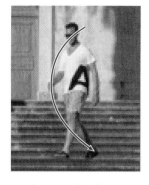) in the Photomerge Scene Cleaner panel.

4 In the Final image, draw a line through the man in the white shirt near the top of the steps, as shown at the right. Make sure your stroke covers both the leading hand and the trailing foot, but try not to extend it beyond his form. When you release the mouse button, the man is removed from the Final image—replaced by detail copied from the Source image. Move the pointer off the Final image onto the surrounding gray background; the yellow line remains visible only in the Source image.

5 In the Final image, draw a second line through the man on the tricycle. Clip the arms and gloves, but don't move further forward or you'll copy the man in red from the Source image. If that happens, or you don't remove as much of the tricycle as is shown at the right below, undo your stroke and try again.

▶ **Tip:** Don't worry about the disembodied head of the broom; you'll remove that with another Source image.

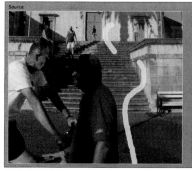
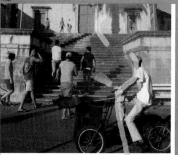
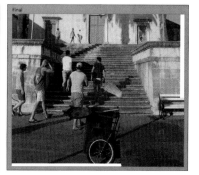

6 If necessary, choose View > Fit On Screen to see the entire image. You can see that this Source image has nothing more to contribute to our composite scene; the left of the photo and the area at the top of the steps are as populated as the Final image. In the Photo Bin, click the third photo (the thumbnail with the green border) to make it the new Source image.

The new Source image has a clear area at the lower left that will enable you to remove three (and a half) more figures from the Final image. You can also copy the area in front of the church door at the right to clear another, but we won't use this Source photo to remove the people at the left of the facade—any stroke in that area of this image picks up the girl sitting on the wall.

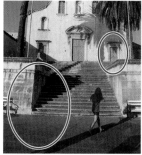

7 In the Final image, draw a line down through the young man at the far left, extending your stroke to catch the trailing foot, as shown below. A mirror of the same stroke should remove the next customer. Draw a short line straight down through the third man; don't go too far at this point or you'll introduce new problems. Click once to remove the extraneous shadow at the lower left, and once more to clear the figure from in front of the church door at the right.

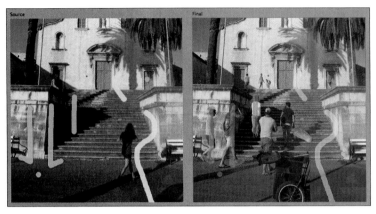 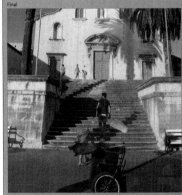

8 Choose View > Fit On Screen to see the entire image. In the Photo Bin, click the thumbnail with the red border to make it the new Source image.

9 Draw in either image to remove the one-and-a-half people from the central fore-ground, together with the wreckage of the street-sweeper's tricycle. If you intend to draw in the Source image, refer to the illustration below before making your stroke. A short horizontal stroke will get rid of the stragglers loitering at the top of the stairs, and a single click will clear the heavy shadow in the fore-ground. If you need to edit a stroke, use the Eraser tool ( ) in the right panel.

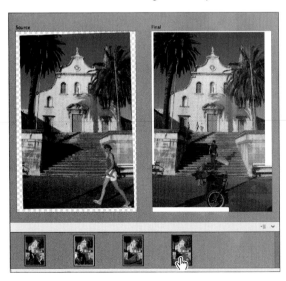 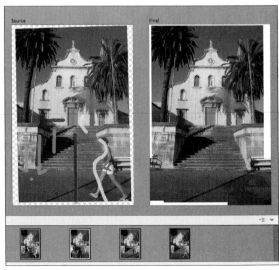

10 Double-click the Hand tool, or choose View > Fit On Screen. To see which part of each image has contributed to the cleared and blended composite, select the Show Regions option in the Photomerge Scene Cleaner panel.

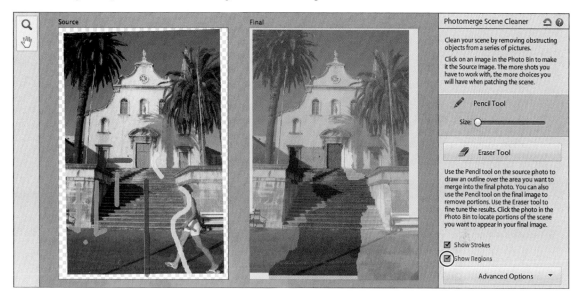

11 Click the Next button at the right of the taskbar; then, under Continue Editing, click In Expert.

12 The image has empty and patched areas around the edges, resulting from the alignment process. Choose Image > Crop. Drag the handles of the cropping rectangle to trim the image; then, click the check mark to commit the crop.

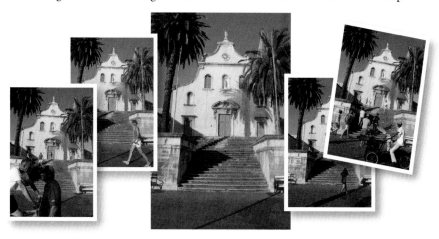

13 Choose File > Save. Name the file **08_03_Depopulated**, to be saved to your My CIB Work folder, in Photoshop (PSD) format. Make sure that the Layers option is selected and that the file will be included in the Organizer. Click Save, and then close all five files.

Blending differently exposed photos

There are many common situations where we (or our cameras in automatic mode) are forced to choose between properly exposing the foreground or the background.

Interior shots often feature overexposed window views where the scene outside is washed out or lost completely. Subjects captured in front of a brightly lit scene or backlit by a window are often underexposed, and therefore appear dull and dark.

Capturing outdoor night shots is another problematic situation; we need to use a flash to light our subject in the foreground, but a background such as a neon-lit street scene, a city skyline, or a moonlit vista is usually better exposed without it.

Photomerge Exposure provides a great new way to deal with photos captured in difficult lighting conditions, enabling you to combine the best-lit areas from two or more images to make a perfectly exposed shot.

For this exercise, you'll work with two photos of a mother and daughter posed in front of stained-glass windows in a dim interior, captured with and without flash.

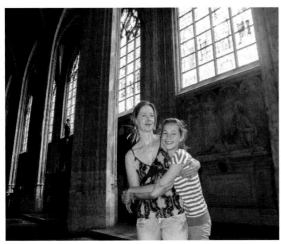 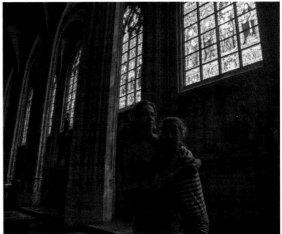

The photo shot with flash has been correctly exposed to capture the figures in the foreground, but the windows appear "blown out"—most color and detail have been lost. The second photo has captured the glowing colors in the stained glass reasonably well, but the rest of the image is too dark, dull, and lacking in detail.

1 If you're still in the Editor, switch to the Organizer now by clicking the Organizer button (⊞) in the taskbar.

2 Click the check box beside the Lesson 08 tag in the Tags panel, if necessary, to isolate the images for this lesson. Ctrl-click / Command-click to select the images 08_04a.jpg and 08_04b.jpg.

3 Choose Edit > Photomerge > Photomerge Exposure. When the Editor has opened, show the Photo Bin.

Using the Photomerge Exposure tool

Whenever you're faced with difficult lighting conditions, you should keep the Photomerge Exposure tool in mind; make a point of shooting two or more photos at different exposure settings, and then let Photoshop Elements align them and blend them together when you get home.

Photoshop Elements can detect whether the images you've chosen to combine are a pair shot with and without flash or photos taken with different exposure settings—for example, a series captured using your camera's exposure-bracketing feature.

The Photomerge Exposure tool has two working modes; it will default to Manual mode for photos captured with and without flash, or open in Automatic mode for a series of exposure-bracketed shots.

Merging exposures manually

The Photomerge tools let you extract content from the Source image and blend it into the Final image. By default, Photoshop Elements places the first photo in the Photo Bin in the Source pane at the left of the Photomerge Exposure workspace.

Tip: If what you see onscreen differs from the illustration below, click Cancel, close both images without saving, and quit the Editor; then, start again from step 2 on the previous page.

1   Click the Manual tab in the right panel if it's not selected. Next, click the second thumbnail in the Photo Bin to replace the default source photo with the image 08_04b.jpg. Drag the first thumbnail (08_04a.jpg) from the Photo Bin into the Final image pane on the right. Make sure that the option Show Strokes is activated, and then activate the Edge Blending option.

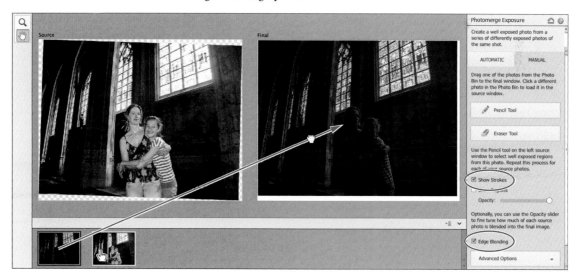

2   Use the Zoom and Hand tools to focus your view on the figures in the foreground; then, select the Pencil tool (✏) in the right panel. You won't need to change the default brush diameter.

3 Starting near the woman's right eye, draw carefully around the top of her head, staying as close to the outline of the hair as possible without moving the brush outside it, and then drag down the line between mother and daughter.

Tip: If you've copied unwanted background detail from around the woman's head into the Final image, use the Eraser tool from the right panel to remove that part of the line. Reduce the brush size for the Pencil tool by pressing the left bracket key ([ ) and try again, making sure that you stay within the outline of the woman's hair.

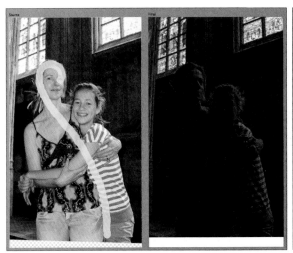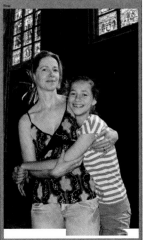

4 Zoom in on the daughter's head. Reduce the brush size a little, if you haven't done so already, and draw around the top of the girl's head, taking care not to move the brush outside of the outline, but making sure that you pick up the highlighted areas of the hair. If your stroke introduces unwanted background detail, click or make short strokes with the Eraser tool (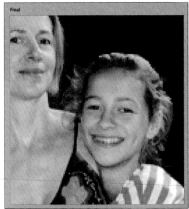) to correct it.

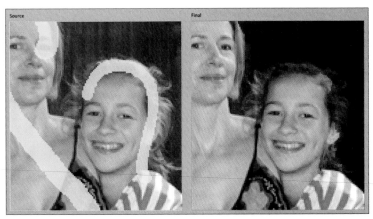

Tip: To more easily move the cropping handles by small increments, zoom in: press Ctrl / Command with the plus sign key to zoom, and press the spacebar to switch to the Hand tool.

5 Double-click the Hand tool, or choose View > Fit On Screen. Don't be concerned about the legs of our subjects' jeans—you'll crop that part of the image in the next step. Click the Next button at the right of the taskbar, and then, under Continue Editing, click In Expert.

6 Double-click the Hand tool; then choose Image > Crop. Drag the handles of the cropping rectangle to trim the image; then, commit the crop.

The merged image is a far better exposure than either of the original photos, but there is still plenty of room for improvement.

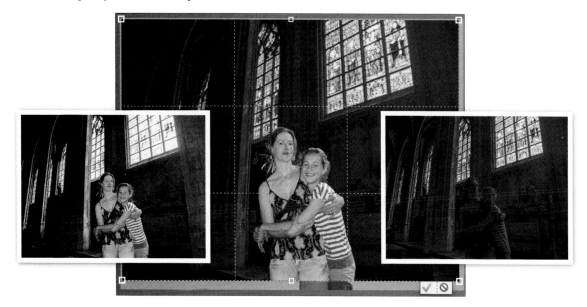

If we had much more time, we could add some detail from the flash-lit photo to the wall and columns, or try reversing the process by making the underexposed shot the Source image and copying the stained glass into the flash-lit photo instead.

7 Choose File > Save. Name the file **08_04_Merge_Manual**, to be saved to your My CIB Work folder, in Photoshop (PSD) format with Layers activated, and included in the Organizer. Click Save. Keep the file open for the moment.

Merging exposures automatically

Even in Automatic mode, Photomerge Exposure gives you a degree of control over the way that the source images are combined.

1 Click an empty area in the Photo Bin to deselect all the thumbnails. Ctrl-click / Command-click to select the two original photos in the Photo Bin, and then switch to the Photomerge category in Guided Edit mode. Click the interactive preview for Photomerge Exposure.

2 Click the Automatic tab at the top of the Photomerge Exposure panel; then, drag the Shadows slider all the way to the right to set a value of 100. This will lighten the shadows in the blended image, improving definition. Click the Next button at the right of the taskbar, and then, under Continue Editing, click In Expert.

3 Crop the image; then, choose File > Save. Name the file **08_04_Merge_Auto**, to be saved to your My CIB Work folder, in Photoshop (PSD) format with Layers activated, and included in the Organizer. Click Save. Keep the file open.

4   At the top of the Edit pane, click back and forth between the name tabs for the two merged images, 08_04_Merge_Manual and 08_04_Merge_Auto, to compare the results of the two blending modes. For our base images, the manual blend achieved a better exposure for the foreground subjects, while the automatically merged image reveals much more of the architectural detail.

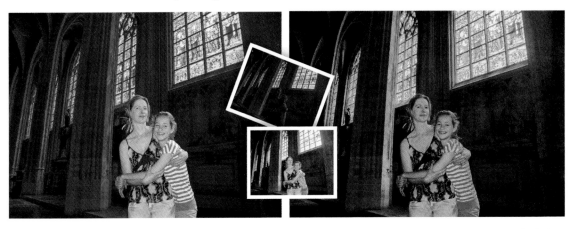

5   In the Photo Bin, deselect all the thumbnails; then, Ctrl-click / Command-click to select the last two images, 08_04_Merge_Manual and 08_04_Merge_Auto. Switch to the Photomerge category in Guided Edit mode and click the preview to launch the Photomerge Exposure process once more.

6   Click the Manual tab at the top of the Photomerge Exposure panel; then, drag the image 08_04_Merge_Auto into the Final pane. Use the Pencil tool to copy the figures from the manually merged photo to the automatically generated image; you won't need to be as careful as you were earlier. When you're done, click Next, move to Expert mode, crop the file, and save it as **08_04_Merge_Remix**.

7   Click back and forth between the name tabs for the three merged images you've produced to compare them. When you're done, choose File > Close All.

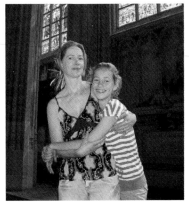
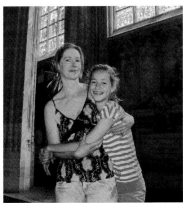
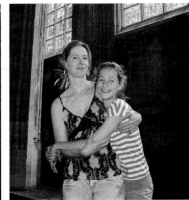

Photomerge Exposure—Manual   Photomerge Exposure—Automatic   Photomerge Exposure—mixed methods

Using layers to combine photographs

In this lesson so far, you've used some of the Photomerge tools to automate the process of combining photos. In this project, you'll take a more hands-on approach, using layers, selections, and masks to take full control over the way several source photos are combined to create a complex composite image.

1   In the Organizer, locate and select the images 08_05b.jpg and 08_05c.jpg: a scenic view of the ruins of a Scottish castle and a photo of a seagull in flight.

2   Click the Editor button (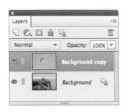) in the taskbar. In the Editor, click in the mode picker at the top of the workspace, if necessary, to switch to Expert mode.

Arranging the image layers

In the first part of this project, you'll arrange these two images on their separate layers, and then blend them to create a composite background.

1   Click the Layout button (▦) in the taskbar, and choose the All Row layout to tile the open image windows horizontally. Click the name tab of the image 08_05c.jpg (the seagull) to make it the active window.

2   Select the Move tool (✛), and hold down Alt / Option as you drag the seagull onto the coastal view. Release the mouse button and then the Alt / Option key. Holding the Alt / Option key as you drag a layer to another file ensures that the layer is aligned the same way in the target file as it is in the source, so that the image appears in the same position in the window. Close the image 08_05c.jpg.

3   If the Layers panel is not already visible, choose Window > Layers. In the Layers panel, make sure the layer with the gull is selected, and then choose Image > Resize > Scale. If necessary, click the Tool Options button (🖊) to show the tool options pane; then, choose View > Fit On Screen.

● **Note:** Depending on your operating system, the seagull layer may be named "Layer 1," rather than "Background copy," as illustrated here.

4   In the tool options pane, make sure that the option Constrain Proportions is selected, and then type **50%** in the W (width) field.

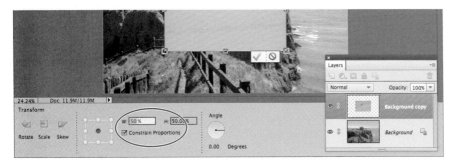

5   Position the pointer in the middle of the seagull photo and drag it to the upper-right corner of the image; then, drag the lower-left handle of the bounding box upward and to the right to reduce the image further. Keep your eye on the Width (W) and Height (H) values in the tool options pane; stop when both values reach 40%. Click the green Commit button on the bounding box to accept the changes.

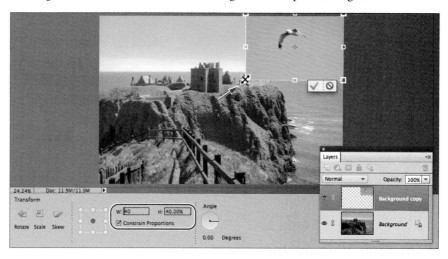

Creating a feathered layer mask

A layer mask allows only part of the image on a layer to show, and hides the rest by making it transparent. Layers lower in the stacking order will be visible through the transparent areas in the masked layer. In the next steps, you'll make a feathered selection and use it to create a soft-edged mask that will make it possible to blend the seagull into the sky in the background scene without a visible edge.

1   Select the Rectangular Marquee tool (⬚) in the toolbar. In the tool options pane, activate the elliptical variant of the marquee selection tool, and then use the slider, or type over the default value, to set the Feather amount to **50** px.

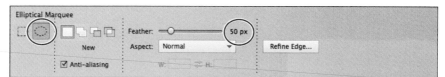

2   Starting from a point below the bird's body, drag an elliptical selection marquee, holding down the Alt / Option key as you drag to draw the marquee from its center. Release the mouse button when you have as much clearance around the seagull as is shown at the right. If necessary, drag the selection in the image window to center it on the bird.

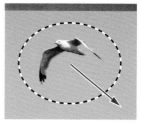

3   With the seagull layer selected, click the Add Layer Mask button (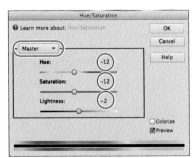) at the top of the Layers panel to convert the selection to a layer mask. In the Layers panel, the layer with the gull now has a black-and-white mask icon; only the part of the image corresponding to the white area still shows in the image.

4   To see the layer mask displayed in the image window as a semitransparent overlay, hold down the Shift key and then Alt-click / Option-click the layer mask thumbnail. Repeat the action to hide the overlay.

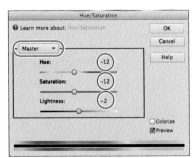

As you can see, the center of the mask is completely clear; the soft edge created by the feathered selection allows just enough clearance for the seagull. Though the selection is no longer active, you could edit the mask, if necessary, by painting directly onto it in black or white.

Although the feathered mask blends the image smoothly into the layer below it, the color in our wildlife photo still needs to be adjusted to match the background.

Matching the colors of blended images

Every color matching problem requires its own solution, but this exercise should at least give you an idea of what kinds of things you can try. In this case, you'll use a blending mode together with several different adjustments to color and lighting.

1   Double-click the colored thumbnail (not the layer mask) on the seagull layer to select the image rather than the mask; then, choose Enhance > Adjust Color > Adjust Hue/Saturation. In the Hue/Saturation dialog, use the sliders or type new values to set both the Hue and the Saturation to −12 and the Lightness to −2.

2   Use the menu above the sliders to switch from the Master channel to the Cyans channel. Set the Saturation value for the Cyans channel to −20. Switch to the Blues channel, and set the Saturation to −20; then click OK.

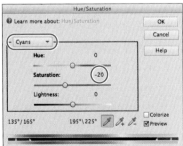
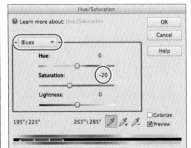

As you can see in the before and after illustration below, this combination of adjustments has not only matched the colors in the blended images but has also reduced the contrast and made the seagull a little brighter, helping it to fit in better with the slightly hazy aerial perspective in the background image.

▶ **Tip:** If you wish to tweak the position of the seagull, make sure its layer is active; then, select the Move tool and drag the bird by its center. The Move tool will not work if you try to drag a part of the image that is masked (invisible). Alternatively, once the Move tool is activated, you can nudge the selected layer with the arrow keys on your keyboard.

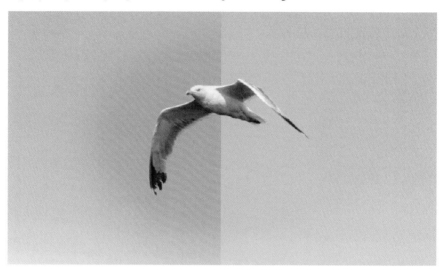

3   Choose File > Save As. Save the file to your work folder, in the Photoshop format with Layers enabled. Make sure that the image will be included in the Organizer but not in a version set. Name the new file **08_05_Composite**, and then click Save. Keep the blended image open for the next exercise.

Cleaning up selection edges

Defringing removes the halo of residual color that often surrounds a selection copied and pasted from one image to another. In this exercise, you'll add a foreground image of four sisters, select and delete the background from that photo, and use the Defringe feature to blend the selection halo into the background.

1   Choose View > Fit On Screen; then, choose File > Open. Navigate to and open your Lesson 8 folder. Select the file 08_05a.jpg, and then click Open.

2   With the image 08_05a.jpg selected as the active window, choose Select > All. Choose Edit > Copy, and then File > Close. Make sure the top layer of the composite image is still selected; then, choose Edit > Paste. The image of the four sisters is placed on a new layer, right above the layer that was selected.

3   With the new layer selected in the Layers panel, select the Move tool (⊹), and drag the photo of the girls to the lower-right corner of the image.

4   Click any of the handles on the bounding box. In the tool options pane, make sure that Constrain Proportions is selected; then, drag the upper-left handle of the bounding box upward and to the left to meet the left border of the image.

5 Click the Commit button at the lower right of the bounding box, then, use the right and down arrow keys to nudge Layer 1 just a fraction down and to the right.

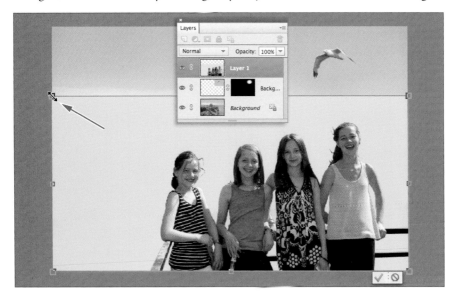

6 Click the Quick Selection tool, or whichever of its variants is currently visible at the right of the Lasso tool (◯) in the Select tools category. At the left of the tool options pane, activate the Magic Wand tool (✻). Set the Tolerance to **5**, activate Anti-aliasing, and disable the Contiguous and Sample All Layers options. Select the yellow background on Layer 1 with the Magic Wand tool.

7 Press the Delete key to delete the yellow background, and then press Ctrl+D / Command+D, or choose Select > Deselect, to clear the selection.

8 Zoom in to the space between the heads of the two sisters in the middle of the group. A yellowish fringe or halo is clearly visible around the girls' hair.

9 Choose Enhance > Adjust Color > Defringe Layer. In the Defringe dialog, type **5** pixels for the width, and click OK. Most of the fringe is eliminated.

▶ **Tip:** The Magic Wand tool (✻) is grouped together with the Quick Selection tool (◌) and the Selection Brush (✎) in the Select category at the top of the toolbar.

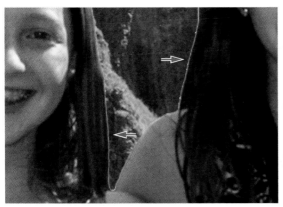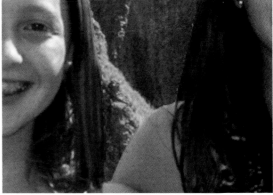

10 Double-click the Hand tool in the toolbox, or choose View > Fit On Screen, to see the whole image in the Edit window.

11 Select the Magic Wand tool (✷) once more, and click anywhere in the cleared area surrounding the girls. Choose Select > Modify > Border, and set a border width of **4** pixels; then, click OK.

12 Choose Filter > Blur > Blur More, and then repeat the command to soften the harder edges of the pasted image. Press Ctrl+D / Command+D, or choose Select > Deselect, to clear the selection.

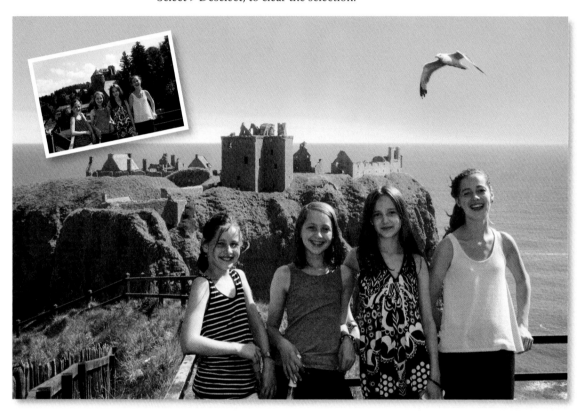

13 Choose File > Save, and then close the document.

Combining layers in Guided Edit mode

Now that you know what's involved in layering a composite image, you'll appreciate another of the latest additions to the Guided Edit mode; the Replace Background guided edit automates much of the process.

1 In the Organizer, select the image 08_06.jpg and click the Editor button (⬀) in the taskbar. In the Editor, switch to Guided mode. Click the preview in the Special Edits category to launch the Replace Background project.

2   Click the Select Subject button in the actions pane at the right. Which tool you use depends on the photo. In this case, Select Subject has done an admirable job of selecting the girl.

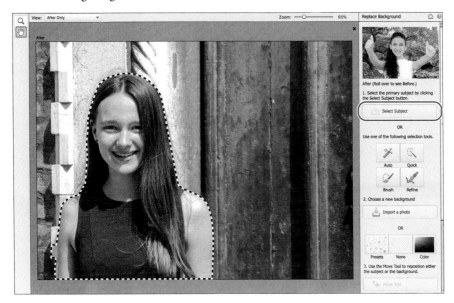

3   Switch to the Selection Brush. In the tool options pane, make sure the Selection Brush is set to Subtract From Selection mode. Set the brush size to 80 pixels and its hardness to 97%. Paint out any unwanted areas that have been selected; pay attention to the outline of the arm at the left, and the top of the girl's head.

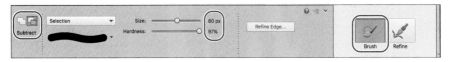

4   Set the Selection Brush to Add To Selection mode. Paint over any unselected areas that need to be included; pay particular attention to the bottom edge of the image, the girl's right shoulder, and the top of her head, left of the parting. You don't need to select the fly-away wisps of hair.

5   In the actions pane, click Import A Photo. Navigate to and open the Extras folder inside your Lesson 8 folder; then, select the image 08_06_Background.jpg and click Place. Switch to the Move tool and drag the background downward as far as you can, without exposing the upper edge. Drag the girl just a little to the right, stopping before the frame of the door behind her becomes visible.

6   If necessary, use the Refine Edge Brush tool to tidy up the girl's outline; look for fringes of the original background around her arms and hair.

7   Click Auto Match Color Tone, the last step in the guided actions pane. Wait while Photoshop Elements analyzes the photos and makes the adjustment.

Photoshop Elements applies a slightly "harder" contrast to the image of the girl, but the color tone still looks a little cool and out of place against the afternoon sunshine in the new background. You can adjust that easily in Expert mode.

8 Click Next at the lower right of the workspace; then, under Continue Editing, choose In Expert. Click to select the image thumbnail—not the black and white mask—on the top layer in the Layers panel.

9 Choose Enhance > Adjust Color > Adjust Color For Skin Tone. Click a neutrally lit area of the girl's skin—neither a highlight nor a shadow; then, drag the Ambient Light > Temperature slider a little to the right, moving it no more than the width of the slider button itself. Click OK.

10 In the Layers panel, click to select the middle layer, 08_06_Background. Choose Layer > Simplify Layer. Choose Filter > Blur > Gaussian Blur; then, set the blur radius to 8 pixels and click OK. The blurred background competes less with the subject and simulates a depth-of-field effect.

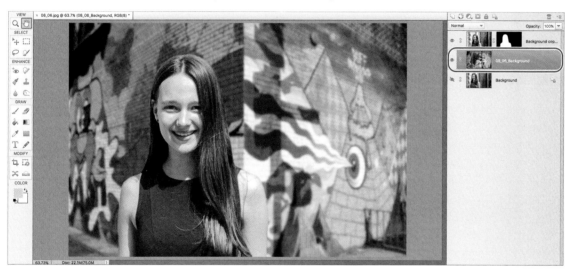

11 Choose File > Save As. Save the file with all its layers in Photoshop format, with an appropriate name and all the usual settings; then, choose File > Close.

Congratulations, you've completed the last exercise in this lesson. You've learned how to create a stunning composite panorama, merge multiple photos into the perfect group shot, remove obstructions from a view, combine elements from two photos, and compose several photos into a single image by arranging layers and using a selection to define a layer mask. You've also gained some experience with solving difficult lighting problems by combining shots taken at different exposures.

Take a moment to work through the lesson review on the next page before you move on to the next chapter, where you'll explore opportunities for unleashing your creativity with Photoshop Elements.

Review questions

1 What does the Photomerge Group Shot tool do?

2 How does the Photomerge Scene Cleaner work?

3 Why is it that sometimes when you think you're finished with a transformation in Photoshop Elements you can't select another tool or perform other actions?

4 Why does Photomerge Exposure sometimes open in Automatic mode and at other times in Manual mode?

5 What is a fringe, and how can you remove it?

Review answers

1 With the Photomerge Group Shot tool, you can pick and choose the best parts of several similar photos and merge them together to form one perfect picture.

2 The Photomerge Scene Cleaner helps you improve a photo by removing passing cars, tourists, and other unwanted elements. The Scene Cleaner works best when you have several shots of the same scene so that you can combine the unobstructed areas from each source picture to produce a photograph free of traffic and tourists.

3 Photoshop Elements is waiting for you to confirm the transformation by clicking the Commit button or by double-clicking inside the transformation boundary.

4 Photomerge Exposure detects whether your source photos were taken with exposure bracketing or with and without flash, and defaults to Automatic or Manual mode accordingly. Manual mode works better for source files taken with flash / no flash.

5 A fringe is the annoying halo of color that often surrounds a selection pasted into another image. When the copied area is pasted onto another background color, or the selected background is deleted, pixels of the original background color show around the edges of your selection. The Defringe Layer command (Enhance > Adjust Color > Defringe Layer) blends the halo away so you won't see an artificial-looking edge.

9 GETTING CREATIVE

Lesson overview

Once you've adjusted and polished your photos, Photoshop Elements offers a multitude of ways to add your own artistic touches; you've already experimented with some of the creative possibilities of the Recompose and Photomerge tools and designed your own custom effects in the Filter Gallery.

In this lesson you'll have some fun with the type tools and explore the Create mode, where Photoshop Elements makes it simple to create stylish, professional-looking projects to showcase your photos, from greeting cards and photo books to calendars and slideshows.

- Locating artwork in the Graphics library
- Setting up a photo project in Create mode
- Adding a creative touch with text and graphics
- Fitting text to an image
- Building a slideshow
- Working with layers, blend modes, layer styles, and effects
- Creating layer masks and type masks

 This lesson will take between 90 and 120 minutes to complete. To get the lesson files used in this chapter, download them from the web page for this book at www.adobepress.com/PSECIB2020. For more information, see "Accessing the lesson files and Web Edition" in the Getting Started section at the beginning of this book.

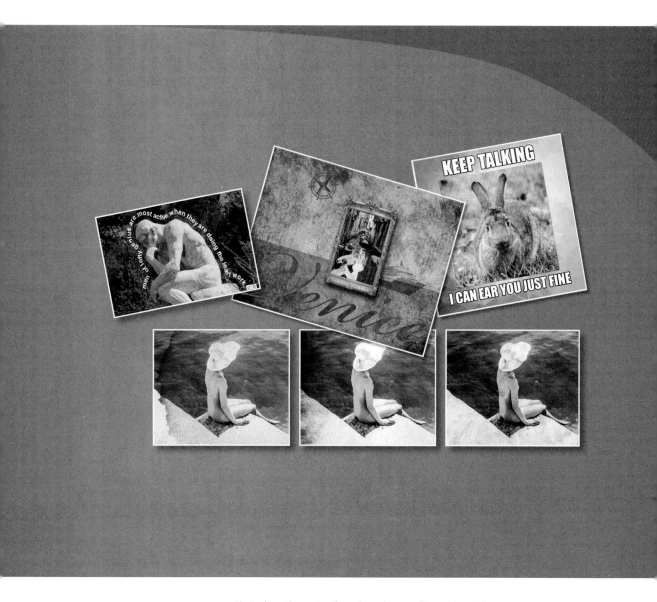

Photoshop Elements offers a huge library of layout templates and clip graphics, and a whole family of text tools that make it easy to produce eye-catching projects to showcase your photos. Show loved ones how much you care with stylish personalized greeting cards; preserve and share your precious memories in a sophisticated photo book; combine pictures, text, and effects to fit your photos to a practical purpose; or tell an evocative story in an artistic photo collage.

Getting started

Note: Before you start this lesson, make sure you've set up a folder for your lesson files and downloaded the Lesson 9 folder from your Account page at www.peachpit.com, as detailed in "Accessing the lesson files and Web Edition" and "Creating a work folder" in the "Getting Started" section at the beginning of this book. You should also have created a new work catalog (see "Creating a catalog for working with this book" in Lesson 1).

Begin by importing the sample images for this lesson to your CIB Catalog.

1 Start Photoshop Elements, and click Organizer in the Home screen.

2 In the Organizer, check the lower-right corner of the workspace to make sure that your CIB Catalog is loaded—if not, choose File > Manage Catalogs, and select it from the list.

3 Click the Import button at the upper left of the Organizer workspace, and choose From Files And Folders from the drop-down menu. In the Get Photos And Videos From Files And Folders dialog, locate and select the Lesson 9 folder.

4 Disable the option Get Photos From Subfolders; then, click Get Media.

5 In the Import Attached Keyword Tags dialog, click Select All; then, click OK.

On the arty side of the Editor

The Photoshop Elements Editor is much more than just a digital darkroom; when you're ready to go beyond simply improving your photos technically, you'll find that the Editor is also a versatile desktop design studio equipped with everything you'll need to give free rein to your creativity.

In Lessons 4, 5, and 6, you saw how even the standard tools for correcting color and lighting can also be used to achieve striking, evocative effects. In Lessons 7 and 8, you discovered ways to reinvent and reinterpret your photos with the image-editing magic of state-of-the-art content-aware editing and Photomerge technologies and by creating your own unique photo effects in the Filter Gallery.

In this lesson, you'll have a little fun with the type tools, practice some interesting creative techniques using layers and masks, and take a look at the Editor's Create mode, where Photoshop Elements can guide you through the process of designing stylish photo projects and presentations, from slideshows and photo books to calendars, greeting cards, and even customized CD or DVD labels.

Exploring the artwork library

Whether you're working with a preset project template in Create mode or building a photo-illustration layer by layer in Expert mode, Photoshop Elements makes it quick and easy to create distinctive photo projects by providing an extensive collection of backgrounds, frames, text styles, clip-art shapes, and graphics in the Graphics library. Although this artwork is also available in the Create mode, we'll start by exploring the Graphics panel in Expert mode.

1 In the Organizer, press Ctrl+Shift+A / Command+Shift+A, or choose Deselect from the Edit menu, to make sure you have no images selected in the Media Browser, and then click the Editor button (⬜) in the taskbar.

2 If the Editor is not already in Expert mode, click Expert in the mode picker at the top of the workspace, and then choose Window > Reset Panels. If you don't see tabs for the Layers, Effects, Filters, Styles, and Graphics panels at the top of the Panel Bin, click the arrow beside the More button (⬛) at the right of the taskbar, and choose Custom Workspace at the bottom of the menu.

3 Click the Graphics tab at the top of the Panel Bin to bring the Graphics panel to the front.

4 Click the menu icon (▼≡) at the far right of the Panel Bin's header bar, and make sure the option Large Thumbnail View is selected.

5 Move the pointer over the left edge of the Graphics panel; when the double-arrow cursor appears, drag the edge of the Panel Bin to the left to increase it to its maximum width.

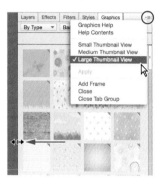

What you see displayed in the Graphics panel depends on the options set in the sorting menus above the thumbnail swatches. By default, the sorting menu at the left is set to "By Type." At this setting, the content of the library is sorted by functional category. The second sorting menu lists the categories: Backgrounds, Frames, Graphics, Shapes, and Text.

6 In the header of the Graphics panel, choose each category in turn from the second menu, and scroll down to see thumbnails of the artwork available.

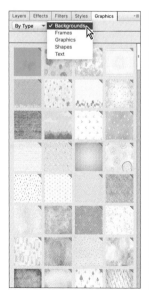
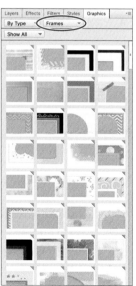
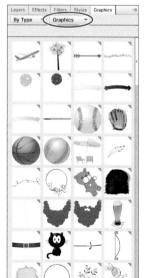
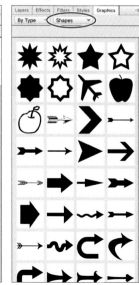

Using the Favorites panel

At first, the large number of choices in the Graphics panel may seem a little overwhelming, but you can easily locate the artwork you need by using the sorting and filtering menus at the top of the panel. These search functions are not available on the Graphics tab in Create mode, so it can save you time to do a little advance planning and assemble the items you want for a project while you're in Expert mode, using the Graphics and Favorites panels in tandem.

1 Choose Window > Favorites. Drag the Favorites tab from the header of the floating panel group to the bottom of the Panel Bin, and release the mouse button when you see a blue line indicating an insertion point below the Graphics panel. Close the floating panel group. Move the pointer over the upper edge of the Favorites panel; then, drag upward with the double-arrow cursor until the Favorites panel occupies about half of the space in the Panel Bin.

2 The Favorites panel already contains a small sample selection of popular graphics and image effects. To clear these items, select each swatch in turn and click the trash can icon in the Favorites panel header. Alternatively, you can right-click each swatch in turn and choose Remove From Favorites from the context menu.

▶ **Tip:** Hold the pointer over a swatch to see the item's name. If you can't find some of the graphics referred to in steps 3 through 7, Photoshop Elements has not yet finished downloading all of the project content that was not installed with the software. Make sure that you are connected to the internet; then, wait for a few minutes before working through these steps again.

3 Choose By Word from the sorting menu in the header of the Graphics panel. If you don't see the filter menu below the sorting menu and the Find button, change the sorting option temporarily to By Style, and then switch back to By Word. Type **paper** in the search box. Choose Backgrounds from the filter menu in the bar below the sorting menu, and then click Find. Drag the backgrounds Handmade Paper 03 and Handmade Paper 04 into the Favorites panel. You'll need these items later in this lesson for your Create mode project.

4 Set the filter to Frames. Locate the Paper Frame swatch and drag it into the Favorites panel. Swipe over the word "paper" in the search box and type **travel**. Choose Graphics from the filter menu, and then click Find. Drag the graphics Compass 02 and Cruise Ship into the Favorites panel.

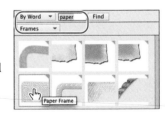

5 Choose By Color from the sorting menu, and then select Black from the colors menu. Set the filter to Backgrounds and add Black Folded Paper to your Favorites. Reset the filter to Frames and collect the Basic Black 40px frame.

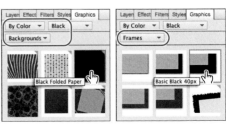

6   From the sorting menu, choose By Style; then, select Comic Book from the adjacent styles menu. Set the filter for Graphics; then drag the graphic named Speech Bubble 05 to the Favorites panel.

7   Change the style from Comic Book to Vintage. Set the filter for Frames and collect the frames Gold Frame Ornate, Gold Frame Round 2, and Old Black & Gold Frame and the background Blue Swirly. Change the style filter from Vintage to Decorative, and add the graphics Gold Flourish Corner and Silver Flower Spray to your Favorites. Check through the preceding steps to make sure that you've added all 14 of the artwork items in the illustration at the right.

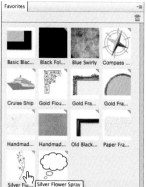

Note: At installation, the Graphics library contains only a small selection of items. Swatches marked with blue in the upper-right corner are *online assets* that will be downloaded to your computer automatically as soon as you place them in a project, so that your hard disk is not cluttered with unwanted items.

The Favorites panel can also store items from the Effects and Styles panels. To complete this exercise, you can now add some layer style effects that you'll use to refine your photo projects later.

8   Click the Styles tab at the top of the Panel Bin. Choose Drop Shadows from the style categories menu and drag both the High and Low drop shadow effects to the Favorites panel.

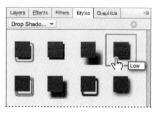

9   Click the Organizer button (⊞) in the taskbar to return to the Organizer.

Producing a photo book

Our exploration of the Create mode will focus on the Photo Book project—the most involved of those offered in the Create menu. The skills and techniques you'll learn for your photo book are applicable to all of the other Create mode projects.

A sophisticated, attractive way to present and share your memories, and an ideal output medium for digital scrapbooking, a photo book can make the perfect personalized gift for a loved one. You can either export your photo book in PDF format and have it printed and bound professionally, or print it yourself at home. For home printing, you'll need high-quality double-sided paper, and depending on the capabilities of your printer, you may need to scale your layout in the print dialog to fit within the printable area.

▶ **Tip:** If you don't see file names below the thumbnails in the Media Browser, select the Details and File Names options in the View menu.

1   Click the Lesson 9 folder in the My Folder list to isolate the images for this lesson. Make sure that the Sort By menu in the actions bar above the thumbnails is set to Oldest. In the Media Browser, select the image photobook_01.jpg; then Shift-click the image photobook_26.jpg to select all the images in the series.

2 Click the Create tab above the right panel group, and choose Photo Book from the Create menu. The Photo Book setup dialog opens.

Tip: You can change the units of measurement used in the Photo Book setup dialog on the Units & Rulers tab in the Editor's preferences dialog. If you don't see all of the themes shown in the illustration at right (the Themes menu should contain more than 30 templates in all), wait a few minutes while Photoshop Elements downloads project content that was not installed with the software.

3 The Sizes pane shows the size options available for your printer; choose the size closest to that shown in the illustration below. Scroll the Themes menu to see the design templates offered; then, choose the Colorful template. At the bottom of the dialog, set the number of pages for the photo book to **8**. For the purposes of this exercise, deselect the option Autofill With Selected Images; then, click OK.

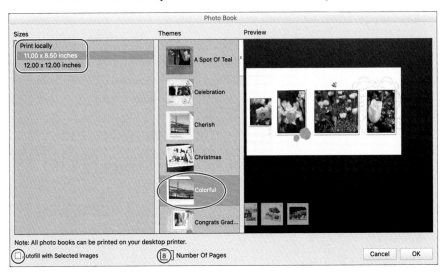

You'll see a series of progress bars as Photoshop Elements downloads online artwork assets, builds pages, and generates previews, and then the title page of the photo book appears in the Editor. The Pages panel at the right displays thumbnail previews for the title page and four two-page spreads.

4 Show the Photo Bin by clicking the Photo Bin button ( ) in the taskbar. The Photo Bin displays the images currently selected in the Organizer.

Tip: If you don't see thumbnails for a cover page and four two-page spreads in the Pages panel at the right, you may need to refresh the view. Click the Layouts button ( ) at the right of the taskbar; then, click the Pages button ( ) to reopen the Pages panel.

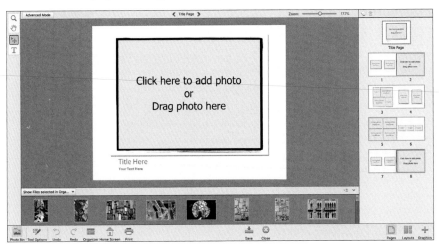

Changing page layouts

When Photoshop Elements generates Photo Book pages automatically, it applies a different layout to each page randomly, varying the number, size, and positioning of photos so that every spread has a unique design, as reflected in the Pages preview.

You can either accept the automatic layout as is or use it as a starting point and customize the design page by page. For the purpose of saving time in this project, we've prepared a tweaked layout designed to fit the lesson images, leaving it up to you to replace the page layout for the title page.

1   Choose File > Close, and then click No / Don't Save to discard the default layout. Choose File > Open. Navigate to and open your Lesson 9 folder; then, select the file Venice_Book.pse and click Open. On Windows, you'll need to select the Venice_Book.pse folder, and then select the Venice_Book.pse file and click Open.

▶ **Tip:** You may see a warning that text layers need to be updated for output. If so, select the option Don't Show Again, and then click Update.

2   In the Pages panel at the right, make sure that the title page is selected.

3   Click the Layouts button ( ) in the taskbar below the right panel. Scroll down in the Layouts menu to examine the variety of page design templates available. Hold the pointer over a layout preview thumbnail to see its name displayed in a tooltip. When you're done, click the arrow at the right of the Different Layouts header to collapse that category.

4   In the One Photo category, locate the template Photobook Landscape Grey-text and drag the layout preview thumbnail to the title page in the Edit window.

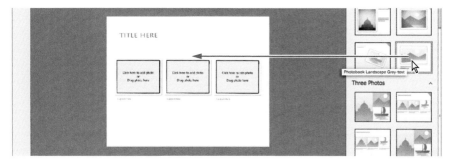

5   Click the Pages button ( ) in the taskbar below the right panel, and examine the completed base layout in the Pages preview. Including the cover page, the design now has the correct number of placeholders for our 26 lesson photos. Three of the placeholder frames may be hard to spot, as they fill whole pages, with smaller frames arranged on top of them (pages 2, 4, and 5).

Rearranging the order of images in a project

When you create a photo book—or any other photo project—and have Photoshop Elements place your photos automatically, the images are arranged in the layout template in the same order in which they appear in the Photo Bin.

For a multipage project such as a photo book, you can save time and effort by arranging your photos before you begin. In the Organizer, you can establish a custom sorting order by creating an album. Once you're in the Editor, the easiest way to change the order of your images is by simply shuffling them in the Photo Bin.

1 If necessary, click the Photo Bin button (⬛) in the taskbar to show the Photo Bin. Make sure the menu at the left of the Photo Bin header is set to Show Files Selected In Organizer. If you don't see file names, right-click in the Photo Bin and choose Show Filenames from the context menu.

▶ **Tip:** If you accidentally open the image photobook_05.jpg, simply close it and then try again, dragging in a single action rather than first clicking and then dragging.

2 Drag the image photobook_05.jpg to a new position to the left of the image photobook_02.jpg so that it becomes the second image in the Photo Bin.

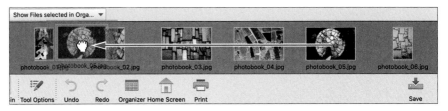

3 Scroll the Photo Bin until you can see some empty gray space at the end of the series of lesson photos. Right-click in this empty space and choose Autofill With Photo Bin Photos. Wait while Photoshop Elements places the images and regenerates the page previews.

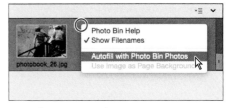

4 Hide the Photo Bin by clicking the Photo Bin button at the left of the taskbar. Choose File > Save.

Working with backgrounds

You can change the page background, like any other element in a preset theme template, as easily as you changed the layout. You can move, rotate, scale, or delete the preset background, just as you can with a frame or clip-art graphic. Unlike with an image in a frame, however, you can't simply select and drag the background image. As the "foundation" of the file, the locked Background layer is a special case: for some operations, it will need to be "simplified"—unlocked and converted to standard bitmapped data—before it can be edited as other layers can.

▶ **Tip:** If the layer names are truncated, move the pointer over the edge of the Layers panel and drag with the double-arrow cursor to make the panel wider.

1 In the Pages panel, click the first two-page spread, pages 1 and 2; then, click the Advanced Mode button at the left of the actions bar above the Edit window. Click the Layers button (⬙) in the taskbar to open the Layers panel. From the panel options menu at the right of the Layers panel header, choose Collapse All Groups. Choose Window > Favorites to open the Favorites panel. Drag the Favorites panel to position it where it won't obstruct your view.

2   Double-click the Black Folded Paper background swatch In the Favorites panel. Wait while Photoshop Elements downloads this online asset to your computer; then, watch both the Layers panel and the preview spread in the Edit window as the Background layer is updated.

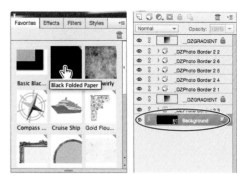

The new background graphic has been scaled to fit across the width of the two-page spread, but the right half is hidden by the full-page image on page 2. The gray strip at the center of the layout is part of the frame around that image.

3   With the Move tool (⊹) selected in the toolbar, right-click the full-page image on the right page of the spread, and choose Clear Frame from the context menu. You now have a clear view of the line where the inside edges of the facing pages meet at the center of the spread.

We could make more of the subtle textural detail in this background by reducing it to cover only the left page. To move, scale, or rotate the background, you first need to use the Move Background command to unlock it on the Background layer.

4   Right-click the background where it's visible on the left page, and choose Move Background from the context menu. A bounding box now surrounds the background graphic, though most of it is out of view because the image is larger than the two-page spread. Test this by dragging the background downward; then, drag the image back to its original position.

5   In order to scale or rotate the background manually, you could drag the image to access the control handles, but in this case it will be more convenient to use the controls in the tool options pane. Click the Tool Options button (🗒✏) in the taskbar, if necessary. In the tool options pane, type **50**% in the Width (W) text box; with the Constrain Proportions option activated, the Height (H) value will be updated automatically. The background image is scaled by 50% from its center.

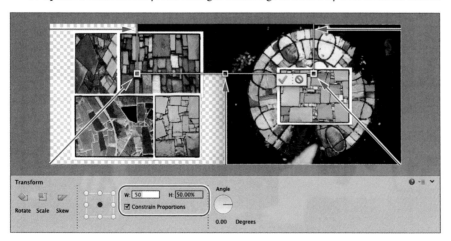

6   Drag the reduced background artwork, and position it flush with the left edge of page 1. Move the image up and down until you're pleased with the placement of the detail, and then click the Commit button (✔) to apply the changes.

7   Without the background covering the entire spread, a thin margin of white shows around the large photo on the right page. Click the image; then, click once on any of the bounding box handles. Rather than drag the handles to scale the image and its containing frame, type **101**% in either the W or H text box in the tool options pane; then, commit the change.

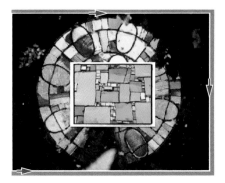

8   Drag the Basic Black 40px frame swatch from the Favorites panel onto each of the five smaller, framed photos in the layout; then, click the background.

9   Choose File > Save. Click the Pages button (▯) in the taskbar to open the Pages panel. In the Pages preview, click the third spread in the photo book: pages 5 and 6.

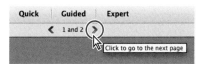

Alternatively, you can navigate to the page 5/6 spread by clicking twice on the right-facing arrow above the Edit window.

Working with photos and frames

You've already replaced photo frames in a page layout by substituting artwork from the Graphics library; in this exercise, you'll learn how to manipulate a photo and its frame as a single grouped design element, and how to modify a photo's position and orientation independently of the frame with which it's grouped.

1   You can start by replacing all seven frames in the page 5/6 spread. If necessary, choose Window > Favorites to reopen the Favorites panel, and then drag the Old Black & Gold Frame from the Favorites panel onto each of the four small images on the left page, and the Paper Frame onto the three photos on the right.

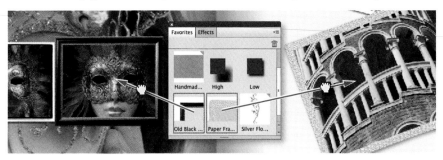

2 Double-click the Handmade Paper 04 swatch to replace the background; then, right-click the full-page image on the left of the spread, and choose Clear Frame from the context menu.

3 To move a framed photo, simply drag it with the Move tool (⊹). Shift-click each of the four small images on the left page to select them. Start dragging the row of photos downward; then, hold the Shift key to constrain the movement as you position them halfway between the girl's eyes and the mouth of her mask.

▶ **Tip:** When the Move tool is active, you can use the arrow keys on your keyboard to move selected project elements in small steps instead of dragging them with the mouse.

4 Click the background to deselect the four photos, and then reselect the image at the left. Hold the Shift key as you drag the framed photo about halfway to the left edge of the page. Move the photo on the right end of the row the same distance in the opposite direction. Select all four images; then, click the Tool Options button (📝), if necessary, to show the tool options pane. Click the Middle button in the right-hand column under Distribute to automatically space the second and third photos evenly between the first and fourth images.

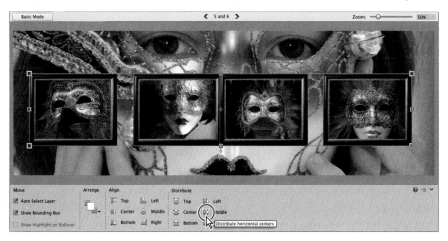

5 Right-click each of the three photos on the right page in turn, and choose Fit Frame To Photo from the context menu for each. The frames are resized so that their outside borders conform to the edges of the images.

6 Click to select the image at the right; then, drag the handle at the lower right of the bounding box to enlarge it—together with its frame—until the right edge of the image extends beyond the boundary of the page. You don't need to use the Shift key; the proportions of the frame group are constrained by default. Click the Commit button (✓).

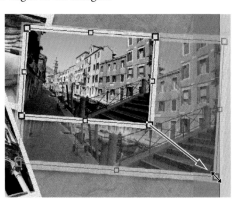

7   Drag or nudge the three tilted photos into a pleasing arrangement, scaling or rotating them as you wish. To rotate a framed photo manually, select the photo and move the pointer close to one of the corner handles, staying just outside the bounding box; when the curved double-arrow cursor appears, drag to rotate the image. Hold the Shift key as you drag to constrain the rotation to 15-degree increments. Always click the Commit button (✓) to commit the changes.

▶ **Tip:** If a photo does not fill its frame properly when scaled or rotated, right-click the photo and choose Fit Frame To Photo. Alternatively, double-click the photo, and resize it within its frame by using the slider, as discussed in the next exercise, "Adjusting a photo inside a frame."

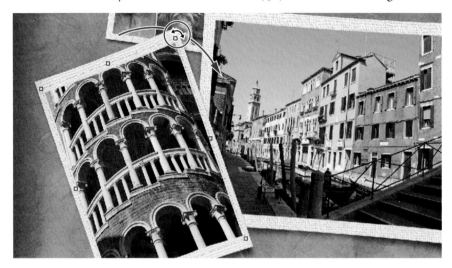

8   Choose File > Save. Click the right-facing arrow above the Edit pane to move to pages 7 and 8.

Adjusting a photo inside a frame

Although a photo frame appears to be overlaid on the image it surrounds, the two elements actually occupy the same layer (by default, a layer for a framed photo even takes its name from the frame graphic). As a result, the standard moving, scaling, and rotating operations affect the photo and frame as if they were a single object. In this exercise, you'll learn how to transform a photo independently of its frame; but first, you'll change the background and frames for the last spread in your book.

1   Reopen the Favorites panel and double-click the Handmade Paper 03 swatch in the Favorites panel to replace the background for the page 7/8 spread; then, drag the Basic Black 40px frame swatch onto each of the four images on page 7. You can keep the default frame for the large photo on page 8.

There are two text frames, at the lower left of page 8, that were part of the preset layout. The white placeholder text is a little difficult to see, but even on a white background, you could easily locate and select the text frames in the Layers panel.

2   If necessary, show the Layers panel. From the Layers panel options menu, choose Collapse All Groups. Shift-click to select both _TXTFrame layers, and press Backspace / Delete on your keyboard. Click Yes to confirm the deletion.

When you move a framed photo, or use its bounding box handles to scale or rotate it, the photo and frame are transformed together.

To move or transform a photo inside its frame, right-click the image and choose Position Photo In Frame from the menu—or alternatively, double-click the photo with the Move tool (⊕). A control bar appears above the photo, with a scaling slider and buttons to reorient the image or replace it with another.

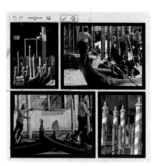

Scale photo

Rotate photo 90°
Browse to replace photo

3   Right-click the image on the right page, and choose Position Photo In Frame from the context menu. Hold down the Shift key to constrain the movement as you drag the image to the left within its frame so that the border no longer cuts off the gondolier on the right. Commit the change.

4   Use the Zoom tool (🔍) to focus on the photos on the left page. We'll deal with the image at the lower right in the next step; for the other three, right-click each image in turn with the Move tool and choose Position Photo In Frame. Use the slider to reveal as much of each image as possible, without resizing the frames. Drag each photo within its frame to arrange the most interesting crop; then commit the changes.

5   You can rotate the last of the four photos within its frame to straighten the blue and white gondola poles. Right-click the image, and choose Position Photo In Frame. To rotate the photo inside its frame, move the pointer close to any bounding box handle; when the pointer becomes a curved double-arrow cursor, drag the handle in either direction. Scale and position the photo within its frame as you did with its three neighbors; then, commit the changes.

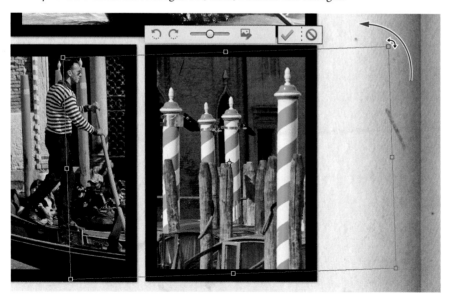

6   Move the large photo on the right downward to align the lower edge of its frame with the group on the left. Double-click the Hand tool to see the entire spread.

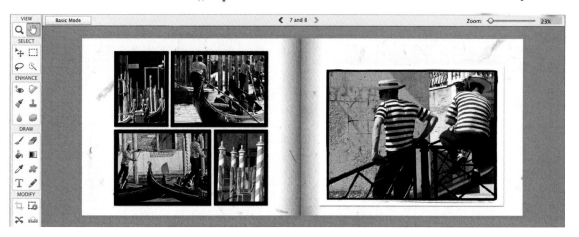

7   Click the left-facing arrow above the Edit pane twice to move to pages 3 and 4.

Refining your photo book layout using layers and effects

In this exercise, you'll begin to polish your photo book design while you refresh some of the skills that you've picked up in the course of this lesson.

You'll start by customizing pages 3 and 4—the last untreated spread—then, you'll add some sophistication to the layout using a little layer magic.

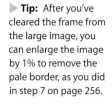

Tip: After you've cleared the frame from the large image, you can enlarge the image by 1% to remove the pale border, as you did in step 7 on page 256.

1   Double-click the Handmade Paper 03 swatch in the Favorites panel to replace the background; then, drag the Paper Frame swatch onto each of the three images on the left page. Drag the Gold Frame Ornate swatch onto the photo of an antique interior on the right page and the Gold Frame Round 2 swatch onto the photo of the couple. Right-click the large backing image on the right, and choose Clear Frame from the context menu. From the Layers panel options menu, choose Collapse All Groups.

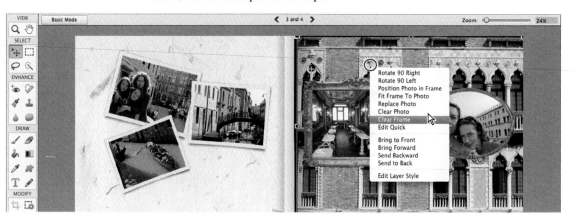

2   Right-click each of the three photos on the left page, and choose Fit Frame
    To Photo from the context menu. Drag or nudge the three tilted photos to
    position them, and scale or rotate them as you wish. If you want to change the
    stacking order of a photo, right-click the image and choose Bring To Front,
    Bring Forward, Send Backward, or Send To Back from the context menu. Scale,
    move, or rotate each photo within its frame as needed, referring to the previous
    exercises if you need to refresh your memory.

3   For each of the two gold-framed photos, first make sure you are happy with the
    scaling and placement; then, select the framed image, right-click its layer in
    the Layers panel, and choose Simplify Layer. Without this step, it would not be
    possible to apply layer styles to these particular framing groups.

4   Drag the High drop shadow swatch from the Favorites
    panel onto both of the gold-framed images on page 4.
    In the Layers panel, double-click the *fx* icon at the
    right of the listing for each of the simplified layers in
    turn to open the Style Settings dialog, where you can
    adjust the settings for the drop shadow effect. For
    both of the simplified gold-framed images, reduce the
    Distance setting to **55** px, and then click OK.

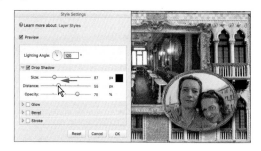

5   Click to select the full-page backing image on the right
    of the spread. At the top of the Layers panel, use the
    slider to reduce the selected layer's opacity to 40%.

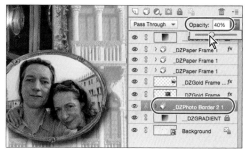

Although this image is no longer grouped with a frame
graphic, it is still contained in an invisible photo-holder
frame, within which it can be moved, scaled, and rotated,
just as you did with the other photos.

6   Revisit the page 5/6 spread, and apply the High drop shadow effect to the four
    small photos on the left page, first simplifying the respective layers in the Layers
    panel, as you did in step 3, and then editing the effect as you did in step 4.

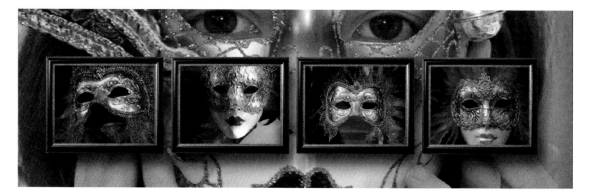

Reordering the pages in a photo book

If you feel that a particular spread would look better placed at a different point in your photo book, it's easy to change the page order.

1 You can start by revisiting the first spread: pages 1 and 2. Move, tilt, and scale the upper-right photo of the group on page 1 to add variety by breaking up the regular arrangement a little (see the illustration below step 3).

2 Double-click the smaller image on page 2; then, click the Rotate Right button to rotate this portrait-format photo to suit its horizontal frame. Use the slider to reduce it to fit the frame. When you're done, click the green check mark to commit the change.

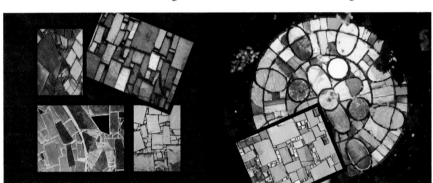

3 Rotate and move the image, together with its frame, to reveal more of the full-page image and hide the out-of-focus foliage at the bottom. Commit the changes.

▶ **Tip:** While you're working on a complex project like a photo book, you should save regularly to avoid losing time and effort.

4 Click the Pages button (⬜) in the taskbar to show the Pages preview. Drag the first spread downward. Release the mouse button when you see an insertion line appear between the page 3/4 and page 5/6 spreads. The first and second spreads change places, and the pages are renumbered. If the Pages panel previews are slow to redraw, click each of the thumbnails in turn.

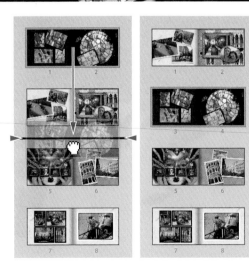

Adding graphics to a project

It's easy to liven up a page design with a judicious use of graphics from the content library. You'll start by adding some atmosphere to the title page, so the front cover of your photo book will create an evocative first impression.

1 Use the left arrow button in the bar above the Edit pane, or click the top thumbnail in the Pages preview, to move to the title page; then, click the Layers button () in the taskbar to open the Layers panel. Collapse the layer groups.

2 The preset text frames included in many page-layout templates are useful for simple titles and captioning, but for this project you'll create your own text layers from scratch. Shift-click to select both of the text frames below the framed image, or select the two TXTFrame layers in the Layers panel; then, press Backspace / Delete on your keyboard, and click Yes to confirm the deletions.

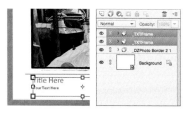

3 Click the Tool Options button (), if necessary, to show the tool options pane. Select the framed photo, and then click any of the bounding box handles. In the tool options pane, type **30**% in the Width (W) text box; with Constrain Proportions activated, the Height (H) value is updated automatically. Click the Commit button under the image frame.

4 While the framed photo is still selected, double-click the Gold Frame Ornate swatch in the Favorites panel; then, right-click the image, and choose Fit Frame To Photo.

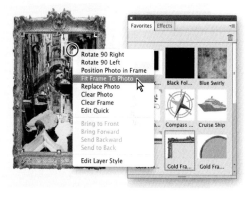

5 In the Favorites panel, double-click the Blue Swirly swatch to replace the background. In the Layers panel, right-click the Background layer, and choose Duplicate Layer from the context menu. Click OK to accept Background Copy as the default name for the duplicate layer.

6 At the top of the Layers panel, set the layer blending mode to Multiply and the opacity to **50**%. In the Edit window, hold the Shift key to constrain the movement as you drag the new layer downward until it covers a little more than one third of the cover page.

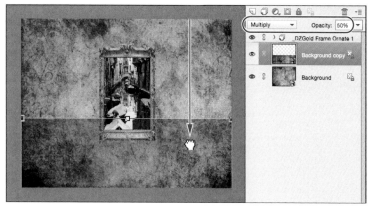

7   Drag the swatch for the graphic Cruise Ship from the Favorites panel to the right side of the page. Watch the W (Width) and H (Height) values in the tool options pane as you drag one of the corner bounding box handles to enlarge the graphic to around 200%. Choose Image > Rotate > Flip Layer Horizontal; then, click the check mark below the bounding box to commit the change.

8   Drag the ship to position it as shown in the illustration at the right. To move the ship behind the photo frame, right-click the graphic and choose Send Backward from the context menu.

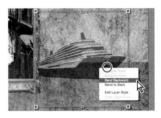

9   Drag the graphic Compass 02 from the Favorites panel to the upper left of the page, placing it as shown below. At the top of the Layers panel, change the blending mode for the new layer to Difference, and set the layer's opacity to **70%**. Change the opacity for the Cruise Ship layer to the same value.

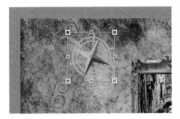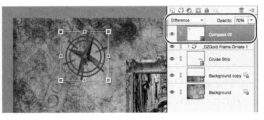

Placing text in a layout

In this exercise, you'll add a title on the cover and a message on the last page.

1   Select the Horizontal Type tool (T); then, choose Bickham Script Pro Regular from the font menu in the tool options pane. Type **460** pt in the font size text box. Click the Center Text option, and ensure that Anti-aliasing is selected so that the letters are smoothed. Click the text color swatch below the font menus, and sample Light Green Cyan.

Tip: If your Color Swatches picker looks different from the one in the illustration, resize it to show 12 swatches per row.

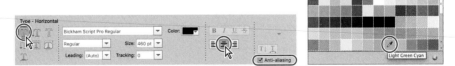

2   Click below the photo, and type **Venice**; then commit the text. At the top of the Layers panel, change the blending mode for the text layer to Difference and the opacity to **90%**; then, drag the text layer downward in the layer order to position it below (behind) the framed photo. Drag the title, or use the arrow keys on your keyboard, to center it horizontally. Select the compass and the photo together and drag them to the right to center the frame above the "n" in Venice.

3 Right-click the layer _DZGold Frame Ornate 1 in the Layers panel, and choose Simplify Layer from the context menu; then, drag the High drop shadow effect from the Favorites panel onto the framed photo. In the Layers panel, double-click the *fx* icon on the frame layer, and reduce the drop shadow's Distance setting to **55** px; then, click OK.

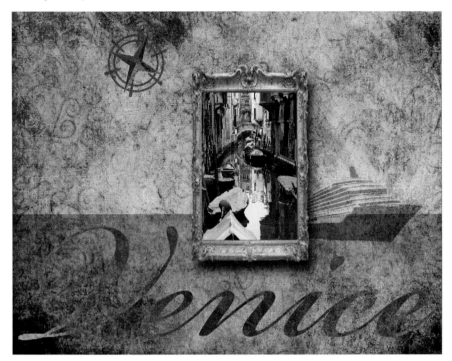

4 Navigate to the last spread in the layout. Drag the Speech Bubble 05 swatch from the Favorites panel onto page 8. Use the handles on the bounding box to scale and stretch the shape; then, position it as shown in the illustration at the right. Commit the changes.

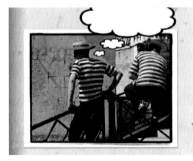

5 With the speech bubble graphic still selected, switch to the Type tool. Use the same font and text alignment setting you chose in step 1, but change the font size to **40** pt, the font style to Bold, and the text color to black. Click the arrow beside the Leading text box and change the Leading setting from Auto to **30** pt. Click in the center of the speech bubble, and type **Gondola: mid 16th century**; then, Press Enter / Return, and type **"to rock and roll."** (including the quote marks and period). Click the Confirm button, and drag the text to adjust its position.

6 Use the navigation buttons above the Edit window preview to move to the page 1/2 spread. Drag the graphic Silver Flower Spray onto the left page. Rotate the artwork 90° counterclockwise, and scale it to almost the width of the page. Move the flower spray so that it extends off the top edge of the page, and commit the change. In the Layers panel, collapse all layer groups; then, move the layer Silver Flower Spray down in the stacking order so that it lies below (behind) at least one of the paper-framed photos and above (in front of) at least one other.

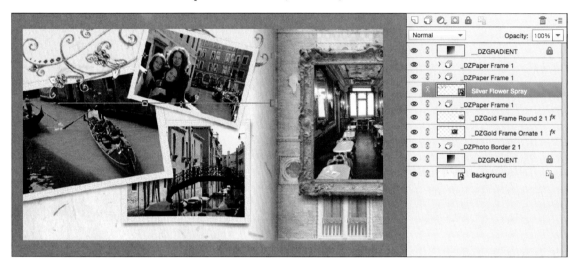

7 Use the navigation buttons to move to the page 5/6 spread. Drag the Gold Flourish Corner graphic onto the right page. Choose Image > Rotate > Flip Layer Horizontal, and then Image > Rotate > Flip Layer Vertical. In the Layers panel, collapse all layer groups; then, change the blending mode for the new layer to Screen. Move the Gold Flourish Corner layer below (behind) all of the Paper Frame layers. Scale the graphic and position it as shown below; then, commit the changes.

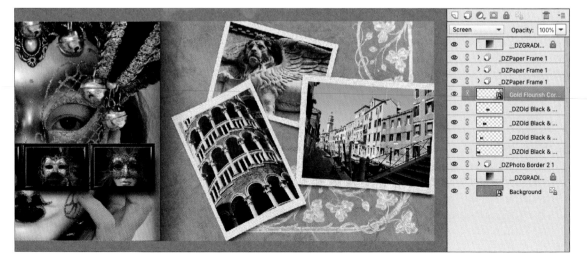

8   The photo book is complete; choose File > Save. By default, photo projects are saved in Photo Project format, a multipage document format that preserves text and layers so that they can be edited later. You could also choose to save the project as a PDF file that can be shared as an email attachment.

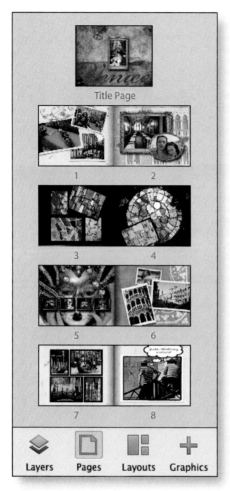

9   Choose File > Export Photobook. In the Export Photobook dialog, choose the PDF format. Click Browse to specify your My CIB Work folder as the Save To Location; then, click OK. Choose File > Close, and close without re-saving.

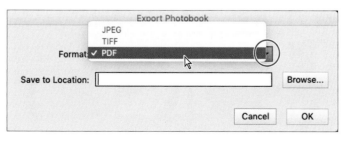

Creating a slideshow

Whether you're sharing memories at home with family and friends, presenting your work to a client, or posting to a social media or sharing site, a slideshow makes a compelling and dynamic way to showcase your photos.

For this project, we'll use a set of photos captured in New York, but if you prefer, you can import a selection of your own photos and then improvise a little as you follow the exercise steps.

1 In the Organizer, isolate the Lesson 9 images, and then set the Sort By option to Name. Shift-click to select just the first nine photos in the Slideshow series. Click the Create tab and choose Slideshow from the menu; then, watch as the default slideshow plays through.

2 When playback has finished, click the Themes button ( ) in the actions bar at the left.

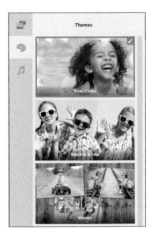

On the Themes tab, the Slideshow Editor offers a choice of preset templates with a variety of slide layouts and transition styles. Once you choose a theme, you can edit the titles, add captions, and change the default soundtrack.

3 Try a few of the templates by double-clicking the thumbnails on the Themes tab. You can interrupt playback at any time by clicking the Themes button. When you're done, double-click to apply the City Lights template.

4 Pause and resume playback by pressing the spacebar, or use the pause and play controls on the playback bar. Use the slider to adjust the volume of the soundtrack music. Click the Media button ( ) in the actions bar.

The Media pane shows the nine photos that you selected, and a preset title screen.

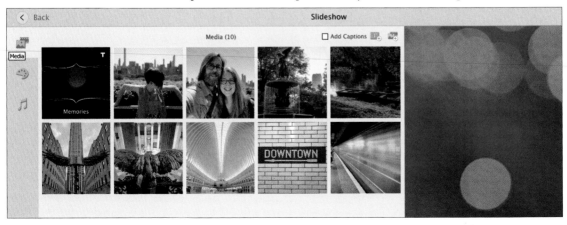

5 Click the Add Photos And Videos button at the upper right of the Media pane and choose Add Photos And Videos From Organizer.

6 Activate the Media From The Grid option under Basic to view only the Lesson 9 images. Scroll down and Shift-click to select the last three of the New York images. Click the Add Selected Media button; then, click Done.

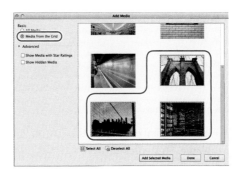

The three new images appear in the Media pane of the Slideshow Editor.

7 In the Media pane, Shift-click to select the last two images in the second row, and then drag them to the left; release the mouse button when you see a blue line in front of the first image.

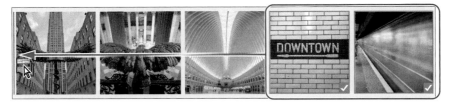

8 Activate the option Add Captions, at the right above the Media preview. Add a caption to every second or third photo in the Media pane by clicking in the text box below the image and typing a short phrase.

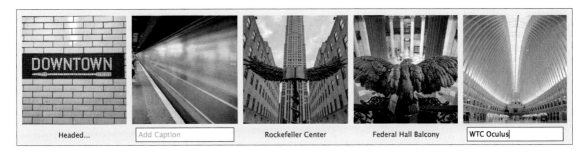

Another way to add text to your presentation is to add a title slide that can help introduce a theme, provide information, or create atmosphere.

9 In the Media pane, right-click the default title slide and choose Edit; then, click the arrow at the right of the text screen preview twice to select the third layout option. Type **Seeing the Sights** in the Title text box, and then click in the Subtitle text box and type **in the Big City**. Click Save to apply the changes.

10 Each theme includes a music track; to replace the default soundtrack, click the Audio button (♫) in the actions bar; then click the minus sign at the right of the track Citylights in the Selected Tracks list.

▶ **Tip:** For a more involved title screen, such as the cover of the photo book in the previous project, create a new slide in the Editor, where you can work with layers, effects, extras from the Graphics library, and a full suite of text tools.

Note: For our lesson project, the presentation includes only 12 photos; for a large selection of images, you can add as many music tracks as you wish.

11 Click the Add Audio button at the upper right of the Audio list. Navigate to and open the Extras folder inside your Lesson 9 folder. Select the file Backslider.m4a and click Open. Click the plus sign to the right of the new track in the Audio list to add it to the Selected Tracks list. Then, click the Audio button in the actions pane to launch the slideshow preview. Watch until playback is complete.

12 Click the Save button (not the arrow beside it) above the preview pane. Type **NY Sights** as the name for the slideshow, and then click Save.

You can open and edit your saved slideshow at any time from the Media Browser to add photos, change the slide order or the music, or update titles and captions.

Exporting the slideshow to YouTube, Vimeo, or disk

Once you've saved your slideshow, you can share it as a video to YouTube or Vimeo—or export it to your hard disk as a high-definition video file. By way of example, we'll share the slideshow to YouTube.

Tip: The procedure for sharing to Vimeo is similar; if necessary, you will first be required to sign in or create an account.

1 In the Slideshow Editor, click the Export button at the upper right. Choose YouTube and wait while Photoshop Elements converts your slideshow to video. In the YouTube dialog, sign in if necessary; then enter a title and description and specify a sharing audience. For now, click Cancel rather than posting the video to your YouTube channel.

2 Click the Export button again, and choose Export Video To Local Disk so that you have a finished version ready to play. In the Export dialog, type a name for your slideshow, specify your My CIB Work folder as the destination, and choose either 720p HD or 1080p HD from the Quality settings; then, click OK to save the slideshow in MP4 video format. When asked if you'd like to import the video into the Organizer, click No.

3 Click Back to exit the Slideshow Editor.

Making your own meme

At some point early in the rise of social media, memes developed a specific visual style: a photo or illustration surrounded by a saying or clever quip overlaid in blocky white letters. They're easy to read, especially as people are scrolling their Facebook, Twitter, or Instagram timelines. You could put one together in the Editor easily, but that would still involve a bit of work. Instead, with the Meme Maker guided edit, you can quickly create a viral image that could spread worldwide—or at least put a grin on the faces of family and friends.

1 In the Organizer, isolate the Lesson 9 photos, if necessary; then, click to select the image 09_meme.jpg. Click the Editor button (⌾) in the taskbar.

2 In the Editor, switch to the Guided Edit mode and click the Fun Edits category. Click the Meme Maker option.

3 Click the Create Meme Template button, which resizes the photo and puts it inside a colorful border; you'll have the chance to change the border soon.

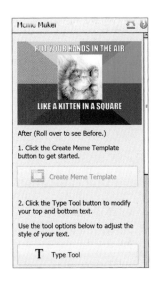

4 Click the Type Tool button, or double-click the top block of text to select it. In the tool options pane, set the Size to **96** pt and type **KEEP TALKING** (in all caps). Although you can type in normal sentence case, memes are usually written uppercase to grab attention. When you're done, click the Commit button (✔). In the bottom text block, which is automatically selected next, set the size to **72** pt, type **I CAN EAR YOU JUST FINE**, and commit the change. Next, drag the top text down so it's not hugging the top of the border.

Note: If you can think of a more memetastic phrase, by all means enter that instead. Your version is no doubt much bunnier than this one.

5 In the actions pane at the right, drag the Zoom control to 130 to make the rabbit more prominent within the frame.

6 A border isn't necessary for a meme—select the Fit Photo To Canvas check box to see what the text looks like overlaid on the photo. Since we want to explore more border options, deselect the option.

7 Click the left-hand box under step 4, (Optional) Choose A New Border. Click any style to preview it, then select the second-to-last version. Click OK.

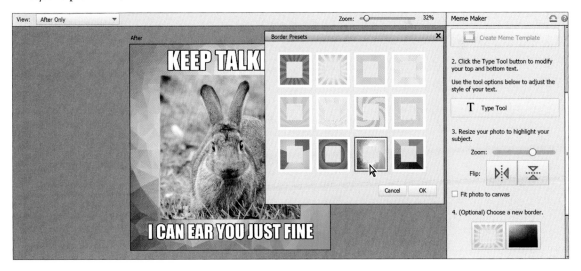

8 Choose File > Save As. Name the new file **09_Meme_Bunny**, to be saved to your work folder in Photoshop format with layers enabled. Include the image in the Organizer but not as part of a version set. Click Save; then, click Next and then Done. Close the file.

Creative framing with layer masks

There are endless ways to use layer masks to edit, blend, and combine photos. In this exercise you'll paint directly into a layer mask to produce a free-form cutout frame—another great way to add creative flair to an everyday image.

1 In the Organizer, isolate the images for this lesson, if necessary, by clicking the Lesson 9 folder in the My Folders list. Select the image 09_Girls.jpg in the Media Browser; then, click the Editor button (⌨️) in the taskbar.

2 If the Editor is not in Expert mode, click Expert in the mode picker, and then choose Window > Reset Panels. If you don't see tabs for the Layers, Effects, Filters, Styles, and Graphics panels at the top of the Panel Bin, click the arrow beside the More button (▦) at the right of the taskbar and choose Custom Workspace from the menu. Drag the Layers panel out of the Panel Bin by its name tab and position it where it won't block your view of the Edit pane.

3 Right-click the image's single layer, the Background layer, and choose Duplicate Layer from the context menu. In the Duplicate Layer dialog box, click OK to accept the default layer name, Background Copy.

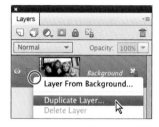

4 Click the eye icon (👁️) beside the Background layer to hide it. With the new layer, Background Copy, selected in the Layers panel, click the Add Layer Mask button (▣) at the top of the panel.

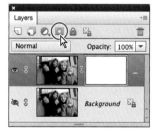

The new Layer Mask thumbnail on the Background Copy layer is highlighted by a blue border, indicating that it is selected—or active—and ready for editing.

5 Choose Edit > Fill Layer. In the Fill Layer dialog box, choose Black from the Use menu, and then click OK.

The solid black fill in the layer mask obscures the photo on the Background Copy layer completely. With the Background layer also hidden from view, the image window shows only the checkerboard pattern that indicates layer transparency.

6 Click the barred eye icon (👁️) beside the Background layer to make the layer visible again. Hold the Shift key, then Alt-click / Option-click the layer mask thumbnail to show the mask as a semi-transparent red overlay.

7 Click the Eraser tool (✏️) in the toolbar to select the tool and access the tool settings. In the tool options pane, make sure that Brush is selected in the eraser's Type options at the right and that the Opacity is set to 100%.

8 Click the arrow beside the sample brush stroke to open the Brush Picker, and choose Thick Heavy Brushes from the Brushes menu. The name of each brush appears in a tooltip when you hold the pointer over the swatch. Double-click the second brush in the set, the Rough Flat Bristle brush; then, press the right bracket key (]) six times to increase the brush size to 300 pixels.

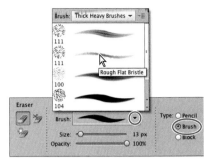

9 With the Eraser tool, scribble a rough line in the image window to quickly clear the red overlay from the faces of all four girls.

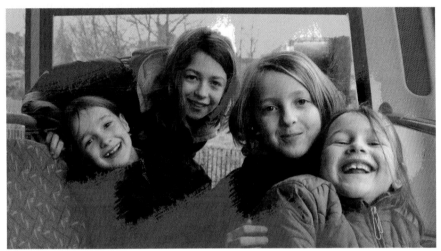

10 Hold down Shift+Alt / Shift+Option and click the layer mask thumbnail to hide the mask overlay; then, click the eye icon to hide the Background layer again. As you can see, the Rough Flat Bristle brush is partly transparent. In the image window, make another short stroke or two over each girl's face.

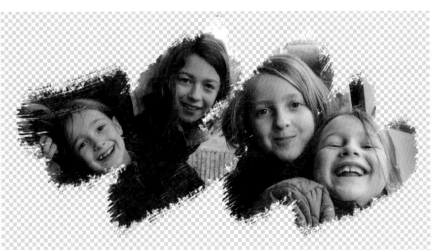

▶ **Tip:** When you wish to make a hard-edged mask, you can use any of the mechanical selection tools (either the Rectangular or Elliptical Marquee tool, or the Polygonal Lasso tool) rather than a brush or an eraser. You could also use any of the bitmapped Shapes options from the Graphics library as the basis for your clipping mask.

You could place a new background on a lower layer, either by pasting from another photo or by choosing from the background artwork in the Graphics library. For now, you'll save your work and look at a related Guided Edit effect.

11 Choose File > Save As. Name the new file **09_Girls_BrushMask**, to be saved to your work folder in Photoshop format with layers enabled. Include the image in the Organizer but not as part of a version set. Click Save; then, close the file.

Making a photo look like a painting

The Painterly guided edit uses layer masks to make a photo look like a work of art, complete with brush strokes, texture, and effects.

1 Open the same image that you used in the previous exercise in the Editor, 09_Girls.jpg, and then switch to the Fun Edits tab in the Guided Edit mode. Click the preview for the Painterly project.

2 Click the Paint Brush button and choose Bold Strokes from the preset menu. Reduce the brush size to **155** pixels and click two faces that are not beside each other. Increase the brush to **170** pixels and use the Brush Angle control to rotate the brush at least 45 degrees; then, click the other two faces. Make a few more clicks to pick up as much of the photo as you like, changing the brush size, angle, and opacity each time. Switch the brush to Hide mode, and vary the size, angle, and opacity as you make a few more clicks around the edges of the image.

3 Choose a basic black or white canvas, or click the Select Custom Color button and use the eyedropper to pick up a color from the image.

4 Choose a texture and an artistic effect to finish the project.

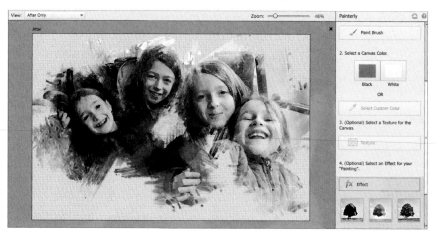

5 Click the Next button; then, click Save As. Activate the option Include In The Elements Organizer and disable Save In Version Set With Original. Name the file appropriately, and then save it to your My CIB Work folder. Close the file.

Applying a watercolor effect

A photo that is turned into a painting can take on an abstract look, as in the previous project, or a more subtle—but no less beautiful—treatment. The Watercolor Effect guided edit turns photos into watercolors that you'd swear were created with paint.

1 In the Organizer, select the image 09_Mediterranean.jpg and click the Editor button (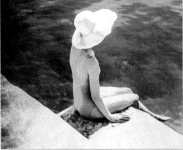) in the taskbar. In the Editor, switch to Guided mode. Click the preview in the Special Edits category to launch the Watercolor Effect project.

2 In the actions pane at the right, the first step is to select from three preset watercolor effect styles; for our lesson image, choose Effect 1, the softest of the three styles.

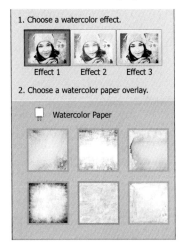

3 Click Watercolor Paper and sample a few of the simulated paper styles; the options range from wet paper styles to distressed and antique surfaces, boosting the watercolor effect by adding the look of natural materials. When you're done, click the second thumbnail in the second row, a wet paper with inky, pastel hues.

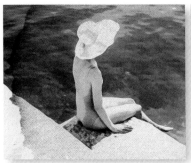

4 Set the opacity of the simulated surface to 80%; as you drag the slider, the numerical value appears in a tooltip above the pointer.

5 Now click Canvas Texture and select the second thumbnail to apply the coarsest of the texture options. You can leave the intensity setting at the default.

6 Click the Refine Effect Brush. Make sure the brush is in Subtract mode and set its size and opacity to **50** pixels and **80%**, respectively. The Refine Effect Brush softens or removes the effect of the watercolor paper overlay in areas where it interferes with the image. Soften the wet paper detail on the crown of the girl's hat and the front of its brim. Set the brush opacity to **100%**; then remove the inky stains from the girl's bare back and arms, and the sunlit parts of her legs.

7 Click the Type tool; the tool options pane opens below the preview. Set the type options as shown below. Choose the font Lithos Pro Regular, and then set the color to white and the size to **48** pt. Type in the text box to set the leading to **40** pt. Click the third of the alignment buttons to right-align the text.

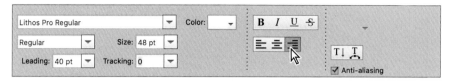

8 Click to set a text insertion point that is centered vertically in the image and a little inside the right edge. Type **dreaming of**; then, press Enter / Return and type **the islands**. Click the green check mark to commit the text; then, drag the text to center it between the girl and the right edge of the image. Align the top of the text with the point where the hat brim intersects the girl's neck.

9 Click the Text Style button in the actions pane and choose Style 2; then, click the Advanced button. In the Style Settings dialog, set the lighting angle to **135°**. Use the Drop Shadow controls to set the size of the shadow to **10** pixels, the distance to **20** pixels, and the shadow opacity to **25%**; then, click OK.

10 Click Next at the lower right of the workspace; then, under Continue Editing, choose In Expert. In the Layers panel, use the eye icon beside each layer in turn to hide and show the layer. Select each layer in turn and inspect its blending mode and opacity settings. Experiment with the layered image in any way that interests you, remembering to undo each change.

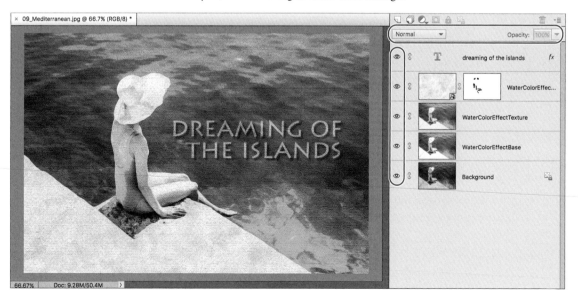

11 Choose File > Save As. Save the file with all its layers in Photoshop format, with an appropriate name and all the usual settings; then, choose File > Close.

Making part of a photo look like a sketch

If you can make an entire photo look like it was created using a different medium, why not apply an effect to just portions of it? The Partial Sketch guided edit uses the Editor's selection and filter tools to make it easy for you to get creative with a sketched photo.

1 In the Organizer, select the image 09_Kayak.jpg and click the Editor button (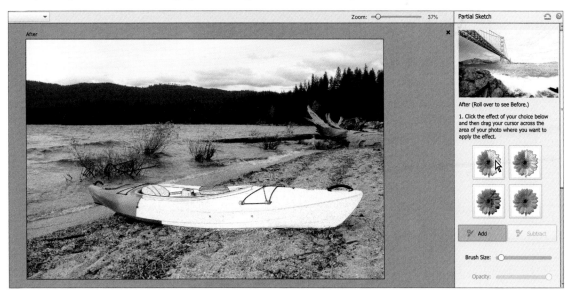) in the taskbar. In the Editor, switch to Guided mode. Click the preview in the Fun Edits category to launch the Partial Sketch project.

2 In the actions pane at the right, select one of the four sketch types.

Doing so activates the Add selection brush below them, but the effect isn't visible until you make a selection. Ultimately, we want the vibrant kayak to remain photographic against the sketched background, but waving the selection brush around the image is more work than you need to do. So at this point, we will apply the effect to the kayak and then invert the selection at the end of the project.

3 Set the Brush Size to **75** and drag within the kayak to select it; the sketch effect is immediately applied to the selected area. Adjust the diameter of the brush using the bracket keys ([,]) as needed to select fine details, such as the handles at the front and back. Use the Zoom slider to zoom the image and get in close to the detail areas. For selections that extend beyond the kayak itself, such as the sand in shadow in the foreground, switch to the Subtract brush or hold Alt / Option as you click. While you're working on the selection, click each of the four effect styles to preview them, ending up at the original Pencil Sketch option.

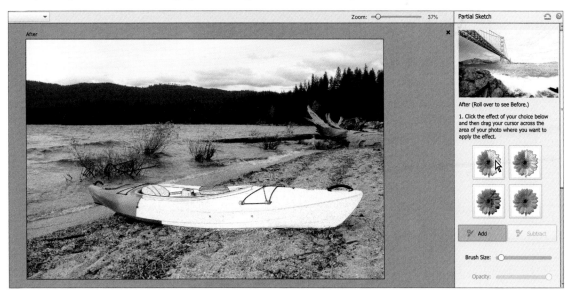

4 If the selection brush isn't giving you the results you want, such as the corners of sand revealed within the front handle, click the Detail Brush button. This brush paints pixels, not selections, which can sometimes help in tight spots like that.

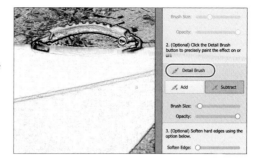

5 Drag the Soften Edge slider to 3.

6 Choose View > Fit On Screen to view the entire image, if necessary. Next, click the Flip Effect button at the bottom of the actions pane to invert the selection.

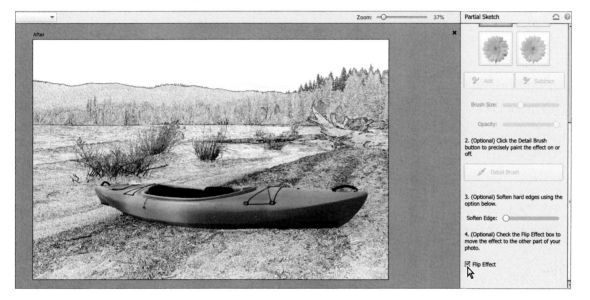

7 Click Next at the lower right of the workspace; then, under Continue Editing, choose In Expert.

8 In the Layers panel, click the layer mask in the Pencil Sketch 1 layer to select it. Switch to the Brush tool (✐) and make sure the foreground color is set to Black. If there are still any areas you want to touch up or display as the original photograph, such as the beach or the sky, paint those areas using the brush.

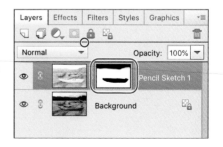

9 Choose File > Save As. Save the file with all its layers in Photoshop (PSD) format, with an appropriate name and all the usual settings; then, choose File > Close.

Creating a photo collage

Photoshop Elements has long been the tool of choice for scrapbookers and people who like to build collages. The recently revamped Photo Collage project makes it easy to assemble and edit a collage using several templates, including ones for Facebook cover photos and Instagram posts.

1   In the Organizer, select the images Slideshow_01.jpg through Slideshow_04.jpg; then, click the Editor button (⌷).

2   Click the Create button above the right panel group, and choose Photo Collage. The Editor opens and builds a simple two-by-two collage.

3   In the pane at right, double-click the Landscape 2 variant to rebuild the layout.

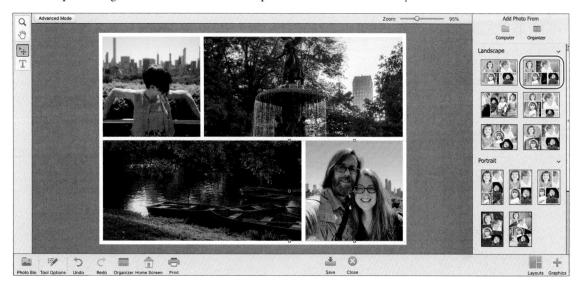

4   Click any photo to select it, and then drag to reposition it in its frame if needed. To change the placement of any of the photos, right-click one and choose Drag To Swap Photo. Then, drag it to another space in the layout.

5   You can add or remove photos; the Editor automatically changes the layout to accommodate. To add one, click Organizer under Add Photo From at the top of the pane. In the Add Photos dialog box, make sure Photos Currently In Browser is active, select the image of the Brooklyn Bridge, and then click Done.

▶ **Tip:** You can change the background and frame styles for each photo by clicking the Graphics button in the side panel and dragging an item to the layout.

6   When you're happy with the results, click the Save button at the lower right. Name the file **09_Photo_Collage**, and save it to your My CIB Work folder in Photo Project (PSE) format, with Layers enabled. Include the new image in the Organizer but not in a version set; then, close the file. Also close the slideshow images you opened.

Making an instant effects collage

Many of the guided edit procedures enable you to apply creative touches that can add style, impact, or humor to any image in just a few clicks. You can highlight your subject with a graphic shape overlay or even make it look like an unfinished jigsaw puzzle! In this exercise, you'll try the Effects Collage project.

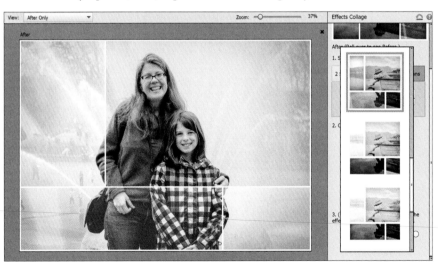

1 In the Organizer, select the image 09_fountain.jpg; then, click the Editor button (⬛). If you're not in Guided Edit mode from the last exercise, switch modes now.
Click the Effects Collage preview in the Fun Edits category to start the project.

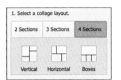

2 The first step is to choose a layout for your collage. In the Effects Collage pane, the layout presets are grouped by number of sections. Click through a few of the options to see how the layouts fit with the lesson photo; then, select a preset. We chose the 4 Sections, Horizontal layout.

3 Click the colored preview thumbnail and sample a few of the style presets, each of which will apply a different effect to each section of your design. Choose a style preset; then, experiment with the Opacity slider.

● **Note:** Every photo responds differently to the effects applied by the various style presets. If you would prefer to replace one or more sections of your collage with an effect you saw in another style preset, run this exercise again using a different style with the same layout, making sure to name the saved file differently. Open both saved files in Expert mode; then, cut and paste from one collage to the other.

4 When you're happy with the results, click the Next button at the lower right; then, click Save As. Name the file **09_Effects_Collage**, and save it to your My CIB Work folder in Photoshop (PSD) format, with Layers enabled. Include the new image in the Organizer but not in a version set; then, close the file.

Getting creative with text

Adding a title or caption is a great way to fit an image to a specific purpose, such as a cover page for a printed document or a title screen for a slideshow, but text can also be used imaginatively to suggest meaning, emphasize context, add humor, or evoke emotion. Photoshop Elements delivers a suite of type tools that provide limitless creative possibilities for fitting text to your images, whatever the purpose.

Fitting text to a selection

One of several type tool variants that enable you to shape your text creatively to image elements in your photos, the Text On Selection tool makes it easy to wrap your message around any pictured object.

1 In the Organizer, select the images 09_Type1.jpg and 09_Type2.jpg in the Media Browser, and then click the Editor button (▨) in the taskbar. Make sure the Editor is in Expert mode; then, choose Window > Reset Panels. If you don't see tabs for the Layers, Effects, Filters, Styles, and Graphics panels at the top of the Panel Bin, click the arrow beside the More button (▤) at the right of the taskbar and choose Custom Workspace from the menu. At the top of the Edit pane, click the name tab for 09_Type1.jpg to bring its image window to the front.

The Text On Selection tool (▧) can make its own selections, but it can also be used with a selection that is already established. For this exercise, you'll first create and fine-tune a selection so that you can have your text follow a path well outside the edge of the selected object, rather than wrapping tightly to its outline.

2 In the toolbar, click the Quick Selection tool (▧), beside the Lasso tool. If you don't see the Quick Selection tool, Alt-click / Option-click its variant, the Selection Brush (▧), to switch tools; then drag inside the sculpture to select the figure, together with his seat. You don't need to be very precise, but if you go too far, hold down the Alt / Option key as you paint to subtract from the selection.

3 When you're done, choose Select > Modify > Expand. In the Expand Selection dialog box, set the Expand By value to **40** pixels; then click OK. Alt-click / Option-click the Quick Selection tool to switch to the Selection Brush (▧). Use a medium brush to round out any tight angles on the selection outline. Hold the Alt / Option key as you paint to remove any obvious lumps and bumps along the edge.

For the sake of comparison, the illustration at right shows the expanded Quick Selection as a dashed line, and the smoothed outline as a red overlay, which is just as you'll see it if you switch the Selection Brush to Mask mode.

● **Note:** Try choosing Select > Subject to make your initial selection. Unfortunately, that command doesn't work as well for this statue. No worries: that's what the Quick Selection tool is for.

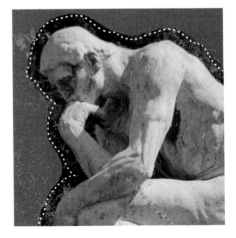

4 In the toolbar, click whichever variant of the Type tool is currently visible. In the tool options pane, select the Text On Selection tool (T) from the seven tool variants at the left. Set the font to Arial Bold and the size to **18** pt; change the text color to white.

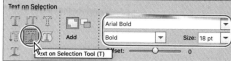

5 Move the tool over the image in the Edit window; the pointer changes to the Quick Selection cursor. Click inside the active selection; then click the green check mark to convert the selection into a path for your text.

6 Move the tool over the newly created path; the pointer becomes a text insertion cursor. Click above the figure's neck and type this quote from Leonardo da Vinci: **men of lofty genius are most active when they are doing the least work**.

7 The tool options pane now shows the full suite of options for horizontal type. If necessary, activate the Center Text (≣) alignment option.

▶ **Tip:** When you're dragging to reposition the text, be careful to keep your cursor on the outside of the outline; otherwise, the text will flip to wrap around the inside of the path. You can add extra spaces between words or letters, where needed, to reduce clumping.

8 Click in the text near your starting point with the text insertion tool. Release the mouse button; then, hold the Ctrl / Command key and drag the text left or right to fine-tune its placement on the path, referring to the illustration below. When you're happy with the result, click the green check mark to commit the text.

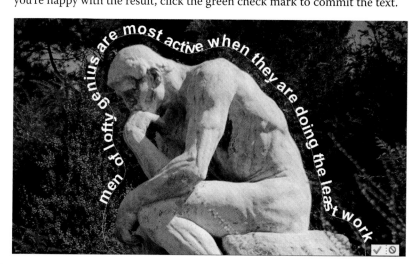

9 Choose File > Save. Name the file **09_Thinker**, to be saved to your work folder in Photoshop format with Layers enabled, and included in the Organizer but not as part of a version set. Click Save, and then close the file.

Wrapping text around a shape

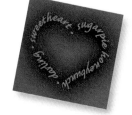

The Text On Shape tool (T) works in much the same way as the Text On Selection tool, except that the first step is to draw a vector shape with one of a selection of shape tools, rather than to make a selection.

1 With the image 09_Type2.jpg in the Edit pane, hold Ctrl / Command and press the minus sign key three or four times so you can see a lot of empty gray space around the photo, as shown in the illustration for step 3.

2 In the toolbar, click the Text On Selection tool, or whichever type tool variant is currently active. In the tool options pane select the Text On Shape tool (⊞) from the variants at the left. Set the font to Brush Script Std Medium and the size to **36** pt. Choose the Ellipse tool from the shape options. You'll apply color to the type in the next exercise.

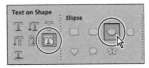

▶ **Tip:** If you don't have the Brush Script font, choose another script typeface, or any font of comparable weight that has a similarly organic feel.

3 Hold down the Alt / Option key so that your shape will be drawn from the center outward. Drag with the Ellipse tool, starting from a point in the gray "artboard" well below the image, and a little right of center. Match the ellipse to the upper curve of the rainbow, making sure to allow clearance so that your text will run parallel to the rainbow, rather than interfering with its edge.

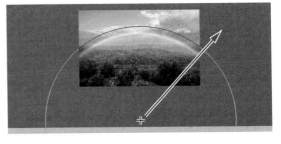

4 Hold down Ctrl / Command and press the plus sign key three or four times so that the photo fills your view. Move the Text On Shape tool over the upper edge of the ellipse and click with the text insertion cursor at the highest point of the curve. Type **Somewhere, under the Rainbow**. Click the green check mark.

▶ **Tip:** If your first attempt at creating an ellipse doesn't match the rainbow's curve, press the Delete key to remove that text shape and then try again.

Once you've committed the text, the Move tool becomes active by default, and the text becomes selected as an object that can be moved, scaled, and rotated on its own layer, just like any other graphic. To edit the content of the text, you would first need to activate one of the type tools.

5 Drag the text, or use the arrow keys on your keyboard, to adjust its placement.

Using preset text styles

You can apply any of the filters and layer styles from the Effects panel to your text, adding bevels, shadows, glows, textures, and gradients to create your own text effects. Some editing operations require that you first "simplify" the text layer to a bitmapped graphic that can no longer be edited as live text. In this exercise, you'll apply a preset text style from the Graphics panel instead.

1 Click the Graphics tab at the top of the Panel Bin. Set the Graphics panel's sorting menu to By Type, and then choose Text from the adjacent categories menu. Scroll down through the swatches to see the many preset styles available in the Graphics library.

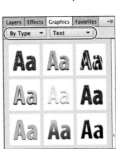

2   Drag the Gradient Blue Medium style from the fourth row of text presets onto the text in the Edit pane; then, click the green check mark to commit the change.

3   Click the Layers tab at the top of the Panel Bin to show the Layers panel. Double-click the *fx* icon on the text layer to open the Style Settings dialog box. Set the Lighting angle to **−90**. Select the box to activate the Drop Shadow effect. Increase the drop shadow Size to **10** px, and the Opacity to **85**%. Click the small color swatch beside the Drop Shadow settings and change the color from black to a deep, saturated blue; then, click OK to close the Style Settings dialog box.

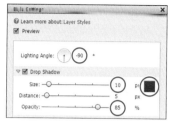

4   As a final touch, you can soften the effect a little by using the slider at the upper right of the Layers panel to reduce the opacity of the text layer to 85%.

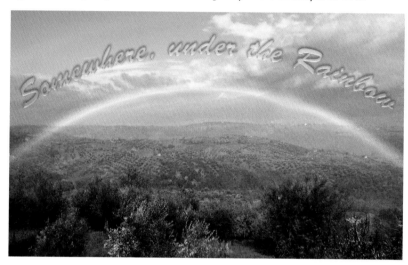

▶ **Tip:** Your text is still "live" and editable. Simply double-click the text to activate the text tool; then swipe over the words you wish to edit, or place the text insertion point and start typing to add to the message.

5   Save the file as **09_Somewhere**, and then close it.

More fun with type

As its name suggests, the Text On Custom Path tool—the last of this group of type tools—lets you draw and tweak a freehand path for your text to follow, providing the perfect solution for images like the example at the right, where creating a path automatically from a selection is not an option.

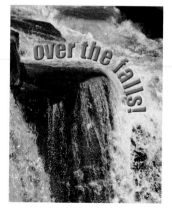

Try clicking the Create Warped Text button at the right of the Type tool controls in the tool options pane to discover how you can warp, bloat, pinch, twist, and otherwise torture your type.

Creating a type mask

The Type Mask tool (⊤) turns text outlines into a layer mask through which an underlying image is visible, effectively filling the letter shapes with image detail. This can create far more visual impact than using plain text filled with a solid color.

● **Note:** The Type Mask tool has one variant for horizontal type and another for vertical type.

1 In the Organizer, isolate the lesson images by clicking the Lesson 9 folder in the My Folders list. Right-click the image 09_Runners.jpg and choose Edit With Photoshop Elements Editor from the context menu.

2 Make sure the Editor is in Expert mode; then, choose Window > Reset Panels. If you don't see tabs for the Layers, Effects, Filters, Styles, and Graphics panels at the top of the Panel Bin, click the arrow beside the More button (◼️) at the right of the taskbar and choose Custom Workspace from the menu.

3 Drag the Layers panel out of the Panel Bin by its name tab and position it where it won't block your view of the Edit pane. Choose Window > Favorites and drag the Favorites panel to a convenient position. Choose Window > Panel Bin to hide the Panel Bin; then, double-click the Hand tool or choose View > Fit On Screen.

4 In the toolbar, click whichever variant of the Type tool is currently visible in the bottom row of the Draw category. In the tool options pane, click to select the Horizontal Type Mask tool (⊤) from the tool variants at the left.

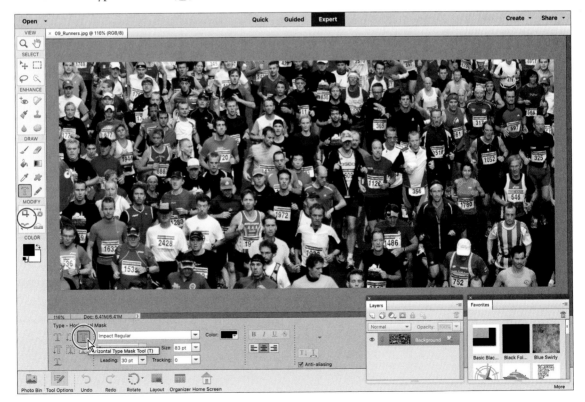

5 Set up the text attributes in the tool options pane: Choose a font from the Font Family menu. We chose Impact Regular, but if you don't have that font, choose any typeface that's blocky enough to let plenty of the image show through the letter forms. Type a new value of **950** pt for the font Size (you may need to adjust that for a different font). Choose Center Text (⊟) from the paragraph alignment options. You don't need to worry about a color for the text; the type will be filled with detail from our marathon image.

6 Click at a horizontally centered point low in the image and type **RUN!**

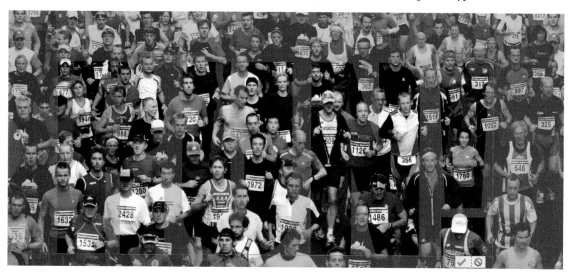

7 Hold down the Ctrl / Command key on your keyboard; a bounding box surrounds the text in the image window. Drag inside the bounding box to reposition the type mask.

8 If you wish to resize the text, hold the Ctrl / Command key and drag a corner handle of the bounding box. The operation is automatically constrained so that the text is scaled proportionally. Alternatively, you can double-click the text with the Type Mask tool to select it, and then type a new font size in the tool options bar.

9 When you're satisfied with the result, click the green Commit button (✔). The outline of the text becomes an active selection. If you're not happy with the placement of the selection, use the arrow keys on your keyboard to nudge it into place.

10 Choose Edit > Copy, and then Edit > Paste. In the Layers panel, you can see that the cutout type image has been placed onto a new layer, surrounded by transparency.

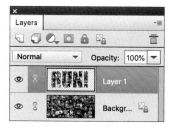

11 Hide the Background layer by clicking the eye icon beside the layer thumbnail.

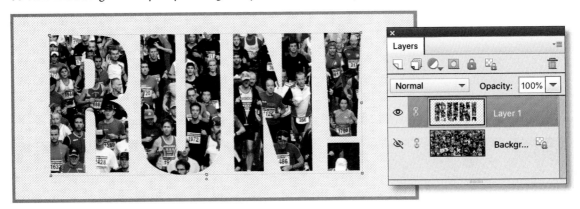

Adding impact to a type mask

The text is no longer live—the mask was converted to a selection outline, so it can no longer be edited with a text tool; however, you can still apply a layer style or an effect to enhance it or make it more prominent.

1 If necessary, select Layer 1 in the Layers panel to make it active. With the Move tool (⊕), drag the type to center it in the image window; then, press the up arrow and right arrow keys eight times each.

2 In the Favorites panel, click the swatch for the High drop-shadow effect.

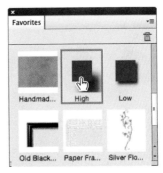

3 In the Layers panel, double-click the *fx* icon on Layer 1. In the Style Settings dialog box, set the Lighting Angle to **45**°. Increase the Drop Shadow Size to **40** px, the Distance to **50** px, and the Opacity to **80**%; then, click OK.

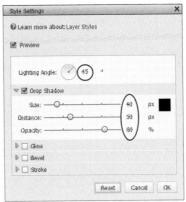

4 In the Layers panel, select the Background layer. Make the layer visible; then, choose Image > Rotate > Flip Layer Horizontal. Click OK to confirm the conversion of the background, and then click OK to accept the default name.

5 Choose Enhance > Adjust Color > Adjust Hue/Saturation. In the Hue/ Saturation dialog box, reduce the Saturation value to **–60**, increase the Lightness to **+60**, and then click OK.

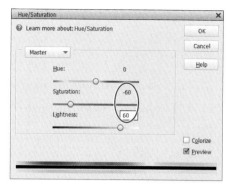

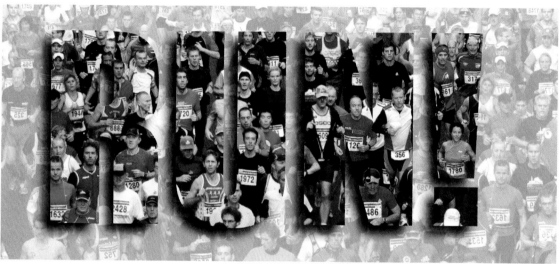

▶ **Tip:** The Photo Text guided edit automates the process of producing a type mask. Try taking the image from this exercise through the Photo Text project to see which method you prefer. When you're done, inspect the new layers in Expert mode.

6 Choose File > Save As. In the Save As dialog box, choose Photoshop (PSD) as the file format, enable layers, and save the file to your My CIB Work folder. Make sure that the new file will be included in the Organizer but not in a version set; then, name the file **09_runners_mask** and click Save. Close the file.

Congratulations! You've completed the lesson. You've explored the Graphics library and become familiar with a variety of methods for locating the artwork you need. You've also learned how to set up a project in Create mode, how to replace and manipulate backgrounds, frames, and text, and the basics of working with layers and layer styles. You've had some fun with type and gained more experience with layer masks.

Before you move on to the next lesson, take a moment to refresh your new skills by reading through the review on the facing page.

Review questions

1 How do you begin a new project, such as a greeting card or photo book?

2 How do you scale and reposition a photo in a photo project?

3 How can you find the items you want amongst all the choices in the Graphics library?

4 What are layers, how do they work, and how do you work with them?

Review answers

1 To create a project, select the photos you want to use in the Organizer, or open them from the Editor; then, choose a project option in the Create tab at the upper right of either workspace. Once you've chosen a theme, the right panel group presents page previews and provides access to layers, layout templates, graphics, and effects.

2 You can scale or rotate a framed photo by dragging the bounding box handles, and move it by dragging. To scale, rotate, or move a photo within its frame, you need to double-click the image to isolate it before using the same techniques, so that the changes affect the photo independently of its frame.

3 You can sort and search the items in the Graphics library by using the menus and text box at the top of the Content panel. You can sort the content by type, activity, mood, season, color, keywords, and other attributes. Use the Favorites panel to assemble a collection of the items you're most likely to use, rather than looking through the entire library every time you want to add an artwork item to a project.

4 Layers are like transparent overlays on which you can paint or place photos, artwork, or text. Each element in a photo project occupies its own layer—the background is at the bottom, and the other elements are overlaid in the order in which they are added to the project. You work with layers in the Layers panel, where you can toggle their visibility, drag to change their order, and add layer styles, effects, and masks. To make changes to a layer mask rather than to the image on that layer, first select the black-and-white mask thumbnail to the right of the image thumbnail. The checkerboard grid areas in the layer thumbnails represent the transparent parts of the layers through which you can see the layers below.

10 PRINTING, SHARING, AND EXPORTING

Lesson overview

In previous lessons you've imported images from a range of sources, explored a variety of ways to organize and find your files, learned how to correct and enhance photos, and then created projects and presentations to showcase them.

In this lesson, you'll learn about outputting your images and creations so that you can share them with family, friends, or the world at large:

- Printing a contact sheet
- Printing a picture package
- Printing individual photos
- Fine-tuning the composition of an image in the print preview
- Sharing photos by email
- Backing up your catalog and media files
- Sharing your photos online
- Exporting images for use on the web

 This lesson will take about 45 minutes to complete. To get the lesson files used in this chapter, download them from the web page for this book at www.adobepress.com/PSECIB2020. For more information, see "Accessing the lesson files and Web Edition" in the Getting Started section at the beginning of this book.

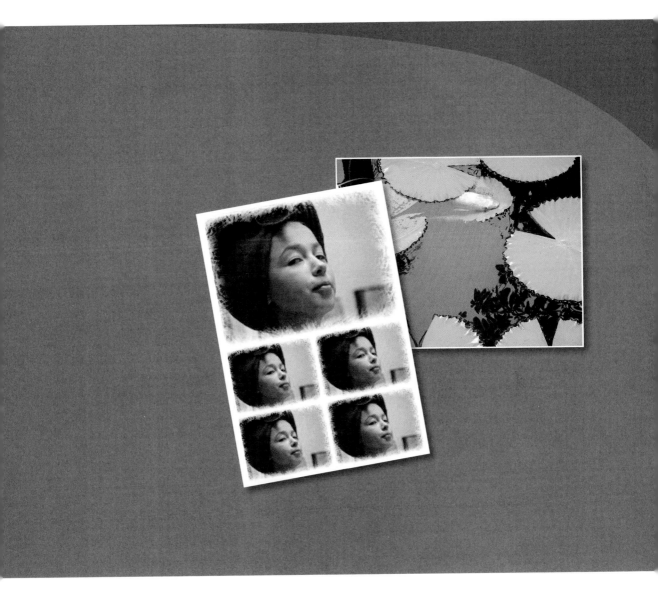

Now that you've organized and searched the images in your growing collection, corrected and enhanced your photos, and created stylish presentations to showcase them, it's time to let Photoshop Elements help you share your images and creations with the world—as printed output, by email, or online.

Getting started

Note: Before you start this lesson, make sure you've set up a folder for your lesson files and downloaded the Lesson 10 folder from your Account page at www.peachpit.com, as detailed in "Accessing the lesson files and Web Edition" and "Creating a work folder" in the "Getting Started" section at the beginning of this book. You should also have created a new work catalog (see "Creating a catalog for working with this book" in Lesson 1).

You'll begin by importing the sample images for this lesson to your CIB Catalog.

1   Start Photoshop Elements, and click Organizer in the Home screen. In the Organizer, check the lower-right corner of the workspace to make sure that your CIB Catalog is loaded—if not, choose File > Manage Catalogs, and load it.

2   Click the Import button at the upper left of the workspace, and choose From Files And Folders from the drop-down menu; then, locate and select the Lesson 10 folder. Activate the option Get Photos From Subfolders, and disable all of the automatic processing options; then, click Get Media.

3   In the Import Attached Keyword Tags dialog, click Select All; then, click OK.

Thumbnails of the images you've just imported appear in the Media Browser. The bar above the thumbnails indicates that you are viewing newly imported files.

About printing

Photoshop Elements offers a range of options for printing your photographs as well as projects such as photo books, greeting cards, and photo collages. You can output any Photoshop Elements print job from your home printer or take advantage of Adobe partner services to order professional prints online.

You can print photos individually (in batches or one at a time), have Photoshop Elements generate a picture package layout that repeats the same image at a variety of sizes on the same page, or preview a selection of photos as thumbnail images arranged on a printed contact sheet.

Printing a contact sheet

Before the advent of digital photography, a *contact sheet* or *contact proof* was produced by laying strips of film negatives directly onto a sheet of photographic paper, which was then exposed in the darkroom to create a printed preview of every shot on the roll. Photoshop Elements offers the option of printing a digital contact sheet—an effective and economical way to print-preview a selection of images at thumbnail size, arranged in a grid layout on a single sheet of paper.

To learn how to set up a contact sheet on macOS, skip ahead to the next exercise.

Printing a contact sheet on Windows

1   Click the Back button (⊙) at the left of the actions bar above the thumbnail grid, so that the Media Browser displays all the images in your catalog.

2   At the top of the left panel, click Folders, and then, in the My Folder list, select the folder To_Print. Press Ctrl+A to select all the images in the source folder.

3 Choose File > Print.

The Prints dialog opens. The column on the left displays thumbnails of all the photos you selected for this print job. At center stage is the print preview.

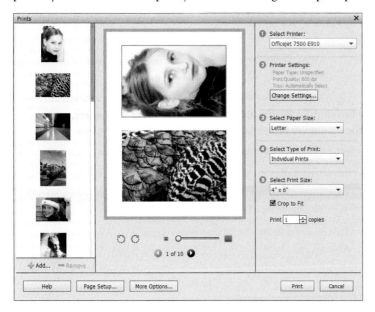

▶ **Tip:** You can also open the Prints dialog in contact-sheet mode from the Create tab above the right panel group. Choose Photo Prints from the Create menu, and then click Contact Sheet. If you cancel a print job that was launched from the Create menu, you'll also need to click Cancel in the taskbar below the Create panel.

4 In the Prints dialog, choose a printer from the Select Printer menu. For the purposes of this demonstration, set the paper size to Letter. From the Select Type Of Print menu, choose Contact Sheet; make sure the Crop To Fit option is unselected. Under Select A Layout, the number of columns should be set to 4, so that all 20 photos will fit neatly on a single page.

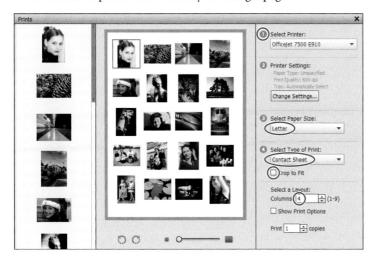

▶ **Tip:** To remove a photo from the contact sheet, select its thumb-nail in the column at the left and click the Remove button (▬) below the menu pane.

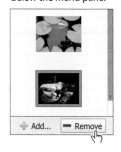

The contact sheet layout includes all the images in the thumbnail column at the left. A page count below the print preview indicates that you are viewing page 1 of 1.

5   Under Select A Layout, click the down arrow button beside the Columns number, or type **3** in the text box. With only three columns, the images are larger, but only nine photos will fit on a single page at this paper size, so the page count below the print preview now indicates that you are viewing page 1 of 3. Use the Next Page and Previous Page buttons on either side of the page count to navigate between the pages. Change the number of columns to nine, which is the maximum. You can see that a single letter-size page can accommodate many photos at this setting. Return the layout to four columns.

6   Click to select any photo in the print preview; then, use the slider below the preview pane to zoom in. Drag the photo to reposition it within the frame of its image cell. Select another image, and then use the Rotate buttons to the left of the zoom slider to change the photo's orientation.

Note: Some words in the text label may be truncated, depending on the page setup and column layout.

7   To print information extracted from the images' metadata below each photo on the contact sheet, first click to activate Show Print Options (just below the Columns setting), and then select any or all of the text label options.

8   Click Print or Cancel, and skip to "Printing a picture package" on the next page.

Printing a contact sheet on macOS

On macOS, you initiate a contact-sheet print from the Editor. For this demonstration, we'll use all the photos in a single folder; it will be quicker to open the Editor without first making a selection in the Organizer. If you want to print a contact sheet with photos drawn from multiple folders, you'll need to select the images in the Media Browser, and then switch to the Editor.

1   Press Shift+Command+A to deselect any images that are currently selected in the Media Browser; then, click the Editor button ( ) in the taskbar. If necessary, click Expert in the mode picker to switch the Editor to Expert mode.

Tip: The alternative option in the Use menu under Source Images fills your contact sheet with whatever images are already open in the Editor. You would use this setting if you had made a selection of images in the Media Browser before switching to the Editor.

2   Choose File > Contact Sheet II. Set up the Contact Sheet dialog as shown in the illustration at the right. Choose Folder from the Use menu under Source Images. Click Choose, and locate your Lesson 10/To_Print folder. Click Open. In the Document settings, specify a size for your contact sheet. Under Thumbnails, specify the order in which the images will be placed. Select Use Auto-Spacing; then, type **4** and **5** in the Columns and Rows boxes, respectively. Your Columns and Rows settings are reflected in the layout preview at the right. Deselect Rotate For Best Fit, and select Use Filename As Caption.

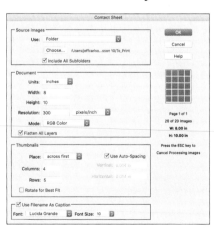

3 Click OK, and then wait while Photoshop Elements places the images and captions.

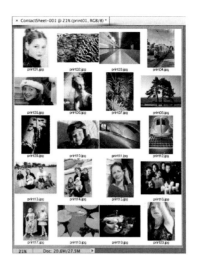

In our example, all 20 images fit onto a single page. When the number of images selected for printing exceeds the capacity of a single page at the layout settings specified, Photoshop Elements generates more pages to accommodate the extra photos.

4 Select the contact-sheet page(s) in the Photo Bin. Choose File > Print if you wish to print the contact sheet. If not, choose File > Close; then, click Don't Save.

Printing a picture package

A picture package layout lets you print a photo repeated at a choice of sizes on the same page, much as professional portrait studios do. You can choose from a variety of layout options and a range of image sizes to customize your picture package print.

To set up a picture package print on macOS, skip ahead to the next exercise.

Printing a picture package on Windows

1 Select two or more pictures in the Media Browser, and then choose File > Print.

2 In the Prints dialog, choose a printer from the Select Printer menu. Your choice of paper size will determine which layout options are available for your picture package; for the purposes of this exercise, choose Letter from the Select Paper Size menu.

3 Choose Picture Package from the Select Type Of Print menu. If a Printing Warning dialog appears, cautioning against enlarging pictures, click OK; for this exercise, you'll print multiple images at smaller sizes.

4 Choose a layout from the Select A Layout menu, and then select the option Fill Page With First Photo. This will result in a page with a single photo repeated at a variety of sizes, according to the layout you've chosen. If you selected more than one photo in the Media Browser, a separate Print Package page will be generated for each photo selected; you can see the print preview for each page by clicking the page navigation buttons below the preview pane.

> **Tip:** You can also open the Prints dialog in picture package mode from the Create tab. Click Photo Prints, and then click the Picture Package button. If you cancel a print job that was launched from the Create menu, you'll also need to click Cancel in the taskbar below the Create panel.

The layout options available for a picture package depend on the paper size specified in the Prints dialog, the page setup, and the printer preferences. To change the paper size, choose from the Select Paper Size menu, or click either the Page Setup button at the lower left of the Prints dialog or the Change Settings button under Printer Settings. Depending on your printer, you may need to look for the paper size options in the Advanced preferences settings.

5 Try some of the options in the Select A Frame menu. We selected the Icicles border to suit the winter holiday theme of our selection. You can choose only one frame per picture package; it will be applied to every picture in the layout.

6 Toggle the Crop To Fit option, and assess the result; the Crop To Fit option may fit the multiple images more closely to the layout to better fill the printable area, especially when your photo is of nonstandard proportions.

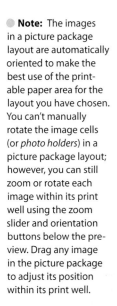

Note: The images in a picture package layout are automatically oriented to make the best use of the printable paper area for the layout you have chosen. You can't manually rotate the image cells (or *photo holders*) in a picture package layout; however, you can still zoom or rotate each image within its print well using the zoom slider and orientation buttons below the preview. Drag any image in the picture package to adjust its position within its print well.

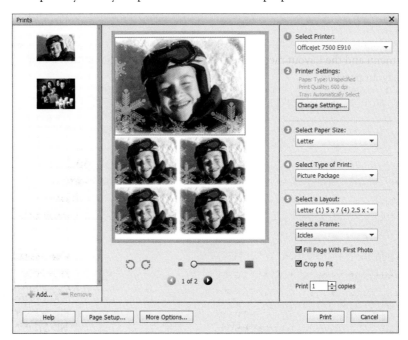

7 Click the Add button ( ) below the thumbnail menu at the left. In the Add Media dialog, you can choose from your entire catalog or from those photos currently visible in the Media Browser. More sources can be accessed by expanding the Advanced options. Choose one or more photos from any of these sets, and then click Done; the selected images are added to the print job and now appear in the thumbnails column in the Prints dialog.

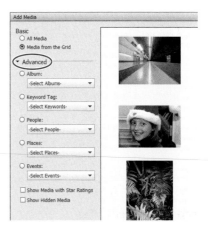

8 Drag the thumbnail of one of your newly acquired photos from the thumbnails column onto any image cell in the print preview; the original image is replaced.

9 Click Print or Cancel, and skip ahead to the exercise "Printing individual photos."

Printing a picture package on macOS

1 If necessary, switch to the Organizer by clicking the Organizer button (⊞) in the taskbar, leaving the Editor window open. Select two or more photos in the Media Browser; then, click the Editor button (⌨) in the taskbar. If necessary, click Expert in the mode picker to switch the Editor to Expert mode.

2 In the Photo Bin, click whichever photo you'd like to print first to make it the active (foremost) image; then, Choose File > Picture Package.

▶ **Tip:** You can open the Picture Package dialog from the Create tab. Click Photo Prints, and then click the Picture Package button. If you do this from the Organizer, you'll see a message asking if you'd like to open the Editor to initiate printing.

3 In the Picture Package dialog, under Document, make a selection from the Page Size menu and the Layout menu, and then click the Edit Layout button below the Layout preview.

4 In the Picture Package Edit Layout dialog, click to select an image in the Edit Layout preview, and then click the Delete Zone button in the Image Zones area at the left. Select another image in the preview, and drag it to a new position on the page preview. Drag the handles on the image's bounding box to scale it or to change its orientation; the image automatically rotates to fit the frame.

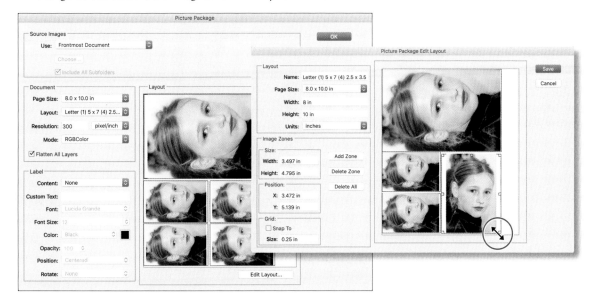

5 Right-click an image in the Edit Layout preview and try out some of the menu choices; then experiment with the other settings and buttons in the Image Zones options. Click Cancel, and then click No to avoid overwriting the default settings for the layout preset you selected.

6 Click OK in the Picture Package dialog, and then wait while Photoshop Elements creates a new document and places the images for your picture package. If you wish to see the picture package printed, choose File > Print; otherwise, choose File > Close All, and then click Don't Save.

▶ **Tip:** If you cancel a print job that was launched from the Create menu, you'll also need to click Cancel in the taskbar below the Create panel.

Printing individual photos

The Photoshop Elements Prints / Print dialog presents all your printing options in one convenient place, and also enables you to fine-tune the placement of each image within its own *photo holder* (its frame in the print preview). You can zoom or rotate an image with the controls beneath the preview and drag to reposition it, so you can get the image placed just right for printing without first editing it.

1 In the Organizer, Ctrl-click / Command-click to select eight or more images.

2 Choose File > Print. Alternatively, click the Create tab, click Photo Prints, and then click the Local Printer button. On macOS, click Yes to continue to the Editor, where printing will be initiated.

3 In the Prints / Print dialog, select a printer, paper size, and print size from the menus at the right. On Windows, choose Individual Prints from the Select Type Of Print menu. If you see a print-resolution alert, click OK to dismiss it.

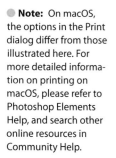

Note: On macOS, the options in the Print dialog differ from those illustrated here. For more detailed information on printing on macOS, please refer to Photoshop Elements Help, and search other online resources in Community Help.

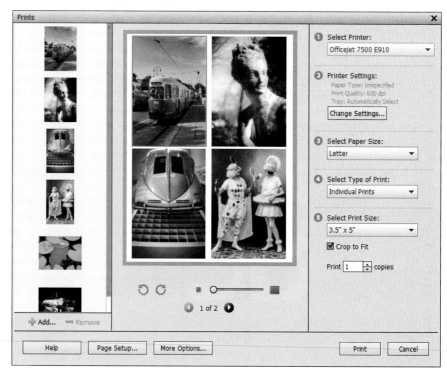

4 Experiment with the controls below the Print preview. Click to select an image in the preview, and zoom in and out inside the image cell using the zoom slider. Use the Rotate Left and Rotate Right buttons beside the zoom slider to change the orientation of the image within its print well. Drag the selected image to reposition it within the frame. Toggle the Crop To Fit option below the Select Print Size menu, and observe the effect in the print preview.

5   Select any image thumbnail in the menu column on the left side of the dialog, and click the Remove button (━).

6   Click the Add button (⊕) below the thumbnails menu. In the Add Media / Add Photos dialog, select an image source; you can choose from your entire catalog, or from those photos currently visible in the Media Browser. Choose one or more photos from any of these sets, and then click Add Selected Media / Add Selected Photos. The selected images are added to the thumbnails column in the Prints / Print dialog, and the Add Media / Add Photos dialog remains open. Expand the Advanced source options, and choose a different source. Select one or more photos; then, click Done to add the photos to your print job and dismiss the dialog.

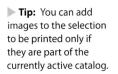

▶ **Tip:** You can add images to the selection to be printed only if they are part of the currently active catalog.

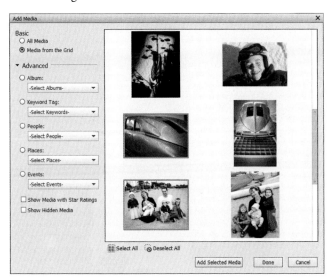

● **Note:** On macOS, many (not all) of the Advanced source options are visible by default in the Add Media dialog.

If you've selected more pictures than will fit on one page at the image dimensions you specified, Photoshop Elements automatically generates extra pages.

7   Check the page count below the print preview. If your print job has more than one page, preview the other pages by clicking the arrow buttons at either side of the page count.

8   Click the More Options button at the bottom of the dialog, and explore the settings available in the More Options dialog. In the Printing Choices section, you can choose to print text details with your images, add image borders or a background color, flip the image for iron-on transfers, and print crop marks to help you trim your images. The More Options dialog also offers Custom Print Size and Color Management settings. Click Cancel to close the dialog.

9   In the Prints / Print dialog, click Print if you wish to see these images printed; otherwise, click Cancel to save your ink and paper for your own prints. On macOS, choose File > Close All.

Sharing photos and videos online

In this section, we'll look at a variety of ways to share your pictures with friends, family, clients, or the world at large. From within Photoshop Elements, you can email photos or upload your images, videos, and presentations directly to social networking or photo- and video-sharing websites by choosing from the Share tab menu in either the Organizer or the Editor. You can also use these services to download media.

Depending on whether you already have an account with the service you wish to use, you may first need to sign up. Some services, such as Flickr and Twitter, will ask you to authorize Photoshop Elements to connect to your online account.

Although the procedure for logging in and sharing may differ slightly for each of these services, the process is essentially similar, and you'll be guided step by step.

Sharing photos by email

Perhaps the most basic way to share a photo is by attaching it to an email. The Organizer's email function makes it easy, automatically optimizing your images specifically for sending via email.

Note: The first time you access this feature, you may be presented with the Email section of the Organizer's preferences. Choose your email client (such as Microsoft Outlook or Apple Mail) from the menu, and then click OK. You can review or change your settings later by choosing the Email pane in the Preferences dialog.

1   In the Media Browser, select a photo to attach to an email. Click the Share tab; then click the Email button.

2   Drag another image from the Media Browser to the Email Attachments pane to add it to the selection to be emailed.

3   Choose one of the smaller size options from the Maximum Photo Size menu, and then adjust the image quality using the Quality slider. The higher the quality setting, the larger the file size will be— and therefore, the longer the download time. Click Next.

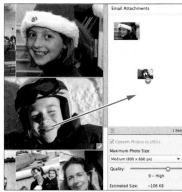

4   Depending on your email setup, you may need to add the recipient as a new contact. Enter a subject and message and click Next to send the message or hand it off to your preferred mail application.

Exporting copies of your photos for the web

The Save For Web dialog box previews the effects of different optimization options; you can choose from a range of file formats for your exported files, resize them, specify color and compression options, and enable transparency or background matting. Use an export preset as a starting point, and then tweak the settings to fine-tune the optimization. In this exercise you'll optimize and export a copy in JPEG format, which reduces the file size and looks good in the majority of web browsers.

1   In the Organizer, click the All Media button (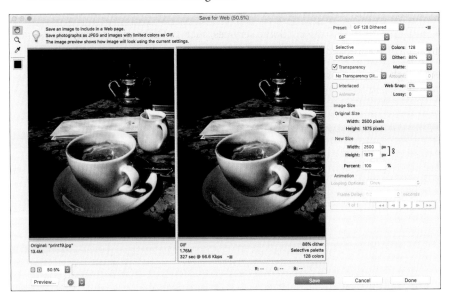 All Media) if it's visible in the actions bar above the thumbnail grid. Select any photo in the Media Browser, and then click the Editor button (⬚) in the taskbar.

2   In the Editor, choose File > Save For Web. In the Save For Web dialog box, choose Fit On Screen from the Zoom menu, just above the Preview button in the lower-left corner of the dialog box.

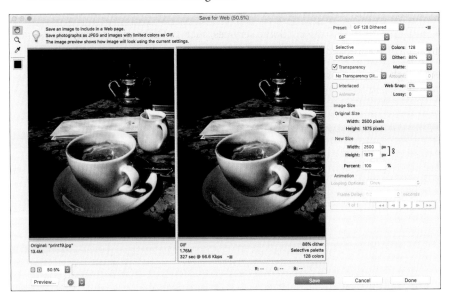

> **Tip:** While you're previewing photos in the Save For Web dialog, you can magnify the view with the Zoom tool ($\mathbf{Q}$) in the toolbox at the upper left of the dialog. To zoom out, hold the Alt / Option key and click the image with the Zoom tool. While you're zoomed in, drag in either window with the Hand tool (✋); the images pan in unison so that both views show the same part of the photo.

3   Watch the change in the file-size information displayed below the export preview on the right as you choose JPEG Medium from the Preset menu at the upper right of the dialog.

4   Select the JPEG Low preset; the file size is reduced even further. Tweak the Quality setting to set a level between the two presets; the default values for the JPEG Low and JPEG Medium settings are 10 and 30, respectively.

5   Under New Size, type **500** in the Width field. The Height is adjusted automatically to retain the image's original proportions. Once again, notice the change in the file size displayed beneath the optimized export preview. Choose Fit On Screen from the Zoom menu to compare the reduced image to the original.

6   Click the Preview button in the lower-left corner of the Save For Web dialog to see the image displayed in your default browser at the current export settings. Scroll down the browser page, if necessary, to see a summary of the optimization settings that were applied. Return to Photoshop Elements.

● **Note:** The JPEG format reduces the file size using compression, which discards some of the image data. The amount of information lost, and the resulting image quality, will vary depending on the photo you're working with and the quality settings.

7   Click Save. Add the extension **_Work** to the original, and save the file to your My CIB Work folder. In the Editor, choose File > Close, without saving changes.

Backing up your catalog and media files

The importance of a good backup strategy is often only understood too late. You can't prevent a disaster from happening, but you *can* reduce the risk of loss— and the time and effort needed for recovery—by backing up regularly.

Backing up the catalog file

The catalog file stores not only the locations of your image files, but the metadata attached to them, including titles, captions, tags, ratings, and album groupings. One technique to protect this information is to save as much as possible back to your original image files. This process serves as a partial *distributed* backup of the catalog.

1   In the Organizer, click the All Media button ((<) **All Media**) if it's visible. Press Ctrl+A / Command+A to select all of the media files in your catalog; then, choose File > Save Metadata To Files. Click OK to dismiss any notification.

Next, you'll make a full backup of your catalog and all the associated media files.

2   Choose File > Backup Catalog. Make sure that Full Backup is selected in the Backup Options; then, click Next. Select a destination drive, and then click the Browse button beside Backup Path to specify a destination folder. When you have chosen a destination folder, click New Folder and name the new folder **CIB Backup [*current date*]**; then, click Create. Click OK, and then click Save Backup. Photoshop Elements will notify you when the backup is complete; click OK to dismiss the message.

Doing incremental backups

An incremental backup saves you time by replacing only the catalog entries and images that have been modified since the last backup.

1   In the Media Browser, add ratings to several unrated photos by clicking the rating stars below the thumbnails. This will serve as the incremental change to the catalog since your full backup.

2   Choose File > Backup Catalog. This time, select Incremental Backup in the Backup Options; then, click Next.

3   Select the same destination drive, and then click the Browse button beside Backup Path to specify the same destination folder. When you have selected the destination folder, click New Folder and type **CIB Backup Incremental [*current date*]**. Click Create; then, click OK.

4   Click the Browse button beside Previous Backup File. Navigate to the folder containing your full backup, and select the file Backup.tly. Click Open, and then click Save Backup. Click OK to dismiss the completion message.

Should you ever need to restore a damaged catalog file or start fresh after a hard disk failure, simply choose File > Restore Catalog, and locate your backup files.

Review questions

1 What is a contact sheet?

2 What is a picture package?

3 How can you fine-tune the composition of a photo for printing?

4 Is the Save For Web command available only in Expert mode?

5 What is an incremental backup?

Review answers

1 A contact sheet is an effective and economical way to print-preview a selection of images at thumbnail size, arranged in a grid layout on a single sheet of paper.

2 A picture package lets you print a photo repeated at a choice of sizes on the same page. You can choose from a variety of layout options, with a range of image sizes, to customize your picture package print.

3 You can fine-tune the placement of each image within its own photo holder frame in the print preview, enabling you to get the image placed just right for printing without first editing it. Zoom or rotate an image with the controls beneath the print preview, and drag to reposition it in the frame.

4 The Save For Web command is available from the File menu in all three edit modes: Expert, Quick, and Guided.

5 An incremental backup copies only those images and catalog entries that have changed since the last full backup.

INDEX

S

Production Notes

Adobe Photoshop Elements 2020 Classroom in a Book was created electronically using Adobe InDesign. Art was produced using Adobe InDesign, Adobe Illustrator, Adobe Photoshop, and Adobe Photoshop Elements 2020.

Team credits

The following individuals contributed to the development of this edition of *Adobe Photoshop Elements 2020 Classroom in a Book*:

Project coordinator, technical writer: Jeff Carlson

Copyeditor: Scout Festa

Proofreader: Jeff Carlson

Keystroker: Becky Winter

Special thanks to Laura Norman, Tracey Croom, John Evans, Katrin Straub, Scout Festa, Becky Winter, Kim Carlson, and Ellie Carlson.

Typefaces used

Adobe Myriad Pro and Adobe Warnock Pro are used throughout the lessons. For more information about OpenType and Adobe fonts, visit www.adobe.com/products/type/opentype.html.

Photo credits

Photographic images and illustrations supplied by Han Buck, Torsten Buck, John Evans, Katrin Straub, Jeff Carlson, and Adobe Systems Incorporated. Photos are for use only with the lessons in the book.

Contributors

 Jeff Carlson is a contributing editor at *TidBITS* and writes for publications such as *DPReview*, *CreativePro*, and *Macworld*. He is the author of the books *Take Control of Your Digital Photos* and *Take Control of Your Digital Storage*, among many other titles, including several editions of *Photoshop Elements: Visual QuickStart Guide*. He also co-hosts the podcast *PhotoActive* and leads photography workshops in the Pacific Northwest. He believes there's never enough coffee, and does his best to test that theory.

 John Evans worked in computer graphics and design for more than 30 years, initially as a graphic designer, and then as a multimedia author, software interface designer, and technical writer. His multimedia and digital illustration work associated with Japanese type attracted an award from Apple Computer Australia. His other projects ranged from music education software for children to interface design for innovative font design software. As a technical writer his work included software design specifications, user manuals, and copyediting for *Adobe Photoshop Elements 7 Classroom in a Book*, *Adobe Photoshop Lightroom 2 Classroom in a Book*, and *Adobe Creative Suite 4 Classroom in a Book*, as well as several editions of *Adobe Photoshop Lightroom Classroom in a Book*.

 Katrin Straub is an artist, graphic designer, and author. Her award-winning print, painting, and multimedia work has been exhibited worldwide. With more than 15 years' experience in design, Katrin has worked as Design Director for companies such as Landor Associates and Fontworks in the United States, Hong Kong, and Japan. Her work includes packaging, promotional campaigns, multimedia, website design, and internationally recognized corporate and retail identities. She holds degrees from the FH Augsburg, ISIA Urbino, and the New School University in New York. Katrin has authored many books, from the *Adobe Creative Suite Idea Kit* to Classroom in a Book titles for Adobe Photoshop Lightroom 2, Adobe Creative Suite 4, and Adobe Soundbooth, and several versions of *Adobe Photoshop Elements Classroom in a Book* and *Adobe Premiere Elements Classroom in a Book*.